T0318256

ROUTLEDGE LIBRARY EDITIONS:
SECURITY AND SOCIETY

Volume 1

SOCIAL ORDER AND THE GENERAL THEORY OF STRATEGY

SOCIAL ORDER AND THE GENERAL THEORY OF STRATEGY

ALEXANDER ATKINSON

LONDON AND NEW YORK

First published in 1981 by Routledge & Kegan Paul Ltd

This edition first published in 2021
by Routledge
4 Park Square, Milton Park, Abingdon, Oxon OX14 4RN

and by Routledge
605 Third Avenue, New York, NY 10017

Routledge is an imprint of the Taylor & Francis Group, an informa business

British Library Cataloguing in Publication Data
A catalogue record for this book is available from the British Library

ISBN: 978-0-367-56733-0 (Set)
ISBN: 978-1-00-312078-0 (Set) (ebk)
ISBN: 978-0-367-60818-7 (Volume 1) (hbk)
ISBN: 978-0-367-60849-1 (Volume 1) (pbk)
ISBN: 978-1-00-310071-3 (Volume 1) (ebk)

Publisher's Note
The publisher has gone to great lengths to ensure the quality of this reprint but points out that some imperfections in the original copies may be apparent.

Disclaimer
The publisher has made every effort to trace copyright holders and would welcome correspondence from those they have been unable to trace.

Social order
and
the general theory
of strategy

Alexander Atkinson

London School of Economics

Routledge & Kegan Paul
London, Boston and Henley

First published in 1981
by Routledge & Kegan Paul Ltd
39 Store Street,
London WC1E 7DD,
9 Park Street,
Boston, Mass. 02108, USA and
Broadway House,
Newtown Road,
Henley-on-Thames,
Oxon RG9 1EN
Printed in Great Britain by
The Thetford Press Ltd, Thetford, Norfolk

Library of Congress Cataloguing in Publication Data

Atkinson, Alexander, 1944-

Social order and the general theory of
strategy.
Bibliography: P 293
1. Strategy   2. Military policy
3. Guerilla warfare
I. Title
U162.A78   355'.02   81-17906

ISBN 0-7100-0907-0   AACR2

Contents

Acknowledgments

The academic and personal debts one accumulates in an endeavour such as this, particularly in the course of my travels twice to Stanford University, California, and Hong Kong to obtain Chinese language sources which, at the time of my research in the early 1970s were not available elsewhere, are really too numerous for me to recall.

The outstanding ones I should mention are due to the Hoover Institution, Stanford University for the generous assistance extended to me as a visiting scholar, and to the Universities Service Centre, Hong Kong. The latter, particularly, was a godsend as the only place students and scholars of China could go in the Far East in an atmosphere of relative freedom and feel they were in the next best environment to actually being there, Without the staff, translators and the many visiting scholars at the Centre who knew so much more about Chinese language, culture and history than I did, this whole project would have died long ago. Finally, I should not neglect the Chinese Cultural Research Institute, Toyo Bunko, in Tokyo, where my kind hosts spent too much of their time trying to fill in for my lack of Japanese.

Of individuals, two stand out for their interest and encouragement. The first is Shelford Bidwell, past editor of the *Journal of the Royal United Services Institute for Defence Studies* for taking an interest in and publishing chapters 2 and 3, giving me the courage to press on when I did need it; the former chapter being extensively rewritten from Vol. 118 (March 1973) *Journal* and the latter appearing in Vol. 119 (March 1974) *Journal.* Second, Philip Windsor, my PhD supervisor at the London School of Economics, I thank for his uncanny ability to be waiting for me at the end of most conceptual avenues I thought so hard to negotiate. I should add my thanks to Peter Paret, Professor of History at Stanford University, for making a number of helpful comments on the finished manuscript, particularly on the discussion of methodology in the last chapter.

Many of the Chinese documents on problems of war, strategy and social order to be quoted have not been readily available, and even fewer have been translated. The translations quoted here, marked throughout with an asterisk (*), are by Mr Hsü Hung-wen as commissioned by me in Hong Kong, November 1973-January 1974.

I should also mention, as regards the differences in English and American rules of style, that since some chapters were written at Stanford and others in London, I fear inconsistencies in style may remain. In addition, I have used the expression frequently throughout the text, along with a few similar expressions, 'the form and movement of armed power *is* conceived' since this form and movement is to be regarded always as a single continuum, or in the case of similar expressions, a single entity.

The author and publishers wish to thank the following for permission to reprint the copyright material listed below:
The China Quarterly for 'Resolutions of the Tsunyi Conference', No. 40, October-December (1969), translated by Jerome Ch'en; Monthly Review Press for *Fanshen: A Documentary of Revolution in a Chinese Village*, copyright © 1966 by William Hinton. Reprinted by permission of Monthly Review Press; Princeton University Press for excerpts from Carl von Clausewitz *On War,* ed. and transl. by Michael Howard and Peter Paret, Introductory Essays by Peter Paret, Michael Howard and Bernard Brodie; with a Commentary by Bernard Brodie (copyright © 1976 by Princeton University Press), pp.75-637. Reprinted by permission of Princeton University Press; University of Washington Press for *The Land Revolution in China 1930-1934: A Study of Documents* (1969) edited and translated by Tso-liang Hsiao.

London 1980

New Preface to the Reissue of 2021

Is there a place left in international politics for the real use of violence as an instrument of policy in the nuclear age? Originally published in 1981, Dr Atkinson attempts to answer this question with new considerations in the presentation of a general theory of strategy. He argues that the classical theory of strategy, so influential for the nineteenth century and for the better half of the twentieth century, was built on a mainly hidden structure of reasoning that still infests theory today. The larger and socially-rooted lessons that insurgent warfare can inform, as best exemplified in the primary sources of the Chinese Civil War period, reveal in a new light this hidden structure of which Clausewitz is the earliest and most eloquent example. By this analysis of the insurgent and classical paradigm opposites the author intends to strip away the blinds of convention still circulating in theory today so that observers and students of international politics may see where new forms of politically motivated violence in the nuclear age seem more than ever to be headed.

Here we have perfect paradigm opposites. In the conventional world battle-field action and ideally 'decisive battle' is the center of all other issues in which such conventional logic in the end sweeps up everything else and runs it back through the logic into success or failure of armed power on the battle-field. Everything hangs on this. In the 'revisionist' insurgent world where social order is weaponized as an object and source of military power through its inherent and valuable (armed) power structures social order replaces narrow battle-field action (ideally focused on 'decisive battle') and alternatively redirects the entire logic and all other considerations, including previously heroic conventional military assets, are remodeled to act against (armed) enemy power structures inherent (as always) in social order for the ultimate object of military victory. Again, everything is on this alone. Which paradigm – one the opposite mirror image of the other – will prevail will depend on the stability and power of the nation state and its institutions, the continued and unhappy collapse on which I base the General Theory.

Within the long process of evolving transitions between underlying social forms and their parallel military organizations during the past 3000 years we have endured a number of distinct evolutionary stages. In each stage the identifying element has been the relationship of a society to its armed forces which has been quite different. The first in Western tradition was that of antiquity, the Greeks and then Romans, which more or less endured until the fifth century and gave way to the 'Romanic – Germanic' period of Germanic kingdoms established within the old Roman Empire. The ninth century saw the arrival of the feudal system (military vassalage; stipendiary tenement-fief) which gradually disintegrated in the course of the fourteenth and fifteenth centuries and was replaced by the Early Modern phase (state formation) embodied in the Peace of Westphalia 1648. We find ourselves now in a new period of rapid transition from the Late Modern age which began with the French Revolution to a completely new era – the collapse of the nation state which had before driven forward the Late Modern age and its great conventional militaries – into a new age of insurgency wherein the combat order, this is, the order of combat infrastructure is indistinguishable from the social order. This new 're-visionist' model, which is the continuation of our long evolutionary descent, is our future for decades to come, perhaps centuries.

Additional material to start Chapter 8

The idea of weaponizing an entire social order as the prime military arm in the war zones wherein the combat order (infrastructure) and the social order are one and the same must seem unthinkable to the conventional mind. See why, in chapter 8.

Clausewitz, even to this day, remains the most eloquent thinker in the world of silent contracts which is why we turn to him extensively in chapter 8.

Introduction

In the nuclear age, is the theory of strategy to be left behind destitute by recent fashion that 'there is no strategy any more — only crisis management' [McNamara]? Are we now destined to believe that 'it is becoming clear that war is not a continuation of policy but a failure of policy' [Rapoport]?

Western observers have almost entirely missed the larger and more general theoretical implications of a recent shift in assumptions underlying the theory of strategy, particularly into its poorly researched social dimensions. In this may be found new life for the notion of violence as an instrument of policy in the nuclear age that can here obtain the results which are otherwise unattainable. If the remarkable success of Maoist insurgent strategy in mainland China had failed to instruct, largely due to the formidable language and research difficulties, if the recent *débâcle* in Indo-China had taught us little, then perhaps Western theorists may be persuaded when the larger theoretical issues these experiences inform are clearly set out. They should, by now, be willing enough to be so persuaded, once their reasoning can be freed from the classical chains of the past that were built on the determination to keep out of theory the greater lessons that insurgent warfare informs. That is one compelling reason why armed groups today, not only in the Far East but also now it would seem in southern Africa, are so easily able to take advantage in the insurgent form, by instruction or intuition, because they can see for themselves the remarkable successes of those who have already done so. The larger theoretical lessons that insurgent warfare can teach the theory of strategy principally about the central problem of social order — generally ignored by our strategic heritage — are in fact fundamental to the theory and practice of war. They strike so deep into the heart of theory that the consequences we can observe seem now more than ever to require the demise of the more obsessive elements of classical theory — although first and most eloquently described by Clausewitz, still rather *covertly* influential today. In its place I shall suggest the free drift of our area of study towards a new theory of strategy that embraces a good deal of sociological theory; *free,* that is, because once the nineteenth-century gentleman's agreement — the one great classical contract that held orthodox theory together — is thrown out then warfare dissolves into its most primitive and elementary social basis wherein the fight to secure social order, once guaranteed by a kind of silent contract, now becomes everywhere critical. This is a plea to take on board a host of the more elemental sociological considerations right into the heart of theory that most of tradition could simply pass over by convention, so that we may come to understand better where new forms of politically motivated violence seem now more than ever headed.

Those who do not have access to the weapons and technology of the nuclear age see a new way in the poorly researched social dimensions of strategy of pursuing their objectives by violence with some hope of success, where before they had little; and those who have access to this weaponry and technology may see an alternative way of avoiding the risks inherent therein and obtain by violence the objectives that they could not otherwise attain.

The problem, however, is that too many present-day students and observers of international politics look, as it were, at the world through rose-coloured glasses unable to see before them the new colours of emerging forms of politically motivated violence in an international environment that seems to be sliding towards a rather dangerous and somewhat violent phase. The reason why Western observers wear rose-coloured glasses without actually knowing it is given here in a rather long and slightly complex theoretical and methodological story that has remained, until now, hidden in the recesses of the history of strategic thinking since Clausewitz.

Abbreviations

CCC: the *Ch'en Ch'eng Collection (Shih-sou tzu-liao shih kung-fei tzu-liao) 1931-7,* microfilm, 21 reels, available at the Hoover Institution, Stanford University
URI: Union Research Institute, Hong Kong
CCP: Chinese Communist Party
CC: Central Committee
KMT: Kuomintang or Nationalist Party

1

Social order and strategic theory

How is it possible that the classical strategists could have
conceived of a theory of strategy which has had quite considerable influence in the last century and in the better half of
this century while too frequently ignoring the real strategic
issue as the proper basis for general theory?

The thrust of the greater part of our strategic heritage
tends to sweep us past an understanding of the very foundation
on which the theory of strategy should always freely rest.
The thinking of classical strategists, being pushed along in a
tide of unnatural obsessions, soon delivers itself to conclusions entirely foreign to realities of the situation theory
attempts to describe.   So long as everyone is irresistibly
swept along in the same mainstream of theory, then the necessity to work one's way back towards its genesis in the process
of reasoning - being altogether too subtly blended into the
fabric of our strategic heritage - simply never would occur.
Theory, unless otherwise compelled, rarely turns itself back
into a self-examination of the assumptions on which it is
founded.   Theorists don't always grasp the basis on which
their work rests, or not infrequently this basis is so well
shared by all that it receives little, if any, attention.   In
practice, none the less, being always the overriding consid-

eration, theory is really no better than the reach of its
underlying assumptions however cleverly concealed from view by
tradition.   It is precisely at this point that the more
obsessive elements of the classical conception of strategy so
familiar to Western tradition are being gradually forced into
dissolution by the free drift of our area of study towards a
new theory of strategy.   It is this rather long and complex
proposition that I shall pursue throughout these pages in an
effort to persuade strategists, in view of recent developments
in the theory of strategy, of the growing poverty of classical
obsession still somewhat influential today, *particularly the
partly hidden structure of reasoning on which it was built.*

The problem is that classical theory ultimately comes round
to putting all its eggs in one basket, indeed, in the one
basket which is, by virtue of the very *social* basis on which
rests the theory of strategy, the least secure.   For all
their differences (and with some exceptions noted later), the
classical strategists from Clausewitz onward possessed in
common a shared conception - indeed obsession - of the manner
in which one pursues the political object by acting on the
opponent's will to resist in war.   The one great obsession in
the classical theory of strategy is the destruction or, in
later forms, neutralization of the armed power of the opponent.   So great, in fact, is this enthusiasm, that the prime
centre of the will to resist in war almost inevitably came to
rest on the armed forces of the opponent, the destruction or
neutralization of which thus being designated as the essential
avenue to the political object.   In essence, the main thread
in classical thinking is reduced to the notion that in the
pursuit of the political object the will to resist in war is,
in the last analysis, primarily a function of the armed
forces.   The paradigm, in its essential formulation being so

inflexible, is simple; compromise the latter and one invariably acts on the former. This obsession with armed power as
the prime instrument of strategy and thus the main centre of
the will to resist tends to direct reasoning towards quick
classical solutions typified by 'decisive battle'. This kind
of solution in war, which has dominated the classical view and
thus been its real avenue to the political object, had generally to find itself tied to this particular centre of the
will to resist. The drive in theory and practice to 'decisive battle' and quick solutions in war from which the political decision is issued is only made possible, in the first
place, by the classical mentality that eulogizes armed power
as the last word in the theory of strategy - a legacy which
has been passed down to us with far too few questions being
raised.

In spite of this rather unnatural intolerance gripping the
spirit of strategic theory, such unyielding obsession crushing
all else out of the theory of strategy must be found to rest,
in fact, on a process of reasoning which somehow persuades the
theorist to sweep out of the body of theory all other considerations which would otherwise moderate or question the original obsession. Only then in this somewhat twisted process of
reasoning are 'outside' considerations invited back into the
arena of theory only in so far as they are now deemed relevant
to the mainstream of thinking - set up almost entirely by
denying these due access in the first place. This is especially a problem peculiar to theory because it relies on the
reduction of an otherwise unbearable weight of discrete phenomena into a few simple propositions. The tool of reasoning
which makes this possible is almost invariably an underlying
assumption or set of assumptions which, as it were, sets the
train of thought on a particular track of reasoning rather

cleared of all potential obstacles.   But there is a distinction here between good and bad theory.   One criterion of this
is the weight of one's initial assumptions and extent to which
this weight propels theory into unyielding obsession.

What I suggest, therefore, is that we work our way back
into the theoretical structure of our classical heritage, at
which point we find that it rests largely on an implicit
assumption subtly concealed in the fabric of tradition.   Here
we have not only a question of faulty logic proceeding from
faulty assumptions but the more fundamental problem of identifying and revealing an idea which rarely presents itself as
the genesis in classical thinking, being too cleverly hidden
by the cloak of tradition.   The one gate through which theorists must pass into the classical arena is the underlying
assumption of the real stability of social order, or what I
shall later refer to as the relative security of social resources.[1]   The classical theory of strategy, in particular
its obsession with armed power as the prime instrument of
strategy and thus the main centre of the will to resist in
war, can only rest on an everywhere present determination
largely to ignore the very basis which the theory of strategy
automatically seeks out once free from narrow classical
assumption.   This basis to which a *free* conception of
strategy should always return is the problem of social order
which, in the past, was so firmly denied its rightful place by
an implicit convention entered into by the classical strategists.   Only if all simultaneously agree by way of a silent
contract to sweep considerations of social order out of the
theory of strategy (which is, in effect, arrived at by assuming that social order is regarded as absolutely stable, hence
inviolable) can everything come to rest on the only other gen-
eralized basis for the theory of strategy, being the classical

obsession with armed power as the prime instrument of strategy
and thus the main centre of the will to resist in war.   It is
really impossible to arrive at the latter without first, consciously or otherwise, entering into the grand assumption of
the stability, hence inviolability, of social order as an implicit convention deeply embedded into the fabric of a good
part of our strategic heritage *not* to formulate a pattern of
strategy entirely contingent on the continuing subversion or
invasion of the opponent's social order.   Only so long as the
sanctity of social order obtains under the great weight of
tradition, then the delicate classical balance is maintained
in which its implicit convention, having so firmly expelled
social order, throws the mainstream of reasoning into the only
other avenue left, being the obsession with armed power and
classical solutions thus typified by quick 'decisive battle'.
It has been too frequently the luxury of the inviolability of
social order which has jettisoned strategic theory overboard
into the 'decisive battle' mentality so central in classicalism.   This theory that celebrates the obsession with armed
power strikes the conception of strategy from its natural
social basis.

I shall pursue this as we progress.   Suffice it to understand here that it is this genesis in thinking from which the
structure of classicalism has sprung.   The classical tradition, first matured in Napoleonic warfare and so eloquently
expressed by Clausewitz, may well have come from the new
social and political conditions which the French Revolution
had created in France and Europe as a whole.   Before this,
there had prevailed an international and domestic society that
was largely hierarchical, from the rigid, or at least pro-
claimed, status allocation of domestic social order to 'the
relative dignity of the monarchs and republics of Christen-

dom'.[2] Until the French Revolution, the notion of legitimacy
attached to the states-system was dynastic, concerned with the
status and rivalries of rulers who enjoyed prescriptive
rights. The dynastic principle operated through the connections between alliances and marriages, territorial claims and
dynastic claims, and the attempts at foreign disorders by cul-
tivating dynastic pretenders. With the exception of the
'Great Republics' that had elective, not hereditary constitu-
tions, this essentially was the mode of politics up to the
time of the French Revolution. After this a new principle of
legitimacy was to replace the old dynastic form, a 'popular'
principle founded on the claims and consent of the governed
wherein sovereignty passed from the individual ruler to the
nation he ruled. The popular principle of legitimacy was a
product of ideology in which prescriptive rights gave way to
an inherently more powerful, yet unstable system. The classical theory of strategy could only ignore the newly emerging
problems of social and international order and legitimacy,
the changes in which may well have made its practice possible,
by a wholly independent convention, woven deeply into its
fabric of reasoning. Whatever the case, our present purpose
must leave this rather oversimplified discussion for historians or strategists with an eye for the past because our
interest lies in contemporary theory that possesses little, if
any, recollection of the detailed historical conditions in
which our classical heritage was born, but does suffer from
the system of reasoning that this same heritage still rather
surreptitiously insists on forcing into our way of thinking.

In contrast to the chameleon-like pursuit of existence
through intended illusion, unspoken conventions, however
subtly blended into the fabric of our strategic heritage,
cannot very long survive the collapse of the narrow basis from

which they proceed.   This must be so especially for convention which robs theory of its true social basis, because this
process of theft only continues so long as the convention
obtains either through universal agreement to ignore this
basis or, far more importantly, through the mutual inability
of strategists to recognize the social bedrock from which
their theories derive.   Given time, any heritage can blend
familiarity into unquestioned fact, and from this, into simple
forgetfulness.   We only begin to remember the roots of our
reasoning when it becomes too painful to do otherwise.

Now at first sight, and as I continue along the central
thread of this analysis, a reaction may develop in the mind of
the reader that, after all, theory has little, if any, value
for the actual practice or conduct of war.   Theory, being in
the first instance, mostly a systematically organized or related set of general ideas, is not always easy to follow.   It
is not infrequently the case that a theorist is the last one
to make what he is trying to get across simple, clear and
carefully organized, that is to say, with the least amount of
unnecessary mystery possible.   Quite apart from the disin-
clination of theorists to pace their thinking to the ability
to absorb and interest of others, there remain peculiar to
theory a host of potential pitfalls.   It is not necessary to
discuss these here except to say that the theorist is continuously struggling, whatever his faults, to press a complex and
seemingly unwilling world into a systematically organized set
of ideas, which can render his attempts to persuade difficult
to digest.   Not infrequently theory is thus viewed with suspicion, disinterest or confusion, the result of which is that
the intended convert is lost to the conclusion that theory is
inherently recondite and specialist, being little more than an
intellectual exercise with nothing to say about practical

necessity (in this case, the relevance of social order to
armed conflict in international and social relations).

The fact is, quite simply, that this could not be utterly
further from the truth of the matter.   Theory, like anything
else of human endeavour, can be corrupt or silly, and its
effects even harmful.   But the crucial consideration here is
that intelligent theory can speak with some vision and influence because its capability, especially in the social subject
matter at hand, can be to sweep an area of the reality in
which we live into a new arrangement of understanding.
Theory performs this service because it can deliver to our
understanding not only this new arrangement but a driving
instinct and inner vision lying beyond the mere rearrangements
of facts, which otherwise would be lost to a spiritless and
dimly perceived reality.   The latter is precisely the state
of affairs in which Western strategists may find themselves
presently.   The firm conclusion here is really very simple.
To push aside theory in favour of the so-called 'real world'
or practical necessity can lead to error simply because this
'real world' especially in war, being before all else a wholly
integrated social activity, is made up of people in the first
place who carry with them a general vision or 'theory' about
its conduct and nature, however articulate.   So none of us
can escape consideration of theoretical questions, even those
who forget the importance of theory in favour of the 'actual
practicalities of war'.   In effect, the latter can play this
mental trick on themselves by passing over theory only to fall
back on to the level of 'practicalities' in which is always
concealed an implicit theory about their nature - the very
thing they seek to escape.   Whether one wishes to admit it or
not, one simply cannot sweep out of the larger consideration
of war the general vision about its nature that people carry

into it - including those who, consciously or otherwise, make
the misleading disclaimers of the value of theory in war.

If then the reality of war is largely, but by no means entirely, a result of the general vision or 'theory' (at whatever level of reasoning) of its nature that people carry into
it, then the theory of strategy is utterly vital - even to
those who are disinterested, if not hostile.   Indeed, these
sceptics of theory can only get away with their craft so long
as everyone agrees on an *implicit theory of strategy* cleverly
concealed in the fabric of tradition - the favourite breeding
ground of such miscalculation.   It is easy for the point
about 'practicalities' to be made when everyone visualizes
these in terms of a shared theory through which we come to
terms with the real world in the first place.   Having employed the services of theory to come to a common understanding of reality it is then tempting but ultimately catastrophic
to forget or discard the structure of reasoning that largely
determines which 'practicalities' we choose to recognize and
ignore.   For example, as I shall discuss later, there is
nothing in reality which demands that armed power should
always be the one prime obsession of the theory of strategy.
The 'practical' problems of armed power as an independent and
the prime instrument of strategy are largely there in the
first place because shared reasoning of classical strategists
has made armed power the last word in the theory of strategy
by agreeing to sweep problems of social order under the rug.
So the real answer is that what one is wholly convinced is a
practical obsession in war - a consideration firmly lodged in
the reality of war to be ignored only to one's own extreme
peril - is largely a consequence of implicit convention, a
gentleman's agreement which might be tossed out at any time.
This is only 'reality' so long as the agreement with which it

is supported obtains.   When this convention is broken the
entire matter comes right back to the question of general
theory.   It is then that the whole problem of the theory of
strategy comes crashing down on all heads.   It is my overall
task to argue that this has already occurred in the theory of
strategy which I shall suggest, using the Chinese example, has
broken loose from its old obsession with armed power supported
by a rather thin convention and taken on its natural obsession
with social order.   I propose to re-examine the general
vision or 'theory' of war that the human element carries into
its nature.   I therefore beg the acceptance that my line of
reasoning delivers (or at least attempts to) a down-to-earth
grasp of the importance of social order in armed conflict endemic in international and social relations, this organized
violence being the prime basis of distinction with which the
theory of strategy remains an area of analysis unto itself.
If the concern of strategy is the theory of the use of violence as a real instrument to fulfil moral and political ends,
that is to say, the conception of strategy is and must always
remain distinguished by the occurrence of violence in relation to the pursuit of ends of a moral and political nature,
then what I shall suggest is that the growing basis for general theory can be the notion of social order.   Otherwise, to
lose this distinction (violence) is to deny the existence of
this area of study - one which ignores the objections about
the unsavoury nature of this distinction founded on the belief
that it is the natural extension of social life and thus of
lasting merit.   To this I shall return shortly.

Finally, at this point I should make clear that what I
shall be pursuing is the discussion of paradigms of two forms
of thought about war, and these, for our present purposes, are
not to be taken as historical contradistinctions but as para-

digm opposites in the method of shedding light on structures
of reasoning that can play a vital role in the conduct of
armed conflict.   There may well be some relationship between
various periods in the history of armed conflict and the paradigms that influenced its conduct; that is to say, classical
theory can normally be associated, in varying degrees, with
the nineteenth and the first half of the twentieth centuries,
and the new more socially orientated considerations I suggest
are beginning to play an ever-increasing role within the
theory of strategy may well correspond to periods of armed
conflict in the future.   Nevertheless, it is central to the
present analysis to keep in mind at all times that, whatever
historical relations may exist, what I am proposing is the
discussion of paradigms of two forms of thought about war as a
means to persuade that the theory of strategy ought now to
take on board a host of social considerations it was built in
its classical formulation largely to ignore.   This is to help
strategists see past the blinds of convention that continue to
obscure theory today straight into where politically motivated
violence seems now more than ever headed.

Moreover, within our strategic heritage it is not difficult
to arrive at the impression that classical theory was very influential indeed, but this should not lead to the conclusion
that the social context of war had always been totally ignored
in the past by use of the classical device of contractual-like
assumptions.   Lenin and Douhet provide examples of theorists
who did dwell on this aspect of strategy.   Although neither
are within the scope of our present purposes, it is worth reminding that Lenin did see an intimate connection between the
social and state structure on the one hand, and the organization and application of armed power on the other.   He, as a
revolutionary, was indeed aware that the conduct of war was

only part military but also social, psychological and economic
in nature.   The possibility was appreciated that revolution,
which is fundamental changes in the social order, and war
could go hand in hand.   Now, the exact relationship between
social revolution and war that Lenin visualized need not
detain us here because he did not go to the theoretical
lengths of giving a formal redefinition of strategy expressed
in terms of social order (to be presented shortly) in which
all of the distinctions in time, space and form that desig-
nate the organization and application of armed power slip on
to a social basis never before experienced in the conduct of
war.   In any case, as explained, the present method to persuade strategists to take on board social considerations right
into the heart of theory by posing paradigms of two forms of
thought about war need not, and does not here, include a comprehensive consideration of the past history of strategic
thought.   For similar reasons, Douhet should not detain us
except to remind that his writings on the importance of offensive air power in the paralysis of the enemy's capacity (along
with the opposing population's will) to wage war did touch on
the relations between the conduct of war and its social context.   This is in spite of the fact that his notion of 'a
complete breakdown of the social structure' largely rested on
the assumption of the comparatively fragile quality of civilian morale that has not always been shown to be accurate.
Again, Douhet does not meet our present requirements because
the theoretical lengths were not contemplated whereby a formal
redefinition of strategy was expressed fully in terms of
social order - only possible by first identifying the contractual assumption at the genesis of classical theory and then
rebuilding a new theory of strategy from this insight.

Now, if my judgment is correct that a *free* conception of

strategy tends to turn itself back into its natural social
basis (that is, problems of social order become the prime
obsession of strategy) as swept out of the classical theory,
then strategists must direct their attention to the notion of
social order, however foreign to their classical sense of pri-
ority. This must be so simply because once the old convention to sweep problems of social order out of the picture by
agreeing on its inviolability thus leading to the obsessions
with armed power and 'decisive battle' has all been tossed
out, then theory must seek a new basis. This must be the
prime notion of social order on which a new and general theory
of strategy is constructed. This general theory of strategy
can only come to rest on the conception of social order from
which all other considerations issue in war simply because
there is no other item that can similarly serve the construction of such theory without unnatural and sometimes easily
ignored conventions. General theory, if it is to be real,
must lie beyond the confines of a gentlemen's agreement,
otherwise it would generally face being too easily tossed out.
Such theory must find its roots in the very nature of war
itself rather than implicit convention.

To pause for a brief diversion into general theory, I
shall, for the moment, pass over such considerations as its
assessment according to the range and precision of its expla-
nations and predictions, the adequacy of its empirical foundation, ability of the conceptual framework to reflect the complex realities of the social world, to reach here a certain
understanding. The theory of strategy must obviously rest on
a thread which is the most central to the nature of the subject at hand. There may, of course, be a whole series of
critical issues circulating throughout the actual conduct of
war; indeed these can at irregular times and circumstances

determine the outcome itself.   But they only circulate in
varied intensity of importance and timing at the sufferance of
the central thread dominating the very nature of the phenomenon theory seeks to grasp.   It is here that the deeper strategic provisions are found to be everywhere present in war, to
which all other issues are attached.   To say that real general theory can only therefore rest on its natural social basis
in which the prime strategic issue is the obsession with
social order is not to dismiss from the confines of theory all
other issues.   Rather, it is simply to re-order the avenues
of reasoning so that everything is no longer left dangling in
a state of false or contractual independence, but is newly
attached to what is always the first strategic consideration.
Here, it is the very rare, if any, general theory which is
truly universally applicable.   Nor is such theory intended as
a truly comprehensive theory of strategy.   To make the error
of viewing the former as necessarily involving the latter is
to ignore the possibility that the complexities of the real
world may well produce new combinations and considerations
that cannot be foreseen today, given the present state of the
empirical foundation on which this study is forced to rely.
*In fact what distinguishes general theory is that it rests on
the far deeper strategic provision than any other presently
visible, and, in particular, the reach of this throughout all
corners of the subject to which theory is addressed.*

   There also may be the not infrequent corruptions of extraordinary circumstances and false obsessions which seduce
theory from its natural social basis.   But these only come
into play in the first place, given present data, in so far as
the real social foundation of theory is frozen, and, as such,
cannot obviously prevail over the deeper strategic provisions
to the position of a general theory intended as a tool to per-

suade theorists to take on board the broad social considerations as the more elemental ones. This social foundation,
being the great hand that wields the instrument, is always
afforded prior consultation. In the first instance, the
'freezing' of theory so that its social roots are forgotten
can be given false life by implicit convention nursed along by
the poor habits of tradition, as already discussed. Here
again, this process of hardening must first start, as is
always the case, with the neutralization of the one cardinal
issue to which a free conception of strategy should always
return. Second, although contractual-like reasoning may well
have considerable influence in 'freezing out' the elemental
considerations of social order from the very heart of theory -
and this can continue so long as all agree to honour this
arrangement - real conditions can also freeze out, as it were,
considerations of social order from the actual conduct of war.
So that questions of social order may prevail in the conduct
of war, its social basis by which all is held together must
not remain frozen behind a wall of inaccessibility; that is
to say, the social resources by which the enemy conducts war
in the first place must be accessible. One can think of such
examples as the First World War and the Korean War in which,
regardless of how contractual the reasoning of strategists was
in the influencing of the conduct of these wars, the formulation and application of a strategy wholly based on the bleed-
ing dry of the enemy's social resources necessary for the conduct of war was in any event largely impossible. In the
former war, advances in weapons technology giving the frontal
defence a temporary but overwhelming advantage made it impossible for either side to reach out and destroy the social resources and order of the enemy and fashion an ongoing pattern
of strategy around this objective. The latter war, being

waged on a rather confined peninsula, rendered it difficult
for the opposing sides to engage in large-scale manoeuvring of
guerrilla forces widely dispersed behind the lines of the
enemy in the assault on the enemy's social resources. Not
only is this lack of adequate space a potential hindrance, but
most importantly, it is possible to imagine situations in
which there is not available a *sufficient mass of social resources or weight of social order* through which mass guerrilla
warfare is waged and sustained. This is conducted so as to
absorb or counterbalance the armed power of the enemy and this
mass-based guerrilla warfare is then extended into his social
order to bleed him dry of the capacity to wage war. In such
sparse conditions there is just not sufficient mass of social
resources and weight of social order in which insurgent forces
can be concealed and into which the opposing armed forces sink
as though in quicksand. Here, it would appear, there are few
options but to attempt to pursue a pattern of strategy that
makes use of the notion of the will to resist as a function of
armed forces in the hopes of a quick 'decisive battle' solution. All of this should become clearer as we progress.
Suffice it to say here that these rather special hindrances,
which may or may not prevail at any given time, should not
invalidate our desire to raise questions about the poorly researched social dimensions of strategy that may play a vital
role in the future if only because the old contractual reasoning inherent in classical theory that helped sweep out these
same dimensions from the conduct of armed conflict is now
beginning to break down. Hindrances may come and go but the
primal and social roots on which war is always conducted
remain the first strategic consideration in the realm of general theory. This leads to the larger question of mature
theory in which this study is intended simply as a *ballon*

d'essai. For mature theory, a much broader historical basis
is needed than the one on which I am obliged to rely in referring shortly to the Chinese experience with the insurgent
invasion of social order.   In the extension of the basis of
general theory, the exchange is always between the raw experience of war from which theory draws substance, and the elaboration of general theory from such experience to which this
theory should always return and enrich, especially in that we
become aware of the more elemental social considerations that
our heritage was largely built to ignore.

I now return to continue with the notion of war as an
articulate social activity deeply embedded in the question of
social order, in an attempt to give an entirely new life in
the nuclear age to the Clausewitzian conception of war as 'a
real political instrument, a continuation of political commerce, a carrying out of the same by other means'.[3]   There
are certain inalienable elements lodged in the foundation of
the theory of strategy which cannot be for ever liquidated in
theory or practice, even by the most clever of subtleties
nursed by tradition.   These elements lie in the notion of
social order, in the absence of which the idea of war simply
vanishes into the random chaos and violence of every man
against the other.   Strategists, being thus compelled to view
war as an articulate social activity, can only turn their
attention to armed power as the prime instrument of strategy
if some prior provision is made for the inviolability of
social order.   So long as everyone embraces, consciously or
otherwise, this convention, then social order simply fails to
appear as any consequence to the theory of strategy.   This
classical convention can indeed uproot the realities of war
and strategy from their everywhere prominent social foundations, leaving theory to embrace an obsession which is not its

natural one.   In contrast to this singularly thin convention,
it is really impossible to concentrate one's strategic reasoning on the instrument of armed power in the absence or compromise of the very social order which always must stand
behind this instrument of strategy.   In other words, theory
which prescribes the organization and application of armed
power as the instrument of strategy is unthinkable in the
demise of the very social order on which such application
ultimately rests in the first place.   Here is the natural
obsession of theory which is everywhere present in war and to
which all other issues are attached.   In sum, it is the great
hand of moral and social order that everywhere wields the
instruments of strategy and if the former is compromised the
latter must follow.

Beyond this, the larger conception of war finds its roots
firmly lodged in the nature of social order itself.   This is
germane to the considerations of strategists because general
theory, as already suggested, cannot ultimately come to rest
on thin convention and its unnatural obsessions with armed
power but on the very nature of the subject at hand.   The
theory of strategy and its instruments simply must not be
divorced from the very social and political context in which
they are intended to serve.   War (and the employment of
organized violence which delivers its theory and practice into
the special considerations of strategists) is the natural
extension of social life.   So must be the reasoning central
to the theory of strategy as an essential description of its
nature and conduct.   The roots of violence do not so much
draw substance from the raw nature of man but from that of men
cast into *social relations*.   It is the conception of social
relations, established patterns of which are the essence of
social order, that gives rise to the twin notions of power and

morality.   In terms of these two, war is the natural extension of the substance of social life.

The pursuit of power as a uniquely moral activity is made
necessary by the very nature of social relations.   *It is
inherent in the nature of these relations that the actions of
men are the potential means to the ends of others, power being
for our purposes the ability to command the actions of others.*
The temptation to command the actions (recognition and services) of others as the prime means to one's own ends only
arises in the course of entering into social relations in the
first place.   Thus social relations are, in the first
instance, power relations.   The root of all substantive power
is the casting of men into social relations in which everyone
is potentially a prime means to the ends of others, and
through which some gain the ability to reach out along the
established fabric of these relations and draw unto their
pursuit of ends the actions of others.   Only through social
relations are the recognition and services of individuals rendered transferable, in any substantive way, to the ends of
others.   Here, it is only within the conception of social
order that the notion of power is truly consummate.

If power is a product of the relation itself without which
considerations of power would simply vanish, the conception of
power is a relative one because, having issued from a relation, the measure of one centre of power can be conceived in
terms of no more than the measure of another.   However uni-
lateral the exercise of power may seem, it is always a relative consideration.   This is to say, since the notion of
power is only alive in a relation or set of relations, the
ability to command the action of others is little more than
the *excess* over this same ability of others.   Moreover, I
pause to acknowledge the existence of varied notions of power

employed throughout the spectrum of sociological theory,
while setting out, for the purposes of explanation, in brief
and general terms the notion of power that best serves our
specialized interests.   By this arrangement we avoid a host
of sociological minutiae surrounding the many, often paradoxi-
cal, aspects of power that would divert and may confuse the
present interests that this notion is intended only to serve.
What matters is that strategists have a general grasp of the
notion of power that best enables them to pursue an understanding of the fundamental alterations which have recently
taken hold of the theory of strategy.   Power can be regarded
as the coercive ability to command the actions of others, particularly so in the theory of strategy held apart from the
rest of reasoning about social life by the conception of violence as an instrument of policy.   Power can also be regarded
as the legitimized ability to command the actions of others,
that is to say, authority is that form of power in which the
actions of others are articulated because this articulation is
regarded as legitimate.   Here is felt the weight of moral
order, a unified system of social values and norms by which
the ability to command the actions of others is upheld and
exercised.   The distinction here is an analytical one, since
empirically authority as one form of power and coercion as
another exist together in many combinations throughout social
life.   Although it is necessary to recognize that both may be
exercised in conflict with one another, in theory they should
not be, and this is precisely the notion of power I shall
employ.   Classical theory could well ignore all of this, particularly bringing considerations of authority into the notion
of power, because the submission of the enemy, or at least
some political advantage, was largely thought of in terms of
bludgeoning him through 'decisive battle' or the lesser com-

promise of his armed forces by some minor act of violence,
wherein problems of authority, moral and social order had
little place in the conduct of war and in relation to the
enemy.

The instant a number of individuals or groups are cast into
relations with one another then the problem of power springs
to life as each discovers the real potential of the actions of
others in the pursuit of ends. Now the judicious individual
sees that, although he may not desire power, he must pursue it
simply to preserve what powers he already possesses. He,
like all others, finding himself unable to do without the
amenities of social life, is thrown into a fabric of social
relations and a general pursuit of power behind which lies the
assumption (and fear) that although not all are desirous of
power by nature, there exist or may exist sufficient numbers
of individuals or groups with an insatiable desire for power
that all are compelled into a like pursuit simply to retain
what power they already possess. Otherwise, the real danger
is everywhere present in social life that the configuration of
social relations through which power is remitted will shift in
such a way as to facilitate the transfer to the ends of others
a portion of one's own recognition and actions. The worst
enemy of society is the principles on which it is founded.
Built into the nature of social relations and through this
into the notion of social order is this incessant pursuit of
power which, being a relative consideration, can never freely
admit, on its own, the notion of limitation, and thus tends to
the extreme in which violence is the prime instrument. The
unlimited hence violent struggle for power is the natural
extension of social life. Violence is rooted in the nature
of society fuelled by the relative essence of power and a fear
concerning the appetites of others that can arise only in the

course of entering into social relations.   The fact that the
very nature of social relations gives rise to the notion of
power condemns society to the spectre of a violent and general
struggle for power.   War, as an articulate social activity in
the pursuit of power by means of violence, is an extension of
the problem of power inherent in social life.   It is a continuation of the social pursuit of power by other means.   The
classical theorists were simply unable to carry through with
their fundamental insight into the political nature of war and
connect the pursuit of power with its inalienable social
roots; and how could they, having condemned themselves to a
scheme of reasoning which, by nature, ignored these roots in
the first place.   We have inherited the same difficulty which
still haunts contemporary theory.

In the first instance, what distinguishes war from social
life is the notion of 'other means', as we know the whole conception of the latter to be far more than a mere struggle for
power in which the employment of violence reigns supreme.
The great dam that denies the flood of social relations their
natural route of decline towards violence and anarchy is the
fact that in the course of entering into these relations
towards a state of social order, not only is power pursued
over others, but social values and norms are fixed into some
form of consensus.   By necessity, social life is a moral
life.   Like the thread that binds a string of beads, it is
only this moral fibre in which is found a consensus on social
values and norms embracing a shared conception of ends which
society should pursue along with a propriety of means (among
which are the actions of individuals) that prevents society
from falling into its natural consequences.   Here reigns the
vital propriety of means which subdues the use of violence
and, equally important, upholds established social relations,

this is, the moral conditions under which power is remitted through these relations with some measure of order and peace. This moral order at the centre of social life literally saves society from itself.

Moreover, not only is social morality founded on the need of organizing and upholding the general transfer of recognition and services from some individuals and groups to the ends of others being inherent in the very nature of social relations, but this moral order uplifts social life from a mere summation of its separate parts. Beyond the tragedy of social life - and its extension into war - that only here are recognition and actions rendered alienable giving rise to the conception of power, the social world, having thus for ever to suffer the principles on which it is founded, is driven into a moral necessity from which emerges a superior moral world. If society were only the sum, it could possess no larger moral value than its component parts which, by themselves, know neither the discovery of power nor the superior consciousness of social morality. Social life suggests to the consciousness of men moral appetites of which they would otherwise know nothing. In this morality is the assembly of all things to which men attach the highest price - a price which is in excess of the moral necessity from which it derives. Social morality is never simply a crude consequence and reflection of the problem of power inherent in social life but, having started here, raises society to participate in higher forms of moral life. Moral and social order goes beyond the needs of moral necessity. It has its own nature distinct from this necessity and those individuals who constitute it. Social order, then, fulfils the one real condition for serving as the object of moral behaviour. This order, being an established fabric of social relations throughout which power is peacefully remitted and resting on a conception of morality which gives this remittance moral value, constitutes by itself a moral end. It is our present conclusion, then, that social action is moral when it has for its end the notion of social order through which men participate in higher forms of moral life. Since the prime direction of social action is also by necessity the pursuit of power, which is the attachment to the notion of social order through which power is remitted and its maintenance and protection, such power does indeed constitute a moral end. The pursuit of power is a uniquely social and moral activity which is, at once, everywhere present in moral life, that is, in the social order through which men participate in higher forms of moral life, and, at the same time, it is a real end of moral purpose. If the conception of power is, by necessity, a moral one, then the higher forms of moral life are also rarely free from disturbance by the struggle for power through which they are given expression. The relationship between social morality and power will be further discussed in later phases of the analysis of my discontent with classical theory.

For the moment it must suffice to consider our present conclusion in the light of war as the natural extension of social life. War is the supreme expression of social morality because this morality has taken into its hands the real use of violence for ends of a moral nature. It is the natural extension of social morality into an act of violence through which is expressed the collective need for attachment to a particular social and moral order, its protection, maintenance and extension. *War is the natural extension of the social pursuit of power by other means of which social morality is the principal author.* This morality is, by necessity, everywhere entwined with the pursuit of power, that is, the pursuit

of social order through which power is remitted, and it gains
supreme expression when this pursuit is, at once, directed to
the larger considerations of social order through which men
participate in higher forms of moral life and moreover intensified by the real use of violence.   Strategists could claim
no area of study were it not for the fact that the conception
of war, unlike the normal run of social life, is an act of
violence as an articulate social activity of which social
morality is the principal author.   That is why strategists
should see this conception in terms of a truly complete social
science loosely referred to as that group of disciplines whose
interests are in man and society.   The nature of war is
shaped by the moral force which gives it purpose and design.
Violence, although endemic in the nature of social life,
being firmly rooted in the principles on which it is founded,
is so volatile an instrument that it can acquire a reason and
force of its own and thereby violate the moral will which
brought it to life and the moral ends to which it is directed.
Violence, if left to itself, simply follows a random and
excessive path for ever grasping in all directions for an
increment of power which by nature rarely satisfies the fear
inherent in power relations about the appetites of others and
its relative and unlimited essence.   Here, violence ceases to
be the *moral* instrument (having normally been taken up by this
morality for ends of its own nature) and random destruction
takes over with a design rooted in the contrary nature and
conditions of violence itself.   War draws its nature from its
real author, never from the instrument alone.   It is only
thin classical convention which turned the eyes of strategists
from the former to the latter.   It is the moral character of
social order which is the great hand that wields the instruments of war.   The will to wage war is everywhere the moral

consideration as a function of moral and social order.   This
will is a real social and moral force.   Social order through
which men participate in higher forms of moral life is the
genesis from which war derives its moral fabric and essential
design.   The conception of war as an articulate social and
moral activity with moral intent, end and instrument can only
be founded in its unifying thread issuing from the moral
fabric of social order.

To end now with a final word of introduction: any exposi-
tion of theory is usually a mixture of philosophical assumptions, theoretical insights and empirical observations.   Our
present conclusion is that war is an articulate moral and
social activity as the natural extension of the social pursuit
of power by other means, of which social morality is the principal author.   Gained from this philosophical exordium is the
relevance of social order to general theory - the theoretical
insight that I suggest for the consideration of strategists
who find a growing poverty in classical reasoning.   The means
by which I hope to persuade of this fact is the collection,
translation and discussion of Chinese Communist documents
dealing with problems of strategy, tactics and social order.
The empirical observations made through, as best can be done
under prevailing circumstances, these writings of Chinese
strategists on insurgency are used solely for the purposes of
theoretical generalization.   For all its difficulties, I am
obliged to use the Chinese case of protracted war simply
because it is, as yet, the first and most carefully reasoned
example of the real practice of the points about general
theory to which I draw attention.   Before commencing this
discussion it is vital to caution that in order to build my
case I shall be shifting ground continuously between the level
of general theory, that is, the social insight into the theory

of strategy, and on the other hand, the empirical observations
of its practice made through selected writings of Chinese
strategists.   The premise from which I do so is, of course,
the one discussed above.   The method here is to employ the
services of the Chinese experience solely for the purposes of
theoretical generalization in such a manner that the central
thread of the argument directing attention to the relevance of
social order to general theory is not lost in a body of source
material that is too comprehensive for the limited service it
is intended to deliver.   Finally, the difficulties of using
the Chinese case would entail a considerable study in itself.
I shall only refer to some of these later.   What is necessary
to mention at present is that I draw out of the not infrequently undocumented and misleading details of the Chinese
case (that remain vital to general theory whatever state of
real documentation they suffer) the general principles which
I suggest are entirely applicable to general theory.   This is
my one interest which, having employed the observations made
through the writings of Chinese strategists, is intended to
arrive at a set of conclusions concerning the nature of general theory.   Otherwise, interminable complications, most of
which may never be resolved given the present state of Chinese
source materials, would lose the general conclusions of this
proposal in a mass of unresolved detail which (whatever its
interest to students of China) would cost our purposes more
than it serves.

I have already concluded introductory comments on the relevance of social order to the theory of strategy, and outlined
the broad assumptions on the basis of which this discussion
shall be conducted.   The following chapter examines the
theory of protracted war as outlined by Mao Tse-tung in order to
show that armed power as the prime instrument of strategy and

the main centre of the will to resist in the classical sense
has undergone a radical formulation. This change is illustrated by demonstrating that the distinctions in time, space
and form with which the organization and application of armed
power is formulated are, for the first time in war, socially
based; that is, these distinctions are based on the invasion
of social order which the instrument of armed power now simply
serves. If this prime instrument of strategy is no longer
independent of immediate considerations of social order as it
is in the reasoning behind the classical view, then under certain conditions the whole problem of social order becomes the
prime obsession of general theory on which a free conception
of strategy should always come to rest.

If social order is indeed relevant to the theory of strategy, then chapter 3 shows through the discussion of paradigm
opposites how, in theory, it must also be compelling. This
is to say, classical theory and its very thin convention
should always give way to a pattern of strategy based on the
armed invasion of social order. This is discussed by setting
up two opposing patterns of strategy, examining their underlying assumptions, the interplay between these, and the nature
of the outcome to the fatal disadvantage of classical theory.

Having opened the door to social order in chapter 2 and
then discussed its fatal consequences in terms of conflicting
strategic assumptions in the third chapter, I turn to a
theoretical expansion of this new conception of strategy and
develop further the discussion of paradigm opposites. I
refer to this new strategy in chapter 4 as *revisionist* theory
because it returns the theory of strategy back into its
natural social basis so firmly assumed out of classical
theory, in addition to so giving new life, in the nuclear age,
to the Clausewitzian conception of war as a real political

instrument. Beyond providing a theoretical expression to
strategic revisionism, I examine its applicability to general
theory and discuss why classical theory could never so
qualify. I conclude with suggestions on the limitations of
general theory.

Chapter 5 returns the analysis to additional empirical
observations on the Chinese case made through the writings of
Chinese strategists to support further the purposes of theoretical generalization. This involves an illustration of the
prime means of the invasion of social order, being, in this
case, effectively applied in terms of land revolution. The
object is to show how the Chinese themselves viewed the notion
of land revolution (designed specifically to meet unique
strategic and social conditions) as an invasion of the fabric
of the opponent's social order, that is, social relations
through which power is remitted into his hands for the conduct
of war. This is later tied up with the previously discussed
reformulation of the organization and application of armed
power given in the theory of protracted war as the armed servant of this invasion of social order. I thereby conclude
that the instrument of armed power, through the movement of
its internal distinctions in time, space and form, has now
shifted on to an entirely new basis of formulation and servi-
tude in which social order and its invasion through land revolution is now the one great obsession. This compelling
obsession with social order is thus woven along the central
thread of my entire analysis to its natural place in general
theory. Although the pattern of reasoning woven into a revisionist cloth may, and indeed must, embrace many different
combinations designed to meet varied strategic and social conditions, these new designs should rarely stray from the central thrust of general theory. This should be so simply

because such theory is firmly rooted in the very nature of
social life itself, rather than in thin classical convention.

But to return to the minutiae of the Chinese case, the experience of the Chinese strategists was never so simple as the
shorthand form of reasoning sketched in above.   They found
themselves continuously embroiled in long and bitter disputes
about the nature of strategy, tactics and social order.
Whatever mixture of personalities and Party politics was involved, these disputes had real strategic content to the considerations of the Chinese Communist Party, faced with the
first problem of survival and, beyond this, the avenue to victory.   The most illustrative of these for our purposes was
the division over the role of guerrilla warfare versus classical or regular warfare to meet the KMT innovation of block-
house strategy first used in the Fifth KMT Encirclement Campaign (September 1933-November 1934).   The successes of this
campaign led to the defeat of the Red Army and the Long March.
The dispute examined in chapter 6 over the origins of this
defeat was in essence formulated, on the one side, in revisionist terms, and on the other, in classical or regular terms,
and thus is of very special interest because it draws out of
the real practice of war the sorts of conclusion I suggest in
terms of paradigm opposites and the more elemental considerations of general theory.

Having more or less won the day as a result of the lessons
of this defeat, the later writings are examined in chapter 7
of the Chinese strategists who favoured a revisionist pattern
of strategy in which the form and movement of armed power as
an instrument of strategy is conceived largely with regard
to the invasion of social order - this being a wholly compelling shift from the assumptions and obsessions of classical
theory, and contributing to the striking successes of its

inventors. What this involved was the formulation of guerrilla warfare, being a dispersal of armed power into the
fabric of the opponent's social order, so as to conduct a
thorough programme of land revolution through which the invasion of social order is consummated. Our conclusion is that
the instruments of strategy in protracted war, of which armed
power is only one, form a continuum in which these instruments
embrace new form and movement at precise points in time and
space. At the roots of this continuum is the obsession with
social order which armed power now only 'polices', thereby
initiating on the level of theory a simple shift in strategic
assumptions through which general theory finds its real basis
in social order. The shift is so fundamental to the conception of strategy that the classical assumptions concealed in
the fabric of our heritage for so long are simply thrown away,
leaving theory, once free from narrow classical convention, to
find its natural social basis and obsessions with social
order.

The final and longest chapter is introduced by a brief discussion of where revisionist theory is likely to be placed in
the mainstream of contemporary strategic thinking; in particular, with regard to the notion of violence as an instrument
of policy in the nuclear age. More and more, the realization
will come that the pursuit of moral and social objectives by
real violence can here obtain in the poorly researched social
dimensions of strategy the results which this pursuit is
otherwise unable to attain. If strategists are to grasp and,
equally important, be persuaded of the primal shifts that are
freeing the conduct of war into its natural social state
wherein the very social considerations classical theory could
pass over by convention now prevail everywhere, then they
must return to the roots of classical reasoning, first

expressed most eloquently in Clausewitz.   So that present-day
strategists may see into the beginnings of how their reasoning
may have come to be shaped and still is influenced in one
degree or another by the undercurrents which continue to flow
today, I use the skeleton of revisionist theory developed in
the prior chapters to analyse Clausewitz in a way that no
classical theorist could do so.   By this route, in which the
theoretical writings of Clausewitz are employed as an expository aid to represent certain elements in classical theory, I
seek to free strategists from the chains of the past by the
further discussion of paradigm opposites so that they might
appreciate where politically motivated violence seems more
than ever headed in the nuclear age.   In this analysis of
Clausewitz's theoretical writings there are two considerations
worth mentioning right away to avoid misunderstanding in this
last chapter, along with the intervening chapters that lead up
to it.   As a way of illustrating how all classical theory
has, in one manner or another, rested on the mishandling of
assumptions on which it was constructed by examining this
structural defect in Clausewitz's work, it is worth reminding
that there may well be considerable differences between this
work and later interpretations of Clausewitz by successive
generations of strategists.   This need not detain us since
the present method is not an historical comparison but, as
earlier explained, a posing of paradigm opposites in which
Clausewitz's theoretical writings have an illustrative role to
play.   Moreover, while examining the above-mentioned structural defect in his work we should recognize that Clausewitz
did not claim to have presented a finished or unified theory
of war.   Our concern will be the manner in which he under-
took theory construction, in whatever state of unity and completion, where he sought to build a model of war in the

absolute form by use of assumptions that were mishandled or
forgotten when new considerations were introduced which con-
flicted with these original assumptions. In short, such
assumptions in the heart of theory construction became an
embarrassment best forgotten that can lead readers of his
theoretical work astray even today. This is illustrative of
all classical theory in one degree or another. Although it
is not necessary for this purpose of illustration of the way
classical theorists mishandled or ignored the assumptions on
which they were working, one can take this notion of forgotten
assumptions inherent in Clausewitz's theoretical writings a
little further and suggest that here is the hitherto unnoticed
thread that does provide a kind of structural unity that the
author himself did not see and which is the single common
factor in all classical theory, however much this body of
theory may seem disjointed, multifaced and structureless.

What is also important to our conclusion of general theory
is a reminder of its limitations as discussed, the interplay
of strategic assumptions on which it hinges, and most important, the philosophical exordium set out above. If my position is correct that the essence of the conception of war is
that it is an articulate social and moral activity, the
natural extension of the social pursuit of power by the real
use of violence of which social morality is the principal
author, then there should remain little other more firm basis
for strategic theory than its natural obsession with social
order. Otherwise, strategists may become lost in the political absurdities of nuclear war, the denial of the real use of
violence in deterrent theory, and the fatal insistence on a
classical convention still influential in regular warfare and
far too thin for the weight of general theory. Once the
theoretical issues are clearly set out, this should engender

little surprise because the struggle for power by means of
real violence, being endemic in international and social relations, if blocked from full expression on some avenues, inevitably finds others.   If this built-in need for collective
violence is held to be untrue, then the very nature of social
life and the principles on which it is founded would have to
be somehow denied.   Here is where the firm guarantee of our
area of study resides while drawing from the resources of a
complete social science loosely referred to as that group of
disciplines whose interests are in man and society.

For those whose orthodox training encourages them to handle
such philosophical considerations as though they had little or
nothing to do with the theory of strategy, here are explained
- through the notion of violence and where it comes from, the
problem of power and from where it springs, the moral threads
running through both and finally, how all of these come together in social order with which all theory construction must
somehow deal - the first building blocks (along with their
rather special mix) of our area of study.   Strategists in the
past too often could pass over all of this by way of a silent
contract embedded in classical tradition that virtually held
theory together.

2

The social premise of protracted war

Western strategists are by now familiar with the strategy of insurgency first developed largely by Mao Tse-tung, later imitated by revolutionary movements in South-east Asia and, one fears, now engulfing southern Africa.   The overall pattern is generally the same.   The insurgents attempt to establish secure bases wherein (for all practical purposes) the rule of the government is overthrown and insurgent rule substituted, the social and political structure altered to conform with revolutionary principles, and the people re-educated.   The government naturally cannot tolerate these autonomous islands and sets out to crush them using military force.   The counter-insurgent forces are then drawn into a debilitating war of attrition in which the insurgent forces use guerrilla tactics to harass them continually and in depth.   A long struggle ensues in which the counter-insurgent forces are gradually worn down and the insurgents extend their areas of influence and establish fresh bases.   Finally, when the time is ripe, the insurgents abandon purely guerrilla tactics for conventional warfare, being strong enough to challenge the opponent's regular forces in open combat with large formations.

The West is also familiar with two basic elements of the

strategy of Maoist guerrilla warfare.   The first is that success in the struggle goes to the side which succeeds in
mobilizing popular support (embodied in Western manuals is the
cliché about the need to win the 'hearts and minds' of the
people).   The second is the element of time.   Implicit in
any guerrilla strategy, regardless of ideology, is the tactical scheme of evasion and withdrawal, of attacking weak enemy
elements and avoiding confrontation with strong ones.   The
insurgent leaders must be endlessly patient in building up
their strength and in the wearing down of the opponent's will.
(The British in Malaya, for instance, enjoying a number of
military and political advantages, were kept in play for
eleven years by the Communist insurgents, who even now are
still in being in cadre form, ready to operate on a larger
scale if opportunity offers.)   Western strategists plan hope-
fully for short campaigns and quick decisions.   The insurgent
is prepared to use time as a weapon and prepare and plan for
protracted war.

So far insurgency and classicalism are on common ground.
The principles of war in the classical sense as understood by
Clausewitz, Jomini or Liddell Hart are as yet unaltered by new
strategies.   There is nothing novel about alternating disper-
sion with concentration, patiently building up a superior
force and finally going over to offensive action which alone
can secure a military decision.   As a result, this aspect of
insurgency has been readily grasped, but the deeper and fundamental strategic provisions concerning the nature of the mass
mobilization of the people into new social structures have
been overlooked.   The fact is that from the Chinese Communist
point of view this mobilization of the masses into a new moral
and social order is the cardinal principle of Maoist guerrilla
warfare.   The way that the strategy of such a war is unfolded

is entirely determined by the rate and extent of its progress.

In other words, Maoist principles of protracted war form a continuum in which the instruments of strategy, of which armed power is only one, embrace new form and movement at precise points in time and space. In order to grasp the reasoning behind this strategy and the way it has exposed the one fatal catch in classical theory, it is necessary to appreciate that at the roots of this continuum is everywhere the obsession with social order which armed power now simply 'polices'. This initiates on the level of theory a simple shift in strategic assumptions through which general theory finds its true basis in social order. What I propose is to start unfolding my discontent with classical theory by examining the notion of armed power as an instrument of strategy in the theory of protracted war. I do so simply because, as already mentioned, in classical theory this instrument is pre-eminent, independent of immediate considerations of social order, and the main centre of the will to wage war. If it is the case that this pillar of traditional theory has suffered a radical formulation, then traditional assumptions are suspect. This may indeed provide some answers for the intense frustration of the recent *débâcle* in Indo-China and the considerable success of Maoist insurgent doctrine in mainland China. What is now more important, Western strategists must learn from these experiences, which cannot help but persuade further imitation that feeds on a violation of a nineteenth-century convention already far too thin for comfort. Once the door - behind which the poor habits of tradition breed - is flung open to the obsession with social order, it is very difficult to force it shut again.

The Chinese strategists were the first to appreciate a substantive reformulation of the employment of armed power as an

instrument of invasion of social order.   Now, the employment
of this instrument is generally expressed in terms of various
distinctions in time, space and form delineating the form and
movement of armed power in the field.   My present concern is
that these distinctions are no longer independent of immediate
considerations of social order, as in the classical obsession
with armed power and quick military solutions, but have indeed
slipped away from classical principles on to a social premise
which is common to all of them.   This premise is the distribution, rate and depth of revolutionary mass mobilization in
the field on which these distinctions in time, space and form
are socially based in a manner never before experienced in
war.   They are given life in the first place by considerations of social order, that is, by a notion of revolutionary
mass mobilization which rests entirely on the destruction of
established social order.   Moreover, these distinctions move
against each other in relative importance as the strategic
continuum progresses through its various phases.   That is to
say, not only are these distinctions based on considerations
of social order, but the way they are reshuffled in relative
importance at varied times rests entirely on changing conditions in the invasion of social order which they serve.   At
first sight this may seem difficult to visualize, but it is
really very elementary, simply because the distinctions in
this line of reasoning are so well connected.   All connections in time, space and form which express the form and movement of armed power as an instrument of strategy lead directly
to a social premise involving the distribution, rate and depth
of the invasion of social order.   In short, social order is
the prime obsession to which all other considerations are
attached - especially the instrument of armed power.

   To pause briefly for an appreciation of the notion of mass

mobilization, it means something much more than creating a
military and civil organization for the exploitation and
direction of a mass of people for the conduct of war.   It is
a far deeper consideration involving the real destruction of
established order, and the painstaking reconstruction of a new
one in which social and power relations are wrenched out of
the grasp of the opponent through which power is concentrated
into his hands and rechannelled into the hands of the insurgent.   The crucial process is the alteration of the established fabric of social relations through which the opponent
draws the power to wage war so that a mass of people can be
rewoven into a new fabric of social and power relations from
which they cannot escape.   In this the insurgent slowly
builds up behind his will and capacity to wage war a firm
social base and order by virtually consuming that of his
opponent on which, of course, his will and capacity likewise
rest.   The moral side of the invasion of social order - this
invasion being an alteration of the fabric of social relations
through which power inherent in social life is served up for
the conduct of war - is everywhere the key on which balances
the entire strategy.   If the moral order on which rests a
fabric of social and power relations is compromised, then the
fabric it upholds goes with it.   Otherwise, in the absence of
this key, the raw use of violence through the instrument of
armed power can only herd a mass of people into a new social
order *but cannot make this a moral order.*   Armed power is
unable to police every social relation, action and thought;
all this instrument can provide is armed protection to a moral
and social transformation of a mass of people from one social
order into another.   If the process of mass mobilization into
a new fabric of social and power relations does not strike at
the moral heart of established social order, then as the eyes

of violence are not looking, a mass of people simply drifts
back towards the moral attraction of old social and power
relations.   At this point in the argument I must beg the
tolerance of the reader.   We shall leave the notion of mass
mobilization as an armed invasion of social order for later
consideration of a more detailed nature.   For the moment it
must suffice simply to appreciate the real meaning of mass
mobilization in the Chinese sense.   I take this procedure
simply because everything cannot be discussed at once, and it
is the present object to determine the social premise of protracted war in light of the instrument of armed power.   Only
then can a substantive analysis of matters of a social nature
be of any interest to strategists who, having witnessed the
demise of armed power as the last word in classical strategy,
see no solutions save those I intend.

   I attempt now to explain how Chinese insurgent strategy
rests on a reformulation of armed power in the larger terms of
the compromise of the opponent's will and capacity to wage war
through the invasion of social order.   The present method in
this and later chapters is to quote freely from the writings
of Mao Tse-tung and others in the hope that this will trace
the path of this reformulation through what appears, at first
sight, to be a largely unintelligible and rambling series of
documents on matters which have little in common.   In part,
the difficulty lies in a serious language and cultural gap,
not to mention the problem of access to these documents in the
first place.   If this were not enough, these documents by Mao
and other leading Chinese strategists were generally written
under the most appalling conditions at varied times and circumstances within a web of changing motives for an audience
which shared so many assumptions and experiences, that West-
erners find themselves at a distinct disadvantage.   For all

this, a pattern in strategic reasoning does indeed emerge
simply because Chinese strategists had to satisfy real social
and strategic conditions; and that they did so with implicit
clarity and forcefulness, if not outright theoretical precision, is witnessed by their extraordinary successes in the
ultimate test of real war.   This may provide an answer to the
curious lack of substantive concern by Western strategists in
a matter of cardinal interest.

This pattern in strategic reasoning which sadly remains
scattered in its virgin state throughout a number of Chinese
documents can be pulled together into nine overall distinctions in time, space and form which delineate the strategic
employment of armed power.   These are in *time* (stage one:
strategic retreat, stage two: strategic stalemate, stage
three: strategic counter-offensive); *space* (insurgent base
areas, guerrilla zones, counter-insurgent strongholds); and
form (mobile, guerrilla and positional warfare).   In terms
of the unfolding of insurgent operations, time is measured by
little more than the changes in the rate of the mobilization
of a mass of people into new social and power relations.
Spatial distinctions rest on its distribution and depth in
the field.   Distinctions in form may appear to have little to
do with considerations of a social nature but, indeed, have
everything to do with this social premise as, in theory,
mobile warfare is prominent under conditions of low mobilization (stage one), guerrilla warfare blossoms into prominence
in medium conditions (stage two), and positional warfare is
prominent only in conditions of its highest possible level
(stage three).

In a maturing strategic situation through the three stages
in time, the pace, depth and distribution of the invasion of
social order engenders a series of changes in the relative

importance of each distinction which, in turn, serves this
invasion.   Mao Tse-tung describes protracted war in terms of
these stages:

> It can reasonably be assumed that this protracted war will
> pass through three stages.   The first stage covers the
> period of the enemy's strategic offensive and our strategic
> defensive.   The second stage will be the period of the
> enemy's strategic consolidation and our preparation for the
> counter-offensive.   The third stage will be the period of
> our strategic counter-offensive and the enemy's strategic
> retreat.[1]

The idea behind this strategy is to 'attain our goal of
strategic protractedness, which means gaining time to increase
our capacity to resist',[2] simply because, as is further explained, 'revolutionary forces grow only gradually, and this
fact determines the protracted nature of our war'.[3]   In stage
one initial insurgent mobilization attracts enemy attention
and is thus at its lowest level, compelling the weaker insurgent forces to engage in a strategic retreat into more secure
base areas.   During this retreat, mobile warfare is the form
that reflects this weakness and the 'regular' nature and
strength of enemy forces;   that is, they advance in large conventional formations backed by the usual supply columns and
depending on road and (or) rail lines of communication.   The
mobile form in Western terms seems to connote a war of manoeuvre, one in which the object is to draw the opponent's regular forces into the base area where he can be gradually worn
down without risking any major engagement, sacrificing territory for time.   Positional warfare is a secondary form of use
of armed power waiting to be reshuffled into positions of
prime importance in later phases.   The guerrilla form is
growing in importance but, depending on prevailing conditions,

is generally considered to be secondary to the mobile form,
especially in the initial phases of the retreat. The notion
of a strategic retreat or defensive is rarely a rout but
rather a carefully planned fighting withdrawal in which is
necessary a precise appreciation of the trade of territory for
time so as to manoeuvre the opponent's regular forces into the
appropriate expanse of base area. As regards this Mao
explains:

> The primary problem, and a serious one too, is how to con-
> serve our strength and await an opportunity to defeat the
> enemy. Therefore, the strategic defensive is the most
> complicated and most important problem facing the Red Army
> in its operations.[4]

It is simply because 'in concrete terms, and especially
with regard to military operations, when we talk of the people
in the base area as a factor, we mean that we have an armed
people',[5] the drawing in of enemy forces into regions of hostile people and foreign social order is precisely calculated
in terms of how much base area is needed to cushion, absorb
and then bleed the armed power of the opponent in an extended
guerrilla war. As Mao suggests, 'in appearance a fully
planned strategic retreat is made under compulsion, but in
reality it is effected in order to conserve our strength and
bide our time to defeat the enemy, to lure him in deep'.[6]
The dimensions and especially depth of a sea of hostile people
in insurgent base areas are served up to balance the armed
power of the opponent:

> We advocate retreating to the base area and luring him in
> deep, for only by so doing can we create or find conditions
> favourable for our counter-offensive.... The terminal
> points for retreat in a base area can be generally divided
> into three types, those in the frontal, those in the

middle, and those in the rear section of the base
area.[7]

These favourable conditions, for which a military price is
paid in casualties and territory, are calculated in terms of
the time required to secure further depth and distribution of
the invasion of social order through revolutionary mass
mobilization.   Mao explains that such conditions are social,
and determine the passing from one phase to another in the
insurgent organization and application of armed power:

In the light of our past experience, during the stage of
retreat we should in general secure at least two of the
following conditions before we can consider the situation
as being favourable to us and unfavourable to the enemy and
before we can go over to the counter-offensive.   These
conditions are:

(1)   The population actively supports the Red Army.

(2)   The terrain is favourable for operations.

(3)   All the main forces of the Red Army are concentrated.

(4)   The enemy's weak spots have been discovered.

(5)   The enemy has been reduced to a tired and demoralized
      state.

(6)   The enemy has been induced to make mistakes.[8]

While suggesting that 'the first condition, active support
of the population, is the most important one for the Red Army'
since 'it means having a base area', Mao traces the consequences of this largely social consideration to a majority of
the remaining conditions: 'Moreover, given this condition, it
is easy to achieve conditions 4, 5 and 6'.[9]   We can conclude
that the first stage in protracted war is defined by a relatively low level in the invasion of social order which is
expressed by a spatial pattern involving limited base areas of
fully mobilized population, germinating guerrilla zones build-

ing towards the extensive development of guerrilla warfare,
and large counter-insurgent strongholds that are expanding
into the insurgent base areas.   In form, guerrilla warfare is
growing in importance but still secondary, and positional warfare unsustainable, leaving a mobile defence to trade territory for time, and to manoeuvre the opponent into a fatal
guerrilla war which feeds entirely on the consumption of the
enemy's social order.

The position, in theory by now shifting into the second
stage of operations, is that the opponent's armed forces are
becoming deeply involved in the insurgent base areas which
they originally set out to destroy by quick military means,
and in which they now attempt to consolidate their military
positions otherwise.   They rarely find the insurgent armed
forces in sufficient numbers for a 'decisive battle' solution.
If they turn to act on the insurgents' social infrastructure
as extended throughout the base areas now occupied, they are
sure to see that the compromise of one of its links simply
results in its covert repair by the mass of people through
which it is given life in the first place.   The temptation to
engage in the wholesale destruction of a mass of people and
thus the insurgents who are carefully concealed within the
very fabric of social relations with them is a moral and political absurdity, violating the moral considerations in war to
which I have already given attention.   In any case, even if
technically feasible in the event that the conception of war
should forget itself, this course is utterly unnecessary, as
later explained.   In short, the opponent finds his classical
principles failing him as his military situation sinks deeper
and deeper into a sea of hostile people and the foreign social
order through which they engage in a mass guerrilla war.
Everywhere where the opponent's armed forces are not perma-

nently situated and thus firmly in control is debatable territory, that is, zones of guerrilla warfare.

It is necessary to pause here and consider the basis of
distinction between the spatial categories of the base area
and guerrilla zone.   It must be remembered that although
today we are all accustomed to the idea that land operations
may not be exclusively linear in pattern (with the advent of
helicopters, long-range penetration and so on), and can take
place in depth over an area, the idea of a war without fronts
or clearly defined areas of contact (lines of communication
and bases) was a novel one around forty years ago.   In this
case, spatial distinctions almost entirely rest on the depth
and distribution of revolutionary mass mobilization in the
field.   Base areas, for example, are not logistic or supply
bases in the classical sense but those areas where mobilization of the people into a new fabric of social relations and
social order through which they conduct guerrilla warfare has
proceeded far enough for them to become secure havens for insurgents.   They may well be chosen for tactical reasons and
such factors as difficulty of access by regular forces and
ruggedness of terrain, making the area suitable for ambush and
guerrilla tactics generally.   But, as Mao repeats with grand
relentlessness, the prime factor is everywhere the social one:
'In concrete terms, and especially with regard to military
operations, when we talk of the people in the base area as a
factor, we mean that we have an armed people'.[10]   While
cautioning that 'we must not forget the consolidation of the
base areas, the chief task being to arouse and organize the
masses and to train guerrilla units and local armed forces',[11]
simply because 'it is in the matter of "dominating the spaces"
that the great strategic role of guerrilla base areas in the
rear of the enemy is revealed',[12] Mao describes the importance
of this spatial distinction:

What, then, are these base areas?   They are the strategic
bases on which the guerrilla forces rely in performing
their strategic tasks and achieving the object of preserv-
ing and expanding themselves and destroying and driving out
the enemy.   Without such strategic bases, there will be
nothing to depend on in carrying out any of our strategic
tasks or achieving the aim of the war.[13]

Base areas behind enemy lines, although cut off from the
main forces, are regarded as an extension in the invasion of
social order by means of guerrilla warfare from those base
areas or insurgent sanctuaries well outside of these lines.
What they possess in common is the invasion and alteration of
social order through which a mass of people is drawn into the
participation of guerrilla warfare:

> It is a characteristic of guerrilla warfare behind the
> enemy lines that it is fought without a rear, for the guer-
> rilla forces are severed from the country's [the insur-
> gents'] general rear. But guerrilla warfare could not last
> long or grow without base areas [behind enemy lines].
> The[se] base areas, indeed, are its rear.[14]

The real basis of distinction between the notion of base
area and the next spatial category down in the scale of revolutionary mass mobilization is the degree to which this social
consideration has satisfied the overall obsession with social
order.   Mao here explains that 'such places will not be
transformed from guerrilla zones into relatively stable base
areas until the enemy forces are destroyed and the work of
arousing the people is in full swing'.[15]   The essence of the
entire strategy is to extend through guerrilla warfare the invasion of social order in such a way that regions of low insurgent mobilization are transformed into the next superior
distinction in the social scale: enemy strongholds into guerrilla zones, and the latter into base areas:

Territory will fall into the following three categories:
first, anti-Japanese bases held by our guerrilla units and
our organs of political power;   second, areas held by
Japanese imperialism and its puppet regimes;   and third,
intermediate zones contested by both sides, namely, guerrilla zones.   Guerrilla commanders have the duty to expand
the first and third categories to the maximum and to reduce
the second category to the minimum.   This is the strategic
task of guerrilla warfare.[16]

Mao explains that 'in guerrilla warfare behind the enemy
lines, there is a difference between guerrilla zones and base
areas',[17] and in reference to the former we are informed:

They are areas which are held by the guerrillas when they
are there and by the puppet regime when they are gone, and
are therefore not yet guerrilla bases but only what may be
called guerrilla zones.[18]

The depth of the invasion and alteration of the social
order through which a mass of people participates in guerrilla
warfare has not yet satisfied the distinction of a secured,
well-armed and protected base area to which insurgent forces
are firmly attached.   Distinctions in space revolve around
their one great social mentor rather than the pure organization and application of armed power which now simply feeds on
this and, in turn, delivers the vital service of 'policing' it
in the process of guerrilla warfare.   As is always emphasized, the invasion of social order upward in the social scale
of spatial distinctions is central, or 'this transformation of
a guerrilla zone into a base area is an arduous creative process, and its accomplishment depends on the extent to which
the enemy is destroyed and the masses are aroused'.[19]   The
remaining spatial distinction from which insurgent mobilization and consumption of social order draws substance is, naturally, the lowest on the social scale:

In order to confine the enemy invaders to a few strongholds, that is, to the big cities and along the main communication lines, the guerrillas must do all they can to
extend guerrilla warfare from their base areas as widely as
possible and hem in all the enemy's strongholds, thus
threatening his existence.[20]

With the social essence of spatial distinctions in mind,
the obsession with social order, having ordered the meal and
already consumed a good part in the first stage, opens into a
general feast in the second.   In the appearance of a strategic stalemate, this obsession further presses the entire
strategy towards the flow of guerrilla warfare throughout the
guerrilla zones which are, by now, continuing to expand geo-
graphically to the 'rear' of enemy forces.   The central
thread of reasoning - the initial trading of territory for
time, the luring in of enemy forces and the continuously reshuffling nine distinctions with which the use of armed power
is conceived - is wholly motivated by success or failure of
guerrilla and social operations in this and the prior phase.
What is required throughout is a precise appreciation of the
pace, depth and distribution of the invasion and alteration of
the social order through which a mass of people conducts guerrilla warfare.   The protracted or elastic conception of time
stretches here to fit the exact requirements of a social shoe,
as Mao explains that 'the duration of this stage will depend
on the degree of change in the balance of forces between us
and the enemy'.[21]   We are further informed that this balance
of forces is the consideration on which the entire strategy
turns:

This second stage will be the transitional stage of the
entire war; it will be the most trying period but also the
pivotal one.   Whether China becomes an independent country

or is reduced to a colony will be determined not by the
retention or loss of the big cities in the first stage but
by the extent to which the whole nation exerts itself in
the second.[22]

The essential measure in this balance is the growing weight
of insurgent mobilization as guerrilla forces flow into expanding guerrilla zones from which they were thought to have
been cleared in the first stage.   So long as insurgent forces
are able to carve up more and more of the opponent's territory
and social order into a proliferating web of guerrilla zones
behind enemy lines, the insurgents inevitably 'will in that
stage gain the power to change from weakness to strength'.[23]
The only real means of policing an invasion of social order is
to break up the organization and application of armed power
into the guerrilla form carefully concealed in the fabric of
the opponent's society or social base for the conduct of war.
At precise points in time and space insurgent forces abandon
their more regular strategy of manoeuvre into the base areas
and flow back in a dispersed and guerrilla form towards the
prime thrust of mass mobilization behind enemy lines.   We are
informed that 'in the intermediate [second] stage guerrilla
warfare will become primary and regular warfare supplementary',[24] simply because:

Except for the troops engaged in frontal defence against
the enemy, our forces will be switched in large numbers to
the enemy's rear in comparatively dispersed dispositions,
and, basing themselves on all the areas not actually occupied by the enemy and co-ordinating with the people's local
armed forces, they will launch extensive, fierce guerrilla
warfare against enemy-occupied areas, keeping the enemy on
the move as far as possible.[25]

Our guerrilla war will present a great drama unparalleled
in the annals of war. For this reason, out of the millions of China's regular troops, it is absolutely necessary
to assign at least several hundred thousand to disperse
through all enemy-occupied areas, arouse the masses to arm
themselves, and wage guerrilla warfare in co-ordination
with the masses.[26]

This is where the popular notion that 'the Red Army fights
not merely for the sake of fighting but in order to conduct
propaganda among the masses, organize them, arm them, and help
them to establish revolutionary political power'[27] comes into
the fullest play. The real assumption is that the insurgent
can indeed 'mobilize the entire people and prepare for the
counter-offensive [of the third stage]',[28] so that he can
'extend guerrilla warfare all over this vast enemy-occupied
area, make a front out of the enemy's rear, and force him to
fight ceaselessly throughout the territory he occupies'.[29]
In the struggle to satisfy obsessions with social order, the
organization and application of armed power is devised in such
a way as to 'divide our forces to arouse the masses, concentrate our forces to deal with the enemy',[30] which is to say:

These tactics are just like casting a net; at any moment
we should be able to cast it or draw it in. We cast it
wide to win over the masses and draw it in to deal with the
enemy.[31]

If the first stage of protracted war is simply a way of
setting up the second, from which the third derives entirely,
then it follows that the one vital thread of the entire strategy running from conditions of low mobilization, through
medium, into its highest possible level (stage three) rests on
the critical dispersal of armed power into the guerrilla form.
For the purposes of organizing my discontent with classical

theory it must suffice to abandon this notion of guerrilla warfare as an armed invasion of social order for a later and more detailed discussion in chapter 7.   It may seem as if I pass over the very social roots from which insurgent reasoning springs.   I take this path simply because strategists nursed on the poor habits of tradition cannot be expected to entertain any interest in matters of a social nature until the pillars of classical theory are downed, leaving few conclusions save those on general theory.   What is our present conclusion is that the instrument of armed power through the nature and reshuffling of those distinctions with which its organization and application is conceived is looking less and less the independent and prime instrument as the centre of the will to resist in war.   As Mao suggests, 'in the second stage guerrilla warfare will advance to the first place and will be supplemented by mobile and positional warfare'.[32]   Distinctions in space, in obvious contrast to the first stage, now show a further proliferation of guerrilla zones, relatively stabilized, if not expanding, base areas, and a fatal confinement of those areas securely held by the opponent.   The real answer, once again, is that these distinctions in time, space and form can only be rooted in the grand obsession with social order.   Having followed classical principles to their fatal conclusion, the counter-insurgent has indeed driven his armed forces into a social swamp in which the longer he remains he only further drowns his instrument in a foreign social order through which is prosecuted a mass guerrilla war.

I conclude this chapter with a discussion of the third and final stage of operations in protracted war.   The assumption remains that the opponent utterly fails to see what is at the root of insurgent power to wage war, or is unable or unwilling to cast away the very principles of strategy with which he has

led himself into such sad consequences. He continues to hope
for a compromise of insurgent will to wage war by religiously
following the good rules of tradition to a military destruction or neutralization of the insurgent armed forces, their
supply lines and bases. What has escaped his attention is
that the centre of the will to resist and thus the prime concern of strategy has circuitously abandoned classical principles and shifted on to the social order that always stands
behind the organization and application of armed power, and
through which real power is remitted into the hands of those
who conduct war. So long as insurgent operations are able to
expand time and, later on, space in the invasion of social
order through which the classical instrument is simply bled
white, and so long as this instrument insists on pursuing
strategic illusion for the real essence of insurgent will and
capacity to wage war, then there comes a turning-point when
the insurgent falls into the temptation to cast away the very
obsession with social order on which his successes have rested
entirely. Now, knowing that he has already compromised the
opponent's social order - and by this his armed forces in mass
guerrilla warfare - to the sufficient extent, he then seizes
the shorter route to victory formerly denied him along the
classical avenue paved entirely by the opponent's stubborn
misconceptions. It is the classicist who takes a classical
threat in the manner in which it is intended, simply because
he shares the hidden convention which drives his reasoning
into the false notion that armed power is the prime instrument
of strategy and thus the main centre of the will to resist in
war. To topple the enemy's will to resist the insurgent
abandons the strategy to which he owes his survival - indeed
ultimate victory - and seizes the shorter route left open by
classical misconception. This is only applicable in the

first place against an opponent who refuses to learn his
lesson and swears by a tradition which has been ruinous, and
must prove fatal.   Otherwise, the insurgent would never dream
of forsaking the strategy by which he survives.   The insurgent option and temptation for traditional principles of
strategy in later phases of operations is utterly cancelled
out by the clear understanding of his opponent that he must
discard classical theory or face certain defeat.   If this
were the case, in theory the position would be that all
parties to the conflict are then left with the everywhere compelling obsession with social order.   The insurgent, here,
sees no advantage, only ruin, in classical principles, and the
opponent finally grasps that he must abandon tradition and
invade by the same process of guerrilla warfare the very
social order or base through which his enemy conducts war.
For reasons which I shall take up later, once one party in war
discards the convention on which classicalism rests then all
must do so, leading the conception of war into a rarely ending
series of small guerrilla conflicts in which the invasion of
social order is everywhere sovereign.

If the third stage is a consequence of classical misconception, then it is also the fruit of insurgent obsession with
social order.   The original suggestion of this chapter then
survives intact.   The continuum in protracted war in which
the instruments of strategy embrace new form and movement at
precise points in time and space retains its roots in a common
premise.   This assumption is in Mao's own words that the
insurgent is able, in the middle second stage, to 'make further progress in the political, military and cultural spheres
and in the mobilization of the people; guerrilla warfare will
develop further'.[33]   For reasons just observed, and the central fact that insurgent mass mobilization in the process of

guerrilla warfare has by now progressed sufficiently, this
invasion of social order by means of the guerrilla form is
transformed into full regular warfare: 'The strategic role of
guerrilla warfare is twofold, to support regular warfare and
to transform itself into regular warfare'.[34] In more detail
we are informed of the reshuffling of those distinctions in
form with which the organization and application of armed
power is conceived, always, of course, tied to the pace, distribution and depth of insurgent mobilization:

> Our primary form of fighting will still be mobile warfare,
> but positional warfare will rise to importance. While
> positional defence cannot be regarded as important in the
> first stage because of the prevailing circumstances, posi-
> tional attack will become quite important in the third
> stage because of the changed conditions and the require-
> ments of the task. In the third stage guerrilla warfare
> will again provide strategic support by supplementing
> mobile and positional warfare, but it will not be the pri-
> mary form as in the second stage.[35]

The level of insurgent mobilization can now sustain a regular warfare in which the positional form - meaning here deliberate frontal defence and attack of localities on a large
scale - is employed in a counter-offensive by large regular
armed forces: 'The third stage will be the stage of the
counter-offensive to recover our lost territories', and thus
'their recovery will depend mainly upon the strength which
China [the insurgent] has built up in preceding stages and
which will continue to grow in the third stage'.[36] Of
course, the reasoning here is that the 'strategic retreat is
aimed solely at switching over to the counter-offensive', and
thus 'the decisive link in the entire strategy is whether victory can be won in the stage of the counter-offensive which

follows'.[37]   A final reminder by Mao suggests that 'we shall
not be able to recover our lost territory unless we launch
powerful positional attacks in support of mobile warfare', and
that 'the mobile warfare of the third stage will no longer be
undertaken solely by the original regular forces; part, possibly quite an important part, will be undertaken by forces
which were originally guerrillas but which will have progressed from guerrilla to mobile warfare'.[38]   The old sarcasm -
never to wish for anything too religiously or one may get it -
is precisely the situation which the counter-insurgent forces
now suffer, having led themselves into defeat by means of the
illusions inherent in classical theory, now find these same
illusions being used successfully against them.   Changes in
the distinctions in space with which the organization and
application of armed power is conceived again find their genesis in a common social premise, as insurgent base areas are
rapidly expanding through the web of guerrilla zones as extended deep into counter-insurgent strongholds, the last of which
are now toppled by purely regular warfare.

From all of this is plucked a simple conclusion soon to
lead us into general theory.   Once salvaged from its virgin
state scattered throughout Chinese sources of varied periods,
subjects and motives, the theory of protracted war is understood as a continuum in which the instruments of strategy embrace new form and movement at precise points in time and
space.   At the root of this strategic continuum is a social
premise to which all considerations are attached, as Mao Tse-
tung informs with a rude relentlessness, if not theoretical
precision:

Weapons are an important factor in war, but not the
decisive factor; it is people, not things, that are decisive.[39]

This question of the political mobilization of the army and
the people is indeed of the greatest importance. We have
dwelt on it at the risk of repetition precisely because
victory is impossible without it. There are, of course,
many other conditions indispensable to victory, but political mobilization is the most fundamental.[40]

It is here that all of the threads, tactical and strategic,
meet. In so far as this conception of strategy approaches
its abstract form, all other considerations are important only
in the degree to which they relate to this premise.

3

The death of classical theory

If the conception of social order is indeed relevant to the theory of strategy, then it must also be compelling. I now turn to the persuasion of this fact by pursuing classical theory into the implicit and very thin convention on which it rests. I do so by setting up two morally conflicting patterns of strategy: on the one hand those which are rooted in the compelling obsession with social order, and on the other, those which rest on the very thin convention hidden in the roots of classical theory. Of special interest will be the manner in which the weight of the premise behind each pattern throws the logic of theory towards divergent avenues of reasoning, and exactly why, once one party in war travels down the avenue paved by the armed invasion of social order, then all parties must abandon tradition for the same path.

The following proposition can serve to introduce the essential thrust of classical reasoning:

Clausewitz put considerable emphasis on the enemy's armed forces as the 'centre of gravity' - an emphasis which dominates his whole work. To achieve one's political object in war, he wrote, is: 'To conquer and destroy the armed power of the enemy', for 'the direct destruction [in battle] of the enemy's [armed] forces is everywhere predominant'.... This emphasis on the destruction of the enemy's armed forces was based on a simple syllogism:

Major Premise: The object in war is to destroy the enemy's
will to resist.

Minor Premise: His will to resist is primarily a function
of his armed forces.

Conclusion: Therefore, his armed forces must be destroyed.[1]

The accepted theories of classical strategy, whether they
are developed by Clausewitz, Jomini or Liddell Hart, still
possess a silent attraction.   The principal idea in the classical paradigm is the need to destroy or, in later forms, to
neutralize the armed power of the opponent.   This is still
rather accepted without any substantive question, that is, a
deeper questioning of the assumptions by which this paradigm
is upheld.   If the paradigm appears logically elegant, its
elegance masks its growing obsolescence.

The classical structure of reasoning remains deeply rooted
in our strategic heritage, the genesis of which in thought is
an unconscious assumption;   that is to say, an assumption
which has been so natural to this heritage that it did not
overtly enter into the formulation of strategy.   The problem
theory faces today is not only that faulty logic flows from
faulty assumptions but, in a more fundamental sense, one of
revealing an idea which rarely presents itself as the starting
point in classical thinking, being too subtly blended into the
fabric of our strategic heritage.

An illustration of the tricks this assumption can play is
the very point at which Liddell Hart attempts to overthrow, or
at least modify, the weight of 'pure' Clausewitzian tradition
as he perceived it.   This classical assumption was beyond
Liddell Hart's perception, making it very difficult indeed to
challenge its consequences in thinking.   Compromise the

assumption and its conclusions which tend to flow no longer
obtain.   In contrast, Liddell Hart found himself clinging to
the former while attempting to deny the latter, leading the
thrust of his challenge (strategy of indirect approach) into a
striking dilemma.   The undercurrents in his thinking clearly
show that he was, at once, drawn into carrying forth, and yet
on the other hand, was attempting to deny the same logical
conclusions sprouting from an assumption too subtly blended
for the naked eye.   This issue should resolve itself as we
progress; suffice it to mention here that, willingly or
otherwise, Liddell Hart is firmly situated in the 'classical
tradition', his embellishments being, in the final analysis,
questionable because these do not delve into the root of the
problem.   The classical obsessions with 'decisive battle'
which he found so objectionable in his strategy of indirect
approach really derive from a hidden assumption about the
relevance of social order to the theory of strategy - a connection Liddell Hart simply failed to grasp.

The extent to which the idea of a state of *social war* contained in the Chinese and an increasing number of insurgent
patterns of strategy is applicable to a general theory of
strategy resides in the interplay of conflicting strategic
assumptions.   This is the peg on which the entire proposal
hangs.   I became aware of, then questioned, the classical
assumption when I began to grasp the unique Chinese approach
to revolutionary warfare.   At first one finds in Chinese
strategic thought, as it relates to social and military operations in the theory of protracted war, a logic which seems
quite unintelligible.   The source of my initial confusion was
that the Chinese strategists and I, being a product of classical reasoning, were working with morally conflicting assumptions (neither of which are clearly stated) and consequential

patterns of strategy. The question which I now propose to
discuss is the resolution of this interplay of conflicting
strategic assumptions to the mortal disfavour of the structure
of classicalism sweeping all participants into a state of
social war which, touching upon the elemental strategic consideration, is applicable to a general theory of strategy so
long as any one party in war is able successfully to discard
the classical assumption behind operations.

The conclusion of the last chapter was that the continuing
strategic premise behind operations in the pattern of protracted war is *social* in nature, and as a consequence of this,
distinctions in time, space and form designating the organization and application of armed power in the classical sense
have degenerated into socially based distinctions. In terms
of the unfolding of insurgent operations, time is measured by
little more than the changes in the rate of mass mobilization
as an armed invasion of social order, and spatial distinctions
rest on its distribution and depth in the field. Form
appears as if it has no social basis whatsoever, but it must
since, in theory, mobile warfare is prominent under conditions
of low mobilization (stage one), guerrilla warfare blossoms
into prominence in medium conditions (stage two), and positional warfare is prominent only in conditions of its highest
possible level (stage three). Furthermore, not only do all
distinctions in time, space and form derive from a strategic
premise which is largely social in nature, but the way these
distinctions move in terms of relative importance against each
other as operations develop is also derived from this premise.
This is all that one has to know in a general sense about the
pattern of strategy in protracted war because everything else
is completely ancillary. In this symmetry is found the very
compelling logic of protracted war in a static or maturing

strategic situation.   Armed power as an independent and prime instrument of strategy and the centre of the will to resist has now become a part of a general invasion of social order, this being the new centre of the will to resist, the every-where compelling obsession.

If one wishes to grasp the Chinese pattern of strategy in order to understand how it and similar patterns are effective-ly compelling the opponent in war to question the reasoning behind the classical pattern of strategy, then having a clear idea of the former in a static and maturing strategic situa-tion is essential.   The Chinese pattern of strategy is really very simple indeed because it is so well connected: all con-nections in time, space and form leading to a strategic pre-mise which itself derives from the underlying assumption of the *relative insecurity of social resources*.   The way insur-gent operations develop in the field assumes the relative in-security of social resources of the opponent, since each step in insurgent operations is entirely contingent on the ability continually to subvert one's way into the opponent's social base (or social order on which any war effort rests) and bleed him dry of social resources necessary for the ability to act in war.   This means that no party in war, especially one who faces the Chinese or insurgent pattern of strategy, can any longer assume the stability and support of one's own social base or social resources, being a mass of people, their states of mind in terms of deeply embedded values and commitments, and related patterns of behaviour and socialization.   Simply put, to assume the relative security of one's social resources in war against an opponent whose operations and pattern of strategy entirely depend on the reverse assumption is fatal. In theory, the latter is assured of slowly drowning the former in an overwhelming sea of hostile people who have been induced

through a scheme of mobilization to embrace a new social order
and life style in which war-will has been broadened and given
the psychological depth of a state of socialization.

What implications does this Chinese and similar patterns of
strategy, being socially based in a manner never before experienced in war, have for the continued influence of classical
reasoning in contemporary strategic thought?   I hope to persuade that in order to find security, everyone in war shall be
compelled to abandon any hopes in the classical pattern of
strategy.   Statements about this pattern of strategy may look
quite reasonable, and we may even tend to accept this reasoning without real question only because we all share, unconsciously or otherwise, an unspoken assumption.   The following
propositions can serve as examples:

It may help to begin with a definition of 'classical'
strategy.   Liddell Hart has provided us with one which is
as good as any, and better than most: 'The art of distributing and applying military means to fulfil the ends of
policy.'[2]

This pattern of strategy, violent conflict aiming at military victory, is the classic strategy of the Napoleonic
era.   Its principal theorist is Clausewitz, though the
well-nigh Wagnerian romanticism of many of his disciples
has frequently distorted his theories.   This was the
dominant European strategy of the nineteenth and the first
half of the twentieth centuries....

In his analysis of Clausewitz, Lenin produced a much-
quoted dictum which shows clearly that the decisive factor
is the psychological; he said: 'The soundest strategy in
war is to postpone operations until the moral disintegra-
tion of the enemy renders a mortal blow both possible and

easy'. He was, however, thinking as a revolutionary and regarded political action as a sort of psychological artillery preparation - the exact opposite of Clausewitz's classical military concept in which the morale of the enemy was to be broken by military victory.[3]

For over a hundred years the theory of strategy has taught that the object in war is to break the war-will of the enemy and that the method of achieving this object is to disorganize his armed forces by battle....

No fresh methods of acting upon that war-will had, however, disclosed themselves, and therefore these [nineteenth-twentieth-century democratic and scientific] changes, by themselves, could bring about no revolution in strategy.[4]

The interesting thing about the essentials contained in these propositions is that, although one may question their continued validity, we hardly bother to think about this in any substantive way. We are rather *compelled* to accept them in an underhanded way without real question by our prior acceptance of an assumption deeply rooted in our strategic heritage. These propositions look normal only so long as everyone, unconsciously or otherwise, accepts this unspoken assumption which permits the classical pattern of strategy to exist in the first place. It is the assumption of the real stability of social order or the *relative security of social resources* - these being a mass of people, their states of mind in terms of deeply embedded values and commitments, and related patterns of behaviour and socialization. The notion of social resources would vanish if it rested on a mass of people without mention of their moral and social capacities to conform to social order through which they conduct war, along with the process of socialization in which, for our purposes,

these capacities are acquired.   The security of social resources behind any war capability is really the security of
social, economic and political commitments and related patterns of behaviour and socialization, the common assumption of
which makes the classical pattern of strategy possible.   Only
if all the parties in war are free to assume (and do so) the
relative security and stability of social resources, that is,
assume that the subversion of this security has no part in the
contest as the prime means of waging war, is it entirely
normal, and may even be necessary, to emphasize armed forces
as the essential 'strategic centre of gravity'.   In theory,
one is lured into certain types of solutions in war: classical solutions typified by 'decisive battle'.   In short, as
long as all parties in war agree, unconsciously or otherwise,
not to formulate a pattern of strategy contingent on the continuing subversion of the opponent's relative security of
social resources then the common agreement on a classical
pattern of strategy is almost automatic.

Accept any one element of reasoning in the classical
pattern of strategy and the other two tend to follow.   Make
the classical assumption, this is, enter into an unwritten
convention not to formulate a pattern of strategy contingent
on the continuing subversion of the opponent's relative
security of social resources, and the emphasis on the armed
forces as the essential 'strategic centre of gravity' naturally flows.   The propensity to classical solutions typified
by 'decisive battle' is then the most likely consequence.   On
the other hand, embrace the 'decisive battle' tradition and
one, unconsciously or otherwise, embraces its built-in assumption and the emphasis on the armed forces as the essential
'strategic centre of gravity'.

This being the case, in the classical pattern of strategy

the security of a society or social order behind any war effort is essentially reduced to, or is seen as no better than, the security of the armed forces.   One can turn to Fuller for an illustration of this concept of security which looks quite normal but is by no means necessary:

Turning from tactics - the art of fighting - to war as a whole, it will, or anyhow should, at once be seen that it possesses a permanent structure, the three elements of which are - bases, communications and battles.   The first, as the word implies, is built around the idea of stability - something which stands firm; the third around that of mobility, whereas the second is the link between them, as a bow string is between the bow and the arrow - what is held fast and what is released.

Of bases there are three types:
(1)   The Main Supply Base - the country of each belligerent.
(2)   The Administrative Base - that part of an army which does not fight.
(3)   The Tactical or Operational Base - the organization of that part of an army which does fight.[5]

In terms of the relationships between the three types of base, Fuller suggests that 'the first supplied the second, the second fed the third, which in turn protected both the second and the first' (excluding, he points out, complications deriving from 'the advent of cubic warfare' which need not concern us).   The instant one party in war *thinks* to discard the assumption concealed within the classical pattern of strategy then everyone is compelled to alter the basis on which war is conducted since security (including that of the armed forces) is reduced to, or is seen as no better than, the security of the supporting social order.   The consequences,

being so determined, are of such radical proportions that a
reconsideration of the theory of strategy may not be inappro-
priate.

The relative security of social resources can only be
broken by permanently altering the values, commitments and
related patterns of behaviour and socialization of a mass of
people, thereby re-ordering society especially in terms of the
fabric of social relations. Should this security be broken,
war-will becomes a part of a state of socialization not affected by the classical pattern of strategy. This is to say,
since the notion of socialization is a process through which a
mass of people conforms to the social order through which they
conduct war (to be later discussed), the will to resist in war
is no longer primarily a function of armed forces, but indeed
of social order itself as this will is engrained into its very
fabric. In this state of affairs, classical solutions in
war, typified by 'decisive battle', are completely illusory,
as I hope to persuade shortly. However, as long as everyone
is free to accept the unspoken assumption (and they can still
do so while engaging in propaganda directed at the war-will of
the opponent, recognizing the importance of morale and winning
the 'hearts and minds' of the people without having any sub-
versive effect on the opponent's relative security of social
resources in the manner described above) the classical pattern
of strategy still obtains.

The instant one blows away this assumption the entire classical structure in strategic thinking is blown away. The
reason behind this is simple. The classical pattern of
strategy exists so long as all participants in war need not
seriously worry about subversion of the relative security of
their social resources. Everything in the reasoning about
war is then released, indeed somewhat compelled, to focus on

the classical 'art of distributing and applying military means
to fulfil the ends of policy' and the 'disorganizing of the
opponent's armed forces by battle'.   However, the very
instant one opponent effectively discards this assumption the
entire contest in war shifts from the battlefield to a state
of social war in which everyone must scramble to obtain relative security of social resources against the subversion of
the same by the enemy.   Of course, the only way to obtain
such security, as the basis of the ability to act in war, is
to assault those social resources of the opponent through a
scheme of social strategy and tactics seeking to re-order
deeply rooted patterns of commitments, behaviour and social
relations into one's own pool of social resources.   It is
precisely because the classical scheme rests on one thin
assumption that it is so vulnerable to degeneration into a
state of social war in which all else derives from the ability
to subvert the opponent's social order by virtue of which he
conducts war through competitive programmes of mass indoctri-
nation and social reorganization, especially in terms of the
fabric of social relations.   This vulnerability is subject
to the qualifications and also the hindrances blocking the
invasion of social order mentioned in the first chapter.

This *social imperative* - the necessity to achieve relative
security of social resources by subverting and re-ordering
those of your opponent into the fabric of your own social
order - in the conduct of social war is equally compelling to
all.   This must be so because everyone's existence militarily, politically, socially and so on is entirely contingent on
ability to satisfy this social imperative in the first place.
The finding of security means drying up the sea of social resources in which one's opponent survives like a fish, who is
otherwise sure to make his posture in war too elusive to be

acted on in a classical manner.   An opponent who has effectively discarded the classical assumption and who would not
then commit himself to a classical posture deliberately reduces everyone in war to the mercy of the social imperative -
including himself.

I pause here to remind not to confuse guerrilla warfare
with social war.   The former being that 'form of warfare by
which the strategically weaker side assumes the tactical
offensive in selected forms, times and places'[6] is essentially
a part of the classical pattern of strategy.   There is
nothing fundamentally new about the strategy of guerrilla warfare (being a way for the weaker party to avoid a classical
solution in war up to the point when such a solution would be
in his favour), until that instant the thinking behind this
strategy acquires a compelling social content focusing on an
armed invasion of social order.   Guerrilla warfare in this
instance becomes part of a state of social war (as in the
Chinese case) in which the classical assumption of the relative security of social resources has been discarded.   It is
quite true that the 'form of warfare by which the strategically weaker side assumes the tactical offensive in selected
forms, times and places' is particularly adaptable to social
war, as it is the weaker who initially disperses his armed
power into the guerrilla form carefully concealed in the
fabric of society on which he feeds.   This is also the case
in partial variations of a state of social war in which one
participant is attempting to act out a full social war while
facing an opponent who is operating in an essentially classical manner, being rooted in a 'decisive battle' tradition
(encirclement and suppression, search and destroy) with little
or no effective interest in the social imperative.   In
theory, the latter is ultimately doomed to suffer the melting

away of social resources into the hands of the opponent.
But, in the meantime, he is able to force the former party,
the insurgent, into settling for a quasi-social war in a
guerrilla form which, during the last stage, is transformed
into a classical mobile and positional offensive only rendered
effective by the disintegrating classical posture of one
party.

When all parties come to understand and effectively employ
the principles of social war, none will be willing to expose
and waste their war resources in a classical manner for any
significant length of time, since everyone will realize that
classical solutions in war are illusory unless, somehow, the
relative security of social resources is again stabilized.
If this should occur, the relative security of social resources, being subject to common assumption, is simply shuffled
out of the pack of strategic playing cards and the contest, in
theory, goes back to the classical book of rules.   This classical assumption is really the joker in the deck.   As long as
everyone recognizes the peculiar function of this assumption
then everything in the reasoning about war is rather compelled
to direct itself towards either the essentially classical
pattern of strategy or a state of social war.   If all parties
in war are free to assume (and do so) the relative security of
social resources then the pattern should be somewhat classical.   The instant one party successfully discards this
assumption all participants are compelled to attempt to do the
same.

The party who, either because he feels he is unable to act
successfully on a social level or is otherwise simply unable
to see what is happening, makes the fatal assumption of the
relative security of social resources by embracing the classical pattern of strategy against an opponent who has success-

fully discarded it quickly finds his ability to act in war
constantly evaporating through the subversion and melting
away of his social base necessary for this ability. In this
case the former party will be unable to find his elusive
opponent in the regular field formations necessary for a classical solution. He will also eventually realize that to
concentrate on assaulting what he can find of the opponent's
social infrastructure as extended into his own dwindling pool
of social resources is achieving little more than acting on an
illusion for the mass of social resources with which it is
supported. There is simply no way out but to attempt to
satisfy the social imperative. Once the principles of a
state of social war are thrown into operation they are
sovereign because security can only be successfully sought
after in one way. In terms of the mutual theft of the relative security of social resources, it would not be long before
everyone saw survival in such war being reduced to becoming a
thief to catch a thief.

A state of full social war in which everyone has effectively discarded the classical assumption tends to degenerate into
a continuing, rarely decisive guerrilla confrontation in which
distinctions between policy and strategy and military and
civilian are blurred. The reasons for this blurring should
be self-evident, but the particularly interesting feature of a
state of social war is that all parties are compelled to
attempt to control that over which one can never really enjoy
an absolute control. In order to achieve relative security
of social resources everyone in such war is forced to assault
those of his opponent through a scheme of social strategy and
tactics seeking to re-order deeply rooted patterns of commitments, behaviour and social relations into one's own pool of
social resources. But the party who experiences increasing

relative security of social resources finds himself dispatch-
ing continually larger quantities of his own resources in
order to subvert and control progressively diminishing amounts
of those social resources of the enemy, the last of which are
hard-core carefully concealed in the fabric of society.   This
irony of diminishing social returns acts to prevent the realization of a solution in social war which inherently tends to
simmer on indefinitely in a series of rarely decisive guerrilla wars.   Of course, as earlier explained, the actual
experience of war may contain many hindrances in the complex
and irregular undercurrents which can, at times, mitigate,
perhaps entirely reverse the inherent and compelling features
of social war.

Simplified, my line of thinking runs something like the
following in terms of a state of social war:

(1)   The classical assumption of the relative security of
      social resources and the classical pattern of strategy it
      supports no longer obtain .

(2)   Military distinctions designating the organization and
      application of armed power as an independent instrument
      of strategy in the classical sense and supported by this
      assumption have degenerated into socially based distinc-
      tions leading to the obsession with social order in the
      unconditional scramble for relative security of social
      resources.

(3)   The will to resist is no longer taken to be a function of
      armed forces, but indeed of moral and social order, that
      is, the 'strategic centre of gravity' (in the Clausewit-
      zian sense) can only be, for all opponents, the same
      finite pool of social resources on which all depend for
      survival in war.

(4)   Classical solutions in war, typified by 'decisive

battle', remain tempting, but are, in fact, illusory because they obtain in the first place only so long as everyone shares the classical notion of the centre of the will to resist being a function of armed forces.

(5) A scheme of social strategy and tactics in the invasion of social order seeking to satisfy the social imperative in war is the basis on which all else in the conduct of war is rendered operational.

(6) In so far as social war approaches its abstract form, all other considerations are only important in that degree to which they relate to the social imperative.

All of this, at first sight, may seem difficult to digest, but it is really very simple and may provide a way of understanding the intense frustration of the recent *débâcle* in Indo-China and the considerable success of Maoist insurgent doctrine in mainland China.   What is more important, armed groups around the world, particularly, it would appear, in southern Africa, are slowly beginning to wake up to the extreme vulnerability of classicalism and discard the thin assumption with which it is supported, as they cannot help but marvel at the resulting successes of those who have already done so.   Of course, there could not be a more suitable response to the superiority of nuclear and conventional weaponry in which we are asked to find security.   In essence, war, especially in terms of the theory of strategy, should be compelled to move in the direction of a truly complete social science loosely referred to as that group of disciplines whose interests are in man and society.

4 Strategic revisionism

Any notion that 'war in the nuclear age has become a political absurdity'[1] is a nonsense of all reason which cannot pass inspection. The reality of the matter is that armed conflict may be drifting towards a rather new or *revisionist* form in which the Clausewitzian conception of war as 'a real political instrument, a continuation of political commerce, a carrying out of the same by other means'[2] is completely reformulated into a new life, the basis of which is an upheaval in the theory of strategy. The struggle for power, that is, the pursuit by real violence of an order in relationships through which power is always remitted, being endemic in international and social relations, if stalled on some avenues of expression (the nuclear and conventional paths), unerringly finds others. Only here in the poorly researched social dimensions of strategy can its instruments truly fulfil, rather than abandon, the very social and moral context in which they are intended to serve. If my judgment proves correct on the thin nature of classical theory, in the nuclear age the conception of social order is the one firm basis left for the continued survival of a truly political notion of strategy in which the real use of violence is the distinguishing feature. It is the task of strategic theory to consider the nature of this feature and the social and moral roots from which it springs.

The thrust of revisionist challenge to contemporary theory
is centred on the redefinition of strategy as the *formulation
and distribution of social order*, tactics being its detailed
application.   In this, the main idea, as previously discussed, is that the instrument of armed power abandons traditional principles, and through the movement of its internal distinctions in time, space and form comes to serve a general
invasion of social order as the centre of the will to resist
in war.   This is, of course, a critical departure from the
Clausewitzian view of the same, the genesis of which in thinking is an implicit assumption of the stability of social order
or the relative security of social resources:

   According to our classification, therefore, tactics *is the
   theory of the use of military forces in combat*.   Strategy
   *is the theory of the use of combats for the object of the
   War*....

   The combat is the single activity in War, in the combat
   the destruction of the enemy opposed to us is the means to
   the end; it is so even when the combat does not actually
   take place, because in that case there lies at the root of
   the decision the supposition at all events that this destruction is to be regarded as beyond doubt.   It follows,
   therefore, that the destruction of the enemy's military
   force is the foundation stone of all action in War, *the
   great support of all combinations,* which rest upon it like
   the arch on its abutments....

   We have only to refer to the conception of War to be
   convinced of what follows:

   (1) The destruction of the enemy's military force is the
        leading principle of War, and for the whole chapter of
        positive action the direct way to the object.

(2)   This destruction of the enemy's force must be princi-
       pally effected by means of battle.

(3)   Only great and general battles can produce great
       results.

(4)   The results will be greatest when combats unite them-
       selves in one great battle.[3]

This view can reveal no new combinations of strategy which
are not reducible to its one implicit assumption.   To attempt
so would result in a theoretical and, more seriously, operational dilemma (Liddell Hart's dilemma in the strategy of indirect approach of not knowing how far to carry the initial
denial of the 'decisive battle' mentality through to a full
denial of the armed forces as the essential 'strategic centre
of gravity' and the identification of its implicit assumption)
or the total dissolution of the classical form.   The classical assumption of the relative security of social resources
renders its consequences not only operationally correct, but
also methodologically inevitable.

I have previously suggested that if any one party in war is
able successfully to apply the revisionist pattern of strategy
(by discarding the classical theory of strategy at its weakest
point), then all other participants have no choice but to do
the same in order to find, in the first instance, security,
and ultimately to achieve their object whether it is initially
limited or otherwise.   The strategic initiative of one party
towards the formulation and distribution of social order
necessarily sweeps all participants off the 'battlefield' into
a state of social war in which the prime object of strategy is
the continuing invasion of the opponent's social order (hence
will to wage war) and the reformulation or reweaving of these
newly subverted social resources into the fabric of one's own
social order.   In theory, there is simply no other way in

which a revisionist posture in war, being so carefully concealed in the fabric of society, can be effectively compromised and, conversely, secured, the former being a condition
of the latter.

The six general propositions which we can now use to identify strategic revisionism in the form of a paradigm of social
war are: (a) the anti-classical assumption of the *relative
insecurity of social resources* by which a pattern of strategy
formulated on the condition of the continuing invasion of
social order is grasped; (b) strategy defined as the *formulation and distribution of social order*: this is observed by
that state of affairs in which the organization and application of armed power is rarely more than an offspring and servant of the general invasion of social order; (c) the *strategic centre of gravity* for all opponents being the same finite
pool of social resources on which all depend for survival,
that is, the will to resist is a function of moral and social
order; (d) the *social imperative*, being the absolute necessity to achieve relative security of social resources by subverting and reweaving those of the opponent into one's own
fabric of social resources and social order; (e) the *irony of
diminishing social returns* relating to difficulties in
approaching a revisionist solution in war; and finally (f)
the general dissolution of war towards a *state of anarchy* -
ironically a consequence of the mutually conflicting scrambles
for relative security of social resources locked into diminishing social returns. In so far as these six propositions
retain their sovereignty in the practice of war, it does not
matter what initial objects participants may think they
pursue; in fact, they are pulled into a general struggle for
power in which they find it increasingly difficult to avoid a
state of social anarchy in a rarely decisive and continuing
series of small guerrilla wars.

It is these six propositions which provide the skeleton of
revisionist theory, now free from narrow classical restraint
and resting on the natural social basis of general theory.
The first is an assumption which invites the question of
social order back into theory without condition or implicit
convention; that is to say, the premise of revisionist reasoning rests on a free consideration of the very moral and social
phenomena of which the conception of war is the natural extension.   Once this free consideration obtains over classical
restraint, then the one real obsession which necessarily
strikes the theory of strategy is the security and invasion of
social order, which the instruments of strategy now religiously serve.   Such is the reasoning behind the redefinition of
strategy as the formulation and distribution of social order
in which its instruments embrace new form and movement at certain points in time and space to fulfil this obsession.   From
here, we move on to the related notion that, in view of this
everywhere present concern, the centre of the will to resist
for all opponents is the same finite pool of social resources
on which all depend for survival.   The will to resist is
everywhere the social and moral consideration, being regarded
as a function of moral and social order in which the notion
of social resources for the prosecution of war must always
reside.   Now it follows that if all considerations in war are
social before anything else, then it can be said that the one
sovereign condition to which all others are attached is the
necessity to satisfy the social imperative to achieve security
of one's own social order by the only means of substance, that
is, the compromise of the foreign social order through which
the enemy conducts mass guerrilla warfare.   The catch here is
that once the social imperative places all parties within its
firm grip (remembering that reverting to a classical strategy

is fatal) they should, in theory, find themselves held in play
by an irony of diminishing social returns.   Neither party is
willing or able to return to the good rules of tradition once
its convention is broken, and both find as they proceed deeper
into the enemy's social order, being the only avenue left,
that the going gets progressively tougher.   This should prove
so because in the invasion of social order one works one's way
through a range of hostile people and foreign social order the
last of which is hard-core, who will continue violence so long
as there remains a sufficiently intact social order or fabric
of social relations in which they remain secured.   In contrast to the classical ideal of quick military solutions, a
revisionist condition is a long-term and begrudging proposition.   The prospect is an indefinite state of social anarchy
in the form of a rarely decisive series of small guerrilla
wars in which prevails the armed struggle for command and
security of social order.

Now if this is so, and all parties knowing this to be so,
why should any one opponent force the other into such an un-
satisfactory paradigm of war in the first place?   The real
answer quite simply is that revisionist reasoning invokes, as
it were, a Pandora's box: once opened it plays havoc with the
theory of strategy.   In the first instance, the calculation
is that at least one party initially chooses to invade social
order as the prime pillar on which the organization and application of armed power rests and through which war is prosecuted, since the other party possesses an overwhelming prepon-
derance in armed forces.   Or it is the case initially that at
least one opponent, generally being the weaker, has so carefully concealed his posture in war in the fabric of social
relations that his will to resist cannot be acted upon through
any other avenue than the general invasion of social order, of

which this fabric is an essential part.   It should, of
course, be quite normal that both considerations flow together
as the taste for security lodged in the fabric of social order
leads directly to the armed struggle for its protection and
extension.   Beyond this, the fortuitous opening of the Pandora's box leaves precious little choice in the matter.
Western strategists have already witnessed the failure of
classical military principles to deal with the social and
moral roots of insurgent reasoning.   If the lesson remains
unlearned then this failure should stand to simple reason -
when the theoretical issues are properly thought out.   Once
revisionist thinking sweeps away the locker-room conventions
with which war may have been conducted, however sad the consequences it is almost impossible to stick together agreements
which no longer obtain and so fatally penalize those foolish
enough to follow them.   In short, no judicious party can a
priori rest the theory and practice of war on the inviolability of social order, leading all parties to protect vigorously
for themselves that which may have been in the past secured by
the good principles of tradition.   The reasoning about war
slips into a revisionist paranoia rooted in the dark uncertainties on the whereabouts and social appetites of the
enemy.   Having said this, I conclude this prospect to remind
that the real conduct of war is impregnated with false obsessions and irregular undercurrents that can trap the simple
strategist who swallows general theory as pure religion - certainly not the conception of general theory intended here.

What I propose to discuss for the remainder of this chapter
is an elaboration of the initial insight on social order into
broader theoretical terms of strategic revisionism, especially
with strategy defined as the formulation and distribution of
social order in mind, as the all too sadly neglected observa-

tion in recent strategic thinking. In the process, I wish
to deepen and broaden our understanding of a phenomenon which
touches the fundamentals of a general theory of strategy to
the mortal disfavour of the structure of classicalism. It is
always simple in theory, yet so difficult in practice, to
establish the limitations of new combinations in strategy.
But it is too painful to the sensitivities of reason that
unconscious fetters which so often nurse a strategic heritage
should survive a general collapse of the narrow basis from
which they proceed.

The conception of social order that is everywhere prominent
in the revisionist theory of strategy is, in its most general
terms, a unified system of deeply rooted social values and
norms, and related patterns of social interaction and stratification of society, the germane aspect of which for our purposes is a rank hierarchy in status and power. A consensus
on social values and norms is the prime moral basis of social
order which unites a mass of people into one single moral com-
munity or society. In the first instance, although not
exclusively, social order is a moral order as it is the latter
which is the central agency of social life. A consensus on
social values and norms renders it possible for an otherwise
chaotic mass of people to order their existence into established patterns of social interaction, or social relations and
ranking in society. If this consensus is seriously compromised, then the established pattern of social relations and
social ranking it has, in part, brought into existence is
greatly weakened if not compromised. Conversely, if the
fabric of social relations and its rank hierarchy in status
and power through which moral order gains expression is for-
cibly or otherwise fundamentally re-ordered, then the established moral order is slowly impoverished. In its elementary

terms, social order cannot very long persist in the absence
of a closely equilibrated relationship between, on the one
hand, social values and norms and on the other the social
relations and ranking in status and power which these values
inform.   What I propose here, of course, is simply a sketch
of those elements of social order most prominent in the interests of strategists.

To complete this conception of social order we must return
to the very important element of power in the fabric of social
relations.   In the first instance, social relations are power
relations, power being, for our purposes, the ability to command the actions of others.   It is inherent in the very
nature of social relations that the actions (or recognition
and services) of individuals are potential means to the ends
of others.   Only through social relations are the recognition
and services of individuals and groups rendered transferable,
in any substantive way, to the ends of others.   The consequence of this, being universally applicable to social relations, is the general pursuit of power through these relations.   The assumption (and perennial fear inherent in social
life) which leads to the flow of social relations towards a
state of anarchy in which the unrestrained and violent pursuit
of power prevails is that although not all individuals have an
insatiable desire for power over others, sufficient numbers
may do so to force the remainder - if they wish to retain what
powers they possess - to be pulled into a general struggle for
power.   This fear of the appetites of others is rooted in the
relative essence of power, being a measure of the excess of
one centre of power over the same of another.   As such, these
principles of social life give no explanation of why there
should be any limitation to the means by which power is pursued, including, of course, violence - the class of means with
which we are here primarily concerned.

Were it not for a crucial fact of social order, social
relations should thus find that they cannot help but flow
towards a condition of social anarchy in which violence pre-
dominates. The mitigation of these tendencies resides in the
fact that social order is also, in the first instance, a moral
order founded in the consensus on social values and norms.
Like the thread that binds a string of beads, it is only the
moral fibre of social order in which is given a consensus on
social values and norms embracing a shared conception of ends
which society should pursue along with a propriety of means
(among which are the actions of individuals), that checks an
otherwise rampant and violent pursuit of power. Here is
found the propriety of the transfer of the actions of some
individuals and groups to the ends of others that gives this
element in social relations a measure of order and peace by
upholding an established fabric of social relations through
which power is always remitted. As such, moral order is the
great dam that contains the flood of social relations from
pursuing their natural route of decline, the effect of which
is the salvation of society from itself.

At first sight this may seem to have little concern for
strategists, but it stands to reason that it has important
consequences for the theory of strategy - if one can only
accept that things are moving into its poorly researched
social dimensions. Once the subtleties of the classical convention are grasped, strategists are virtually forced to trace
the threads in the theory of strategy back to their social
basis. That these threads should terminate here, in the
first instance, resides in the fact that the employment of
armed power as an instrument of strategy is an absurdity in
the serious compromise or absence of social order. It is, or
ought to be, less than an overwhelming conclusion that social

order is crucial to the theory of strategy, and with the
appropriate strategic assumption, becomes its great obsession.   Both the classical and revisionist theories of strategy start with morally conflicting assumptions involving
social order.   The latter theory, being referred to as revisionist, simply corrects classical anomalies and returns the
theory of strategy back into its natural social basis so
subtly assumed out of the body of the former, in addition to
so giving new life to the Clausewitzian conception of war as a
real political instrument in the nuclear age.

Now, if everything in the theory of strategy is thrown back
to the conception of social order, it is necessary for strategists to grasp its essential features.   The first item in
social order relevant to the theory of strategy is that it is
only through social relations that power over others is pursued in any substantive way.   All individuals are not necessarily pursuers of power over others by nature, but are tempted to become so the instant they are thrown into social relations.   Beyond this, they are driven into the violent pursuit
of power in the absence of its moral chains.   Otherwise the
real risk is that the configuration of social relations
through which power is always remitted will shift in such a
way that one's own actions become the principal means to the
ends of others.   This is so simply because the fabric of
social relations with which society is formed always leads to
the systematic alienation of power, that is, the increase in
the power of some over others by the organized transfer of
recognition and services of some individuals and groups to its
concentration into the hands of others.   Social relations
being, in the larger part, power relations, society must first
of all be recognized as an order in the transfer of power
which is observed in the established pattern of social rela-

tions and ranking in status and power contained therein.

As explained, what makes this order work is the moral element in social order founded on a consensus on social values
and norms embracing a shared conception of ends which society
should pursue along with a propriety of the transfer of recognition and services. Here are found the moral conditions
under which this continuing transfer, being natural to social
relations, may proceed peacefully. Thus, the moral element
gives the pursuit of power inherent in social relations a
measure of order and peace by upholding an established fabric
of social relations through which power is always remitted.
The flood of social relations would otherwise, in the absence
of their moral barriers, simply pursue their natural and violent dénouement. Strategists must grasp the fact that social
order is, at once, a moral order and an order in the everywhere prominent transfer of power observed in the pattern of
social relations and social ranking.

This is of crucial importance to strategists in light of
the relevance of social order to general theory. This
focuses on a simple shift in assumptions, the effect of which
is the redefinition of strategy in terms of social order.
How is this possible? And beyond this, what new place does
the organization and application of armed power find in strategy defined as the formulation and distribution of social
order?

I have argued, and will do so further in the last chapter,
that the classical theory of strategy is a logical closure
resting on an implicit assumption and a partly hidden structure of reasoning that still infests theory today. What I am
attempting here is thinking through the consequences of the
revisionist assumption on the proviso of the irrevocable
breakdown of this classical convention. Behind all of this

is the conception of war as an intelligible phenomenon, 'as a real political instrument, a continuation of political commerce, a carrying out of the same by other means'.[4]   Prior to all else war is an articulate social and moral activity, an extension of the social pursuit of power of which social morality is the principal author, and set apart, in the first instance, by the predominance of armed violence, and which is therefore deeply rooted in the social order.   It must be here that the great support of all combinations and the ultimate strategic issue is found, beyond which the notion of war simply vanishes into the violence of every man against the other.   Social order, being a moral order, is the genesis from which war derives its moral fibre.   Reason insists that the conception of war as an articulate social and moral activity can only be founded in its unifying moral thread issuing from the social order through which men participate in higher forms of moral life.   All of this is reduced, in the final analysis, to the very simple proposition that theories concerning the organization and application of armed power *per se* are rather unthinkable in the absence or breakdown of social order.   In short, the latter is so fundamental to the former that strategy can, indeed, be redefined in terms of social order, given the appropriate strategic assumption. And yet, the classical strategists constructed a theory of strategy founded on a mutual determination, conscious or otherwise, to ignore completely the social underpinnings of their theory.   Such precarious treading on dangerously thin ice lasts only so long as all agree to be equally delicate.

If the first and critical element in the organization and application of armed power is the moral and social order which stands behind this organization and application, then it is possible, and in the right strategic circumstances neces-

sary, to grasp social order as the prime seat of the will and
capacity to wage war. Thus, the formulation, distribution
and application of social order is a strategic and tactical
drive to satisfy the social imperative in war, this is, the
absolute necessity to achieve relative security of social resources by subverting and reweaving those of the opponent into
one's own fabric of social resources and social order. The
compromise of the opponent's social order and will to resist
rests on the compromise through a scheme of social strategy
and tactics of the consensus on social values and norms, patterns of established social relations and social ranking,
along with the configuration of power relations contained
therein. The way one pursues victory over the opponent is
not through the implicit convention underlying the model of
'decisive battle', or the neutralization of armed power, but
through an invasion of the very fabric of social relations
and its vital concentration of power which must always under-
lie the capacity to wage war. Here is found the new centre
of the will to resist in war, this being regarded as a function of moral and social order. The prime avenue in the
invasion of social order is, through a scheme of inducement or
coercion, throwing a mass of people into new patterns of
social relations and social ranking in status and power. The
idea here is to refashion these latter two aspects of social
order, in which is contained the configuration of power, out
of the hands of the opponent and into the fabric of one's own
social order and war capacity. Social relations being, in
the first instance, power relations, this means that the
opponent finds the fabric of social relations through which
power is concentrated into his hands for the prosecution of
war is, in contrast, being refashioned and concentrated into
the hands of others.

The one great hurdle in this strategic combination is the
moral order. If this remains untouched, the formation of
new social relations and social ranking in status and power
either never gets off the ground or faces the perennial
spectre of backsliding towards the moral attraction of established social and power relations. The very process of
throwing a mass of people into new patterns of social relations and ranking in which is contained the vital configuration of power is, in itself, the first step in the compromise
of moral order, since it is the continuing social experience
of this fabric of social life which, in part, implants the
fibres of moral order into the minds of an otherwise chaotic
mass of individuals. This is so because moral order is not,
as it were, simply plucked from the sky, but it is deeply
rooted in this fabric, as it is in the course of social interaction or entering into social relations that not only is
power pursued over others but social values and norms are
fixed into some form of consensus. In play here is frequently the experience of *moral lag* in the social process by
which the pattern of social relations and ranking in status
and power through which the enemy conducts war is denied him
and redistributed. This should be so (and indeed was the
case in the Chinese experience) simply because it is always
the relatively simple and quicker task of initially throwing
a mass of people into new social and power relations by for-
cibly denying them access to established social relations.
(This was, in the Chinese case, introduced in programmes of
land revolution by the liquidation or neutralization of landlords and their agents, accompanied by the initial redistribution of their land.) But the task of the compromise of
social order is exceedingly lengthy, repetitive and laborious
since the established fabric of social relations and the

vital social concentration of power contained therein are not
ultimately compromised by a single act of armed violence but
through the slow destruction of the underlying moral order on
which they both rest in the first place.   The invasion of
social order is for ever bound to its moral basis, for if it
proceeds too far beyond this basis in time, space or form then
it must return to pick up the moral lag or risk sliding along
a social ice which becomes everywhere thinner.   Added to
this, therefore, is a highly pressurized ideological content
injected into the social process by which a mass of people is
thrown into new social relations and social ranking in status
and power, making this process an intense ideological experience concentrated directly at the established moral order to
reduce the effects of moral lag.   In sum, the intended consequence of this strategy is the compromise of moral order,
thus releasing established social relations from their moral
chains from which they are free to pursue their natural route
of decline.   .

The opponent finds at this point in the invasion of his
social order that a debilitating struggle for power is working its way further into the very fabric of social relations
out of which he is attempting to weave a capacity to wage
war.   The nature of this dissipation, in which the violent
struggle for power prevails, being no longer subject to any
established moral propriety, not only denies the opponent the
vital concentration of power into his own hands through a
stable fabric of social relations, but facilitates the dissemination of a new moral order, the refashioning of social
relations and a new social concentration of power.   What we
observe in this is a 'turnover' in social order and the power
relations contained therein.   The core of strategy defined as
the formulation and distribution of social order is precisely

this notion of 'turnover', at least to the extent of the
*minimum of new power relations necessary for the prosecution
of war*.   Simply put, revisionist conflict is a mutually conflicting scramble to find security of social order, each
party employing a combination of armed power with a scheme of
social strategy and tactics in an attempt to invade and alter
the fabric of hostile social relations, status and power
accompanied by a compromise of the moral order on which these
rest.

The reduced place of armed power as an instrument of strategy in the general invasion of social order is none other than
to serve, like everything else, the social imperative.   This
is at once observed by the fact that the basis of those distinctions in time, space and form in which the organization
and application of armed power is conceived has radically
shifted, as I have discussed previously.   As such, the organization and application of armed power is no more than an offspring and servant of the invasion of social order.   It is
this arrangement of armed power as an instrument of strategy
that is the principal feature with which the formulation and
distribution of social order is identified.

Thus in revisionist thinking, unlike the perennial military means-political ends conflict in the classical repertoire, the means-ends schema is simply one long primarily
social and moral continuum, within which armed power loses
all independence of movement and form.   The most highly gen-
eralized means that satisfies the higher objects in social
war is the formulation and distribution of social order which
fulfils the strategic object to compromise the opponent's
social order, hence will to resist.   Primarily on the tactical level is found the application of social order in separate
campaigns or programmes of *mass resocialization* which, when

strung together in a social continuum leading to the strategic
object, serve this object as, largely, a social and moral
means to this object. Social order is applied on the tactical level in separate programmes or phases of mass resocialization, the stringing together of these over time and space in
a social continuum leading to the strategic object is the province of strategy. Mass resocialization is that social process, through inculcation or coercion, in which a mass of
people is induced in some measure to conform to new social
values and norms, social relations and a rank hierarchy in
status and power *relative to the opponent's social order.*
Mass resocialization is used here simply as an expansion of
the notion of mass mobilization previously discussed as an
armed invasion of social order. The basic method in the formulation and distribution of social order is, in essence, a
firm grip on a scheme of social strategy and tactics to
achieve relative security of social resources through the dissemination of new social values and norms, social relations
and rank hierarchy during a process of mass resocialization,
within which the organization and application of armed power
is inextricably bound. We thus observe that the organization
and application of armed power primarily in the mass guerrilla
form is an offspring and servant of the invasion of social
order. Such is the way in which a pattern of strategy formulated on the condition of the continuing invasion of social
order is identified. The strategy is simply boiled down to
the redistribution of social relations, status and power,
accompanied by a radical alteration in the very moral order on
which these rest. This is intended to deny the opponent the
social concentration of power inherent in social order on
which depends the will to resist and capacity to wage war.

Finally, before proceeding to the application of this

strategy in the Chinese case, it is necessary to examine the question of the applicability of revisionism to general theory.   Empirical insights are, in many instances, well ahead of the theoretical and methodological formulations of their implications.   The insight that social order is the cardinal strategic issue (as revealed in the Chinese case from which I argue it is entirely possible to sift out broad strategic generalizations) awaits much further formulation if only because the historical basis for this insight still remains relatively narrow.   And yet, having been swept under the rug for so long by the classical strategists, once free of the theoretical chains of our strategic heritage the insight is at once so simple and compelling.   I have attempted to give further expression to the relevance of social order in contemporary strategic thinking in the form of six general propositions which are, in themselves, applicable to a general theory of strategy for two reasons fundamental to the conception of strategy.

Now it is quite wasteful and unnecessary to pose a variety of scenarios in which strategic revisionism is applicable. Such a large and dubious undertaking can be reduced *in toto* into one simple proposition which is the key to the entire proposal.   Theory depends on the reduction of an otherwise unbearable weight of discrete phenomena into one or more simple propositions.   The first of the above-mentioned reasons is, then, the notion that the applicability of strategic revisionism to a general theory of strategy is, in the first instance, entirely reduced to the interplay of conflicting strategic assumptions.   It is with this key that all strategic contingencies can be expressed.   I have argued that both the classical and revisionist theories of strategy are applicable only in so far as their deeper strategic assump-

tions obtain. Neither can claim absolute universality.
What claim can be made, being crucial to the argument, is that
in a situation of conflicting assumptions the revisionist one
should be compelling simply because it rests on a far deeper
strategic provision in the realm of general theory: the violation of social order. As previously discussed, it should
therefore be inevitable that once one party grasps the revisionist assumption and pattern of strategy all parties in
war are irresistibly swept into a state of social war in
which the classical assumption (as an unspoken convention concealed in the fabric of our strategic heritage) is totally
inapplicable. This should be so simply because the classical
repertoire is founded on an assumption that entirely sweeps
problems of social order right out of the arena of theory in
the first place. It is, at best, a shallow burlesque to
search for a solution to the invasion of social order in
'decisive battle' reasoning. In essence, the question of
the applicability of revisionism - as is the case with classicalism - to general theory is, in the first instance, simply
reduced to the nature of their underlying assumptions and the
notion that the reach of the former does indeed exceed that
of the latter, being little more than thin convention on which
no general theory can rely. Only the first theory rests on a
free consideration of the very social and moral phenomena of
which war is the natural extension.

   Beyond this, we move to the second above-mentioned reason,
which is the question of why any one party in war would grasp
a revisionist pattern of strategy in the first place. As
already mentioned, having seen that classical theory is rather
limited by the weak convention on which it rests, it should
only come into play so long as extraordinary circumstances or
hindrances and false conventions which flow in the experience

and reasoning about the nature of war act to freeze out the
more elemental social considerations.   These circumstances
that may or may not prevail at any given time, being rooted
largely in the unusual and the fleeting nature of chance or
thin contract, should not be allowed to proceed over the
objections of such moral and social phenomena to the depths of
general theory.   But they do have the effect of trapping the
simple strategist who swallows general theory as pure religion.   The prospect is simply that the decaying chains of
tradition may release reasoning towards a grasp of the one
revisionist insight on social order in war, the strategic consideration of which war is always the natural extension.   War
being the extension of the social pursuit of power by other
means of which social morality is the principal author, it
should be compelling for a *free* conception of strategy to
arrive at the understanding that moral and social order is
taken to be the prime seat of the will to resist, the great
hand that wields the instruments of strategy.   In the last
chapter I shall discuss further why armed groups in the
nuclear age see a new way in the poorly researched social
dimensions of strategy of pursuing their objectives by violence that they could not otherwise attain.

I conclude by reminding, therefore, that general theory is
not one which necessarily enjoys a universal application without constraint or condition, nor should it be mistaken for a
comprehensive theory of strategy.   Any theory of strategy is,
in some degree, constrained by the breadth and depth of the
assumptions on which it rests.   This is indeed the case with
the classical and revisionist conceptions of strategy.   What
is the point to general theory is that it should rest on a
consideration which is everywhere present in the subject at
hand, and moreover, this consideration should provide the

deeper provision inherent in the matter theory seeks to formulate.   If poor theory rests on a false or too narrow basis,
this is not to say that general theory is a panacea.   But our
ancien régime and the sharp edge of its implicit convention
will no longer cut back the pursuit of theory of its inalienable social roots.

5   The Chinese theory of land revolution

My discontent with classical theory returns the analysis to further empirical observations on the Chinese case made through the writings of Chinese strategists.[1] To remind once again, in order that these empirical observations may fulfil our present concern with general theory in such a way that they serve, not overburden, this purpose, I shall have to push aside many issues in the history of Chinese Communism. Not the least of these is the problem of to what degree are the documents on strategy, tactics and social order chosen here for discussion precisely representative (over time) of all areas under the control of the Chinese Communist Party (CCP). Requirements of space and procedure insist that my purpose restrict itself to the employment of observations made through an abridged sample of the most explicit writings of Chinese strategists intended to conclude with a set of propositions on the nature of general theory.

Revisionist theory ought to be of such flexibility that it may embrace numerous and varied strategic combinations designed specifically to handle differing social and strategic conditions. Future combinations may likely have little to do with the essential design of land revolution as the basis of the case on which I am at present forced to rely. What is of

first importance is that - however varied the individual designs
woven into a revisionist cloth - these should rarely stray too
far from the central thrust of general theory, that is, the
six general propositions with which such theory is identified.
In order to appreciate these six further, it is necessary to
grasp the essentials of the first and most carefully reasoned
example of any substance - on which we are thus obliged to
rely. This is the distinctive design fashioned by the
Chinese strategists to satisfy the rather special conditions
in which they sought survival and final victory.   With one
exception which I shall note later, the invasion of social
order was here conducted (with little substantive variation
for our purposes) through the essential design of land revolution, as it was the case that land relations were the basic
form of social relations.   Of central importance to the
Chinese strategists was a firm grip on a scheme of social
strategy and tactics by which was consummated, in a continuous process of mass resocialization, the painstaking alteration of the fabric of land and social relations and the moral
order on which these rested.   In this process of resocialization, by which a mass of people was thrown into new land and
social relations, the domain of tactics concerned the detailed
application of social order in a continuum of separate mass
programmes or campaigns directed to land confiscation, redistribution, investigation and reconstruction.   The hunger for
land provided, in varying degrees, the basis by which a continuing and repetitive process of mass mobilization in a
series of mass action or struggle campaigns of one sort or
another was set into motion.   The population was here
initially denied access to traditional social relations by the
liquidation or neutralization of landlords and rich peasants,
their property and institutions.   From this, the promise of

more land in fresh and increasingly pressurized mass mobilization campaigns designed to reinvestigate and once again redis-
tribute land and, in the process, prosecute the hidden and remaining enemies of social order, was used to herd further a
mass of people into an everywhere tighter grip of new land and
social relations.   As is frequently explained, land redistribution is not a gift from heaven but something that must be
'earned' in the process of mass action or struggle possessing
a highly pressurized ideological or moral content.   This concern of tactics in the detailed application of social order
delivers to the province of strategy the degree to which each
campaign or phase has met its objective of fixing new land
and social relations.   The latter province, being defined as
the formulation and distribution of social order, grasps the
separate tactical results of each phase and strings together
these in a social continuum leading to the strategic object of
the larger compromise of moral and social order and the will
to wage war.   The concerns of strategy, having set up the invasion of social order in its varied phases, release into the
hands of tactics the responsibility of realizing its specific
tasks in each phase which either permit the deliberations of
strategy to string the tactical results successfully forward
or compel it to rethink or return generally to pick up the
moral lag.

   This should be made more clear as I now turn to the observations on this scheme of social strategy and tactics made
through the writings of Chinese strategists.   What is essential in this is the method of distinction between strategy and
tactics (that in a fully revisionist state of affairs the
organization and application of armed power in its tactical
and strategic aspects should freely merge into this method of
distinction which it now serves), and that at the root of all

this is the degree to which the fabric of social and, in this
case, land relations is refashioned. I propose to discuss
the theory of land revolution of the Kiangsi Soviet period
(1929-34) as just such a scheme of social strategy and tactics, and as the faint beginnings of revisionism in Chinese
strategic thought.[2] The relationship between land revolution
in rural base areas and the revolutionary movement in 1932 was
viewed as follows: 'When the land revolution is carried out
intensively, it will drive the entire revolutionary movement
forward', and precisely for this reason, those 'regions where
the land revolution was carried out intensively not only met
with the cruel "encirclement and suppression" of the XXX, warlords, local despots, gentry and landlords, but also faced the
direct attack and suppression of the imperialists'[3] (XXX replaces reference to KMT as probably deleted by the KMT sources
reviewing these captured documents). This is, of course,
always distinguished from rural reform programmes in which the
simple reshuffling of land ownership patterns is not fully
extended into a general transformation of social relations,
the social concentration of power and the moral order on which
these rest.

The theory of protracted war (in its December 1936 and May
1938 formulation)[4] was the culmination of a long and controversial development, the genesis of which in terms of a scheme
of social strategy and tactics, Mao Tse-tung admits, was the
land law adopted at Ching-kang-shan (the Hunan-Kiangsi Border
Soviet Area) in the winter of 1928-9: 'This was a product of
the experience of the land struggle waged during the whole
year from the winter of 1927 [-1928] to that of 1928 [-1929].
There had not been any experience [of this kind] before that
time'.[5] Although they might appear today as commonplace, the
assumptions underlying the notion of land revolution in rural

base areas as the main form of a scheme of social strategy and tactics were, in fact, controversial[6] insights into the strategic weaknesses of the establishment, being at once social and rural.   This required a somewhat subtle but vital departure from the orthodox Marxist emphasis on workers in urban centres of revolution: 'For in the revolution in semi-colonial China, the peasant struggle must always fail if it does not have the leadership of the workers, but the revolution is never harmed if the peasant struggle outstrips the forces of the workers'.[7]

I should like to pause here for a brief mention of the two fundamental policies of the Chinese Communist movement: these were the establishment of rural base areas and the development of Red Army operations around these bases.   However poorly integrated in the early days, these policies embraced the somewhat controversial notion of land revolution taken to be the main content of the Chinese revolution.   After the move from Ching-kang-shan in January 1929, southern Kiangsi and adjacent western Fukien - an integrated region constituting the Central Soviet Area - was chosen, according to Mao, as the weakest link in the enemy chain of defence in South China. Lined up against this approach, proposed mainly by the so-called Chu-Mao group, were other schools of thought prevailing in the CCP.   One emphasized roving guerrilla activities in the borderlands of Fukien, Kiangsi and Kwangtung without the consolidation of rural base areas in conjunction with guerrilla operations.   Guerrilla tactics alone were to spread political influence and await the impending revolutionary upsurge without any firm base in the countryside.   Considerably more important, other approaches stood in sharper contrast to the twin policies of establishing rural base areas and related Red Army operations.   Of these, one viewed the twin policies as pure lese-majesty in face of the tradition of the labour

movement and decisive armed uprisings in the cities to which
the Red Army in the countryside would only contribute by
flamboyant assaults on key cities in support of a high tide of
urban uprisings, without securing the rear, that is, the rural
bases.   A later variation of this approach, according to Mao,
also underestimated the decisive role of the peasantry in the
Chinese revolution, but rather than calling for ancillary co-
operation of the (now expanding) Red Army in attacks on key
cities, proposed that it should engage in their premature and
outright seizure as a means of gaining preliminary revolutionary successes.   In contrast, the twin policies put forward
the painstaking build-up of rural bases and political regimes,
in this, the expansion of the land revolution, creation of
armed forces, and development of Red Army operations and political power throughout the countryside in a kind of succession
of advancing waves, in which the cities would ultimately
drown.   As the Kiangsi Soviet period came to a close the
focus of the disagreements had shifted - largely by necessity
- somewhat away from the gaining acceptance of rural base
areas and the central need of land revolution in the development of bases to the exact nature of Red Army operations
around these vital bases.   This was a highly important development in early revisionist thinking to which the next chapter
is devoted.

Now, the earliest and most articulate record available of
the strategy and tactics of land revolution in the development
of rural bases is given primarily by Mao Tse-tung in a series
of documents on the land investigation drive initiated and
organized by him in the Central Soviet Area, 1933.   Land
revolution is viewed as an invasion of social order which progresses through three socially distinguishable stages in time,
the distribution of which in the field is visualized as a tri-
partite social pattern in space:

All past experience has proved that only through the correct solution of the land problem and only through the fan-
ning to the highest degree the flames of class struggle in
the rural districts under the resolute class slogan can the
broad peasant masses be mobilized, under the leadership of
the proletariat, to take part in the revolutionary war,
participate in the various aspects of Soviet reconstruction, and build up a strong revolutionary base, so that the
Soviet movement may gather greater momentum and achieve a
greater development and success.

According to the experience of the development of the
land revolution, the unfolding of the class struggle in the
rural districts has its approximate stages to follow,
namely: (a) the stage of land confiscation and redistribution; (b) the stage of land investigation; and (c) the
stage of land reconstruction. According to the three
stages of the development of the land struggle, there are
approximately three different areas in any Soviet region:
(a) the intensified struggle area; (b) the comparatively
retarded struggle area; and (c) the newly developed area.[8]
Mao Tse-tung affirms that the above spatial distinctions
are not founded on an administrative or geographical basis
since they are independently applicable to any level in the
province-county-district-township-village pattern of Soviet
administration:

In general [therefore], both the relatively advanced townships and the relatively retarded townships can be found in
any district of any county where the Soviets have been
established and where the land has gone through confiscation and redistribution. In a township there are also the
relatively advanced villages and the relatively retarded
villages alike.[9]

In the residue of possible criteria for time and spatial
distinctions in the strategy and tactics of land revolution,
the degree of the alteration of the fabric of land and social
relations is by far the most likely.

STAGE ONE: LAND CONFISCATION AND REDISTRIBUTION

The space-time linkages in sequence which structure the invasion of social order are as follows: the newly developed area
is in the stage of land confiscation and redistribution, the
comparatively retarded struggle area is in the stage of land
investigation, and finally, the intensified struggle area is
in the stage of land reconstruction.   While indicating with
regard to these phases that 'such a state of things *determines* the direction of our work',[10] Mao describes the general
features of land revolution peculiar to the first stage:

In the newly developed area, the unfolding of the land
struggle is still in the stage of land confiscation and
redistribution.   Here the central problems are: the
overthrow of the regime of the landlord class by armed
force;   the establishment of a revolutionary provisional
regime (a revolutionary committee);   the build-up of local
armed forces of the workers and peasants;   the formation
of revolutionary mass organizations;   the confiscation of
the land and [other] property of the landlord class, and
the redistribution of the land of the rich peasants to the
hired farm hands, poor peasants, and middle peasants, while
the rich peasants are allotted only poor land;   the annul-
ment of debts;   and the burning of land deeds and promis-
sory notes.   The struggle of this stage covers the whole
period from the initial fight between the revolutionaries
and the counter-revolutionaries to the defeat of the latter

by the former, coupled with the disposal of the land and [other] property of the counter-revolutionaries.[11]

The procedure of operations in these newly developed areas, or what are initially 'White areas', emphasizes the transformation of land redistribution programmes into the formulation of insurgent political power within a new fabric of land and social relations during three phases. This linking of the latter on to the initial impetus generated in the former, as the *raison d'être* of land revolution, is marvellously reflected in a 1951 directive of a much later period:

We request all government agencies responsible for land reform and all members of land reform work teams fully to understand: we reduce rent not simply for the sake of reducing rent, and we divide land not merely for the sake of dividing land. Our *fundamental objective* is to make use of this [land reform] movement [and forthcoming movements] to raise the peasants' ideological and political consciousness to the level of opposing feudalism and imperialism and thus to form a powerful class army to struggle for this political objective. In order to achieve this objective we have to give the peasants some actual benefits or profits, on the one hand, but, on the other hand and at the same time, we have to develop fully the ideological and political education.[12]

The three phases of mass work in White areas of 'mobilizing the broad peasant masses to fight for the acquisition and protection of the land'[13] are summarized here from the Chinese original.[14] The first, referred to as mass mobilization work, embraces propaganda, agitation and quick distribution of portable wealth of the landlord and rich peasant social classes. Problems of getting the masses to accept the 'fruits' of this distribution were dealt with by a deliberate partial distribution leaving those who did not receive any 'fruits' in the first instance in a disappointed and more receptive disposition, on the basis of which new mobilization programmes were launched to ferret out 'hidden' wealth. Through this 'leap-frog' effect in comparative advantage during initial distributions a continuous mobilization process was slowly generated in which small group propaganda gave way to large mass meetings. Of all portable items grain possessed obvious potential in the build-up process towards a mass consciousness that would condone and, beyond this, comprehend land redistribution:

> As the struggle in the villages develops to the point of violent uprising, when the poor peasants, hired farm hands, and jobless masses are plunged in a struggle of beating village bosses and gentry and burning their title deeds, there will certainly be a struggle for an equal redistribution of the grains, which will be followed by a struggle for an equal redistribution of land. Accordingly, the equal redistribution of the grains is an important item in the struggle in the villages.[15]

The second phase is the vital construction of mass organizations within the process itself: guerrilla corps, secret poor-peasant corps, farm labour unions, Red trade unions and Party and Youth League organizations. Among these, the poor-peasant corps is of particular interest as the prime instrument of land revolution in its purpose of having 'to carry out the land revolution thoroughly and deeply, practice the class struggle, and resist all oppression and exploitation'.[16] It was, in the main part, through the everywhere present build-up and formation of a network of mass organizations in the process of land revolution that the mass of people was placed into new social and power relations.

The third phase of mass work in White areas is the decision
to proceed into: (a) initial land redistribution, and (b) the
formulation of political power according to the foundation
laid in the earlier phases. The essential ingredient in this
decision is the disposition of the masses towards carrying
through with the transformation of the former into the latter.
Timing in land redistribution is crucial in the effort to fix
a process of mass mobilization as a continuous social fact:
'Land must be redistributed very fast in order that a thorough
mobilization of the masses may take place quickly and the
influence of the revolution may spread quickly. Where the
masses have risen in revolt, land redistribution must be completed in not more than two weeks.'[17]

The procedure of the redistribution aspect of the third
phase is: (1) mobilize the masses, (2) hold a land redistribution meeting, (3) hold an investigation meeting of land redistribution (determination of land and social relations or
social class, filling out of forms), (4) carry out redistribution (preliminaries, measuring of land, etc.), (5) list of
names of those to be excluded, (6) put up land markers, (7)
burning of land deeds, and (8) mass victory celebration meeting. Generally, the township was the unit of land redistribution, although this could be replaced by 'using the village
as the unit of land redistribution'.[18] The weaknesses of
the village unit, deriving from the established pattern of
social relations, rendered it less applicable to land revolution: 'It is in the village that the landlords and rich
peasants would easily use clan ties to mislead the masses into
rejection of a thorough division of land'.[19] Woven into this
process of division is the twin aspect of the final phase,
formulation of political power within the changing fabric of
land and social relations, which progressed as follows:

(1) estimation of political power, (2) a revolutionary committee is formed, (3) local laws and tasks ratified by higher
Party levels, (4) qualifications of members of government,
(5) on guiding the work line (instruction meetings), (6) decision on the government's budget, and (7) on methods of trans-
forming local political power (strengthening the mass line).

STAGE TWO: LAND INVESTIGATION

In theory, the strategy and tactics of land revolution are,
by now, shifting into the second phase - all, of course, with
a critical eye on the extent to which the fabric of land and
social relations has been altered.   Mao Tse-tung claimed in
a series of documents concerning the land investigation drive
as initiated by him in the Central Soviet Area (1933) that, of
this entire region, the retarded struggle areas constituted by
far the larger part (80 per cent):[20]

> As to the retarded struggle area, its stage of development
> lies between the above-mentioned two stages.   It is a
> transition from a provisional to a formal regime, but the
> power of the regime is not yet completely consolidated.
> Here the open counter-revolutionary struggle of the land-
> lords and rich peasants has already been crushed by the
> revolutionary masses in the first stage....
>
>   In the second stage, owing to the supervision of govern-
> ments on higher levels and the development of the mass
> struggle, the revolutionary committees have been trans-
> formed into Soviets, the mass organizations and local armed
> forces have gone through the first step of reformation and
> development, and those elements who have pretended to be
> revolutionaries have been partially eliminated.   In many
> places there has been a second, or even a third, or fourth
> redistribution of land....

Moreover, owing to the various deep-rooted feudal
[social] relations in the rural districts such as clan
relations, and so on, it is not easy to expect the general
peasant masses to have such a degree of class consciousness
as to realize the necessity of wiping out the feudal remnants once and for all.   Such a situation requires the
Communist Party and the Soviet government to give a patient
explanation to the peasants, to perform many difficult
tasks, and to have a correct class line and correct methods
of mass work.   The central problem here is the problem of
land investigation and class investigation.   If this problem is not solved, the revolutionary activism of the
peasant masses cannot be fully developed, the feudal rem-
nant forces cannot be completely crushed, the Soviets
cannot be consolidated to the greatest possible extent,
and the enormous tasks of expanding the Red Army, raising
funds for the Red Army, expanding local armed forces,
carrying out land reconstruction and economic reconstruction, promoting culture and education, and so on, cannot be
crowned with the greatest possible success.   Therefore,
the land investigation drive is the most central task of
the greatest magnitude in these regions....

For this reason, these places in the spheres of war
mobilization and economic and cultural reconstruction are
lagging far behind the advanced areas.[21]

A clear conception of class differentiation in land and
social relations lay at the centre of the strategy and tactics
of land revolution.   The land investigation drive, being
designed primarily as an investigation and alteration of
class, status and power, is particularly concerned with the
notion of class struggle in its most intense phase.   Accordingly, 'to analyze the class status correctly in the light of

practical social relations is an important part [of the work
of] carrying out the class line'[22] during the investigation of
land.   The significance of this drive in terms of class
struggle is described as follows:

> The land investigation movement is a deep-going rural class
> struggle to thoroughly solve the land problem and, at the
> end, to eliminate the feudal power and the secret agents of
> the landlords and rich peasants who have infiltrated the
> Party and Soviet power, and thus to consolidate this Soviet
> power.   It is also the most powerful weapon in co-ordina-
> tion with the front lines.   This movement also enables the
> basic peasants and rural labourers to get more land and
> interests from the revolution, to raise their enthusiasm,
> and strengthen the organizations of the poor-peasant corps
> and farm labour unions.   It will temper a large number of
> new cadres during the struggle which will strengthen the
> work of the Soviet power.   This movement, moreover, guar-
> antees the strengthening of the war mobilization force so
> that we will be able to smash the enemy's 'encirclement and
> suppression'.[23]

Although some land redistribution may occur, it is repeat-
edly stressed throughout that land investigation is not simply
another round of mass participation in a series of land redistribution programmes but an investigation of classes[24]
possessing a more intensified social (especially with the
purpose of further re-ordering land and social relations) and
ideological content.   Whatever fresh redistribution occurs
is allowed only after the completion of the various mass campaigns of class investigation in land and social relations[25]
so that their social and ideological content is not lost on
the mass of people as absorbed into this process - initially
if only to protect or change their class status, hence their

allotment of land.   The idea here is to keep the succession
of campaigns in the mass struggle process on the track of
class lines.   Otherwise, the perennial spectre of backsliding
into the traditional clan, family and village patterns of conflict[26] may rob the drive of its social and ideological content, if not reinforce the moral order and social relations of
the opposing social order.   In this purpose, a scheme of
class analysis is crucial as the root of guide lines virtually
determining liquidation or survival and, beyond this, alterations in one's allotment of land, on to which a continuing
'turnover' in land and social relations is bound.   Once the
meaning of the land investigation drive was revealed, few
could possibly afford to resist being absorbed into the class
struggle process in which class analysis finds its *raison
d'être*:   'The land investigation drive is the most fierce
class struggle - all attempts to substitute the mass class
struggle with peaceful and percentage calculation methods [of
simple class analysis] are wrong'.[27]   The problems of applying a scheme of class analysis in the field were as complex
and subtle as the limits of individual ingenuity in avoiding
class investigation and liquidation or confiscation of property.   Simply put, however, the class line in 1933 boiled
down to the leadership of the 'working class', relying upon
the poor peasants while uniting closely with the middle
peasants, so as to launch a determined assault on feudal and
semi-feudal social forces, that is, landlords and rich
peasants (see Appendix A for principles of class analysis).

   The class analysis aspect of the land investigation drive
and the manner in which the former provided the conceptual
structure of the latter in terms of re-ordering land and
social relations is equalled in prominence by its ideological
content.   The strategy is not only one of further altering

social ranking in status and power and social relations out of
which a new social concentration of power is delivered for the
prosecution of war, but one of compromising the moral order
which, in part, maintained these in existence.   The moral
thrust of land revolution into the stability of the opponent's
social order is emphasized in Mao's complaint that 'many of
our comrades in the workers' and peasants' prosecution department do not realize that the unfolding of the land investigation drive is the best opportunity to launch an ideological
struggle'.[28]   The connection between established social
values and norms as the target of the ideological content of
mass campaigns in land investigation and the backsliding into
feudal social relations and social concentration of power is
viewed as follows:

> Ideological struggle in and outside the Party has not yet
> been launched on a large scale.   Therefore, in many places
> not only the masses but also responsible persons compro-
> mised with, and capitulated to the local despots, gentry,
> landlords and rich peasants because of family ties or a
> relationship of being close associates, which are feudal
> type social relations.[29]

The view here is made clear that power flows into the hands
of the opponent through a certain fabric of land and social
relations towards which society is drawn back - unless the
underlying moral order on which all rests is firmly compromised.   It is a short step indeed from this early preoccupation with the highly pressurized ideological or thought
struggle content of mass resocialization to the summation in
1951 that 'all propaganda tasks of the Communists are ideological tasks, that is ideological struggle or struggle in
thought',[30] the purpose of which is the dissemination of moral
order.

As a consequence of the uneven distribution, depth and rate
of mass resocialization in the field, the land investigation
drive is concentrated on the backward districts, townships and
villages in which the masses have not been fully mobilized, by
drawing from advanced areas the most effective of the activist
elements to lead the drive. As not unexpected, the commence-
ment of the drive is a thorough propaganda campaign in all
villages and hamlets highlighted by mass meetings which are
motivated through activists primarily in the poor-peasant
corps and the farm labour unions. The application of propaganda and agitation campaigns was to avoid concentration on
mass meetings at the district or township levels, since it was
only on the village and hamlet basis that contact with the
broad masses was most thorough and repetitive. This propaganda method of seeking out and organizing local activist
elements and, through these, pushing into action the remainder
of the local masses (after which the former are then shifted
to campaigns in other backward areas) is, Mao cautions, super-
ficially very slow 'penetration work' but, in fact, is the
only method which leads to quick results.

Once the meaning and purpose of the land investigation
drive has been initially absorbed throughout the various mass
organizations, the leading one being the poor-peasant corps as
the main instrument of the drive, the crucial development of
the mass struggle to 'investigate the classes' in the light of
practical social relations is unfolded. In this investigation process, as carried out by the masses, four items are
salient:

   (a) To mobilize the poor and miserable masses of a given
   village to investigate the landlords and rich peasants of
   the same village, (b) To hold numerous mass meetings for
   the 'explanation of the classes', (c) To find out active

elements and educate them, and it does not matter even if
there is only one such element available; and through
them, to come into close contact with the local masses, to
develop the poor-peasant corps and to unfold the local
class struggle ..., (e) In places where there have been
struggles between two different clans, there should be
signed a 'reconciliation pact' at a meeting of delegates of
the two clans, admitting their past mistakes and agreeing
to substitute the class struggle for their clan struggle.[31]
It is suggested as vital to maintain the mass investigation
process within the village unit, that is, prevent one class
from investigating another of a different village simply to
restrain campaigns from backsliding towards feudal social
relations and their traditional patterns of village and clan
conflict. Proceeding from this into the more detailed clan
relations, it is 'an important tactic in the land investigation drive to mobilize the poor and miserable masses bearing
a common family name in a village to search out the landlords
and rich peasants with the same family name in the same village'.[32] Within the unfolding of the 'investigation of the
classes', prosecution committees on the township level are
formed to carry out prosecution campaigns culminating in mass
trial meetings. The method here is 'to follow the mass
struggle in class investigation, direct the masses to act as
informers, trace counter-revolutionary clues, and arrest
counter-revolutionary elements'.[33] The function of prosecu-
tions and mass trials is described as being dual in nature,
on one hand to purge 'bad elements' and, at the same time,
utilize participation in the prosecution process to mature
further a mass revolutionary consciousness. The determination of class status is undertaken with an analysis by the
land investigation committee based on the gathering of reports

on the class status of landlords and rich peasants. After
the poor-peasant corps has reached a decision in this determination of class status, the entire matter is submitted to
the township Soviet for decision and the district Soviet for
approval. It was only at the completion of the 'investigation of the classes' that a fresh confiscation and redistribution of the property of those prosecuted took place, making it
very much to the advantage of the potential mass of recipients
to arrive at the appropriate conclusions.

Mao Tse-tung concludes that an important measure of success
in the land investigation drive is the number of complaints
lodged with the township or district Soviet to protest against
the assignment of class status. Contrary to the majority of
ineffective drives during which many landlords and rich
peasants, knowing they could rely on established social relations, challenged their class assignment: 'This time, however, it was not that the landlords and rich peasants did not
want to protest, but that they were in no position to protest.
None of the members of their clan and none of their relatives
would give them support.'[34] In essence, it was the weight of
established social relations that continuously threatened to
turn the land investigation drive back towards the old social
concentration of power:

> Above all, they have not been able to abandon their clan
> and local relations during the violent development of the
> land investigation drive, thus giving shelter to the land-
> lord and rich-peasant elements of the same clan or of the
> same hamlet.[35]

If the KMT sources reviewing captured documents are to be
believed (and there is no reason to suspect their sincerity,
if only because their comments were intended for internal
review), the rather shocking absence of even the most rudimen-

tary insight into the kind of social phenomenon posed by the
land revolution is revealed in the following commentary:

> In June 1933, after Po Ku (namely Ch'in Pang-hsien) leader
> of the Stalin faction in China and some others slipped into
> the bandit area from Shanghai, the land investigation move-
> ment was put forth.   Apparently, the purpose of this move-
> ment was to investigate the classes in the villages and
> thoroughly solve the land problem, but actually they wanted
> to use this movement to increase the government's income.[36]

STAGE THREE: LAND RECONSTRUCTION

Knowing full well that the process of land revolution is
really only as solid as its weakest social links, Mao Tse-tung
rather neglects a discussion of the intensified struggle area
which is in the stage of land reconstruction.   In contrast to
the social weaknesses and instabilities of the comparatively
retarded struggle areas, the third stage is found only in
those areas in which the progress of mass resocialization has
yielded 'solid Soviet regimes' to the degree that the main
problems here are reform of the land with regard to farming
methods and productivity.   Presumably, we can observe here at
least a minimum of new power relations necessary for the prosecution of mass guerrilla warfare in the process of 'turnover'
in land and social relations:

> In the intensified struggle area, solid Soviet regimes have
> been established, local armed forces and revolutionary mass
> organizations have been widely set up, the feudal and semi-
> feudal forces of landlords and rich peasants have been com-
> pletely crushed, land has been thoroughly redistributed,
> and the land struggle of the peasant masses has entered
> upon the stage for the reform of land, the development of

its productivity.   Accordingly, the central problem here
is the problem of land reconstruction.[37]

It is necessary to recall that the insurgent *débâcle* of the
Fifth KMT Encirclement Campaign led to the general collapse of
the Central Soviet Area, little of which had, as a consequence, much opportunity to pass into or remain in this stage.
Understandably, therefore, Mao's interest here is largely, to
my knowledge, confined to the propagation of Soviet work
methods as exemplified by two 'model' townships.   This he did
in one report on Ch'ang-kang township in southern Kiangsi, and
another on Ts'ai-hsi township in western Fukien.[38]   It is, of
course, simply a question of shifting a part of the emphasis
in intensified struggle areas away from acute mass resocialization to land productivity, since the former is never entirely banished from the central thrust of land revolution.   Mao
Tse-tung's 'Ch'ang-kang Hsiang Survey' (December 1933) is
then, for our purposes, not entirely without interest.   Being
in comparison a remarkably detailed piece of research, especially its basis in statistical data, on the nature of a model
base area in the Central Soviet Area, this survey runs through
nineteen topics of analysis: political division and census,
the township congress, the latest election, committees under
the township Soviet, local military units, living conditions
of the masses, adjustment of labour force and the problem of
farm cattle, promotion of bonds, co-operative movement, cultural movement, health movement, social relief, women, children, workers, poor-peasant corps, propaganda teams, shock
brigade and finally, revolutionary contest.[39]

Of these a number of items are worth a brief discussion.
By means of introduction Mao suggests that 'as everybody
knows, all work of the Soviet is executed at the township and
the municipality Soviet'; and furthermore, 'without knowing

how the township and the municipality Soviet work, one just
cannot take up the leadership in Soviet work, or really solve
problems according to the guiding principle: "All Soviet
work obeys the demands of the war of revolution".'[40]   The
strategic consequence of encirclement campaigns of the enemy
is the necessity to expand the domain of mass mobilization:

> Now that our missions have been outlined, and many plans
> ranging from Red Army expansion to road and bridge con-
> struction have been announced, the question is how to
> mobilize the masses to carry out these missions and plans.
> The war of revolution is extremely tense [the Fifth KMT
> Encirclement Campaign] requiring us to find a solution to
> this problem quickly and universally.   The solution is not
> to be found by imagination, but by collecting fresh and
> concrete experience during the course of mobilizing the
> masses to execute various missions, by making such experi-
> ence widely known, and by expanding the domain of mass
> mobilization so as to make it suitable for higher missions
> and plans.[41]

Another item of interest is a point of administrative
structure, that is, the fabric of committees through which the
work of the Soviet is executed.   Mao suggests that there is a
functional distinction between the Soviet committees and mass
organizations in that the former are viewed as part of the
Soviet organization and, presumably, fluctuate in composition
as the work of the Soviet changes direction.   In this regard
it is of particular interest that the land investigation committee is no longer in existence in Ch'ang-kang township.[42]
Accordingly, new committees are required to fulfil the tasks
of land reconstruction.   This survey provides a detailed re-
affirmation in real practice of Mao's earlier principle in
regard to the six time and spatial distinctions in the strat-

egy of land revolution that 'such a state of things determines
the direction of our work':[43]

> The village committees of Ch'ang-kang township (many com-
> mittees exist at village level) have enabled the Soviet to
> associate itself closely with the vast masses.   They are
> very good inventions as the work of the Soviet develops to
> a high degree.   Since each village has a five-man commit-
> tee for each type of work, the corresponding township com-
> mittee needs only five members.   Besides, four of the five
> members of each township committee are the heads of the
> corresponding committees of their respective villages.   In
> this way, a network is built for each work.   This is
> greatly helpful to the work of the township Congress.
> However, the comrades of Ch'ang-kang township look at these
> committees in the same light as mass organizations, such as
> the labour union and the poor-peasant corps, without know-
> ing that they are a part of the Soviet organization.   This
> is not right.   Among these committees, the 'Construction
> Committee' may be abolished.   The 'Land Committee' has
> been changed to 'Experimental Farm Committee' in such
> places as Hsing-kuo county where land struggle was
> thorough.   Besides, such committees as 'Food', 'Census',
> 'Industrial Inspection', and 'Red Curfew' should be
> added.[44]

The remaining item is the scope to which mass ressocializa-
tion is developed in an advanced base area.   This is best
illustrated by the mass organization of children: 'Eighty per
cent of the children from seven to fifteen years old have
joined the children's corps.'[45]   The rationale for concern
with children is made quite explicit in a discussion of the
role of the Youth League which is: '(1) to draw genuinely
poor children into joining the children's corps, (2) launch a

struggle of the broad labouring children to strive for the
total realization of the particular interests of the children
as stipulated by the Soviet power, (3) lead the broad masses
of children in joining the fierce struggles for the Soviet
power and the Red Army and against the rich peasants and old
culture, (4) give the children Communist education in a way
they can understand, that is, a way appropriate to a child's
mind.'[46]   This just serves to illustrate further the revisionist obsession with social order in the theory and practice
of war which is, of course, totally foreign, if not scanda-
lous to the classical mentality.

I should end by reminding that excluded from this sketch
of the theory of land revolution intended as an alteration of
land and social relations and (to be discussed later) for the
prosecution of mass guerrilla war is a host of related considerations.   These include, among others, the structural shifts
generated in the very important social fluctuations (in class
status) during and after land revolution; the making of clear
distinctions, in the first place, particularly as regards the
many border-line cases straddling class lines; and, even more
fundamental, the devising and correct application of appropriate criteria for class differentiation and land redistribution
to prevent the alteration of land and social relations from
alienating too many of the individuals it was intended to
secure.   This last point was particularly important in dealing with those already on the knife's edge of classification
between friend and foe, and especially those who had moved up
the scale of class differentiation sufficiently close to this
knife's edge by acquiring new status and land in the social
fluctuations flowing from land revolution.

6   Block-house and guerrilla warfare

It is one matter to have devised and implemented an effective scheme of social strategy and tactics, and quite another to integrate this fully with the strategic and tactical employment of armed power - especially if the strategists involved are languishing under the weight of classical tradition.   As revolutionaries, they may well see the importance of social order, but as classicists they can still cast aside the notion of the will to resist being a function of moral and social order as the basis for the actual conduct of war.   That is to say, it is not necessary that revolutionaries should arrive at a state of affairs in which the instruments of strategy - especially armed power in perfect unity with a scheme of social strategy and tactics - embrace new form and movement at precise points in time and space to fulfil the obsession with social order.   Once they do so, however, they stumble on to the very social and moral phenomena of which the conception of war has always been the natural extension - making it necessary that what began as a concern of revolutionaries blossoms into an obsession which everywhere raises questions concerning the theory of strategy, for reasons already discussed.   We may well pay now for the anomalies of our classical heritage; strategists, whether they initially proceed from a concern

with social order or not, should find it harder to escape such
questions resting on the fact that war is the natural extension of the social pursuit of power by other means of which
social morality is the principal author.   So long as everyone
is willing and able to sweep this fact under the rug, then
strategists who may well happen to be revolutionaries can,
without penalty, cast aside the notion of the will to resist
being a function of moral and social order in the immediate
conduct of war.

Now, in order to reformulate the theory and practice of war
so that the instruments of strategy embrace new form and movement at precise points in time and space to fulfil the obsession with social order of which the will to resist is a function, requires the entire matter to arrive at a certain understanding on *the social content of guerrilla warfare*.   Not
only must this form of warfare be seen as crucial, but also
the classical notion that 'guerrilla warfare is only an auxiliary form of battle' must be firmly rejected.   In its
place, the dispersal of armed power into the guerrilla form
carefully concealed in the fabric of the opponent's social
order must be employed to police the slow and painstaking
alteration of the fabric of land and social relations in the
process of land revolution.   This is indeed the real basis by
which one can make sense of the theory of protracted war in
its original and Chinese context.   In this case, the true
method of distinction between traditional and revisionist
principles of strategy is the question of guerrilla warfare as
the means of policing land revolution, around which the remaining stages and forms in protracted war revolve.   This
novel formulation, which leads us into the larger questions of
general theory, was the product of long and bitter disputes on
the nature of strategy, tactics and social order.   As already

mentioned, their focus had shifted, as the Kiangsi Soviet period came to an end, somewhat away from the gaining acceptance of rural base areas and the central need of land revolution in the development of bases to the exact nature of Red Army operations around these vital bases.   The culmination of this was the occasion of the Kuomintang (KMT) innovation of block-house warfare first used in the successful Fifth KMT Encirclement Campaign (September 1933-November 1934) lodged against the Central Soviet Area.   Prior to this the Red Army had withstood the first four Encirclement Campaigns by attacking the enemy through mobile warfare and, in co-ordination with this, the expansion of guerrilla warfare behind enemy lines.   But it was the KMT innovation of block-house warfare in the Fifth Campaign that provided the occasion of the celebrated, if little-researched, dispute over the 'simple guerrilla warfare method of the past'.   Whatever mixture of personalities and Party politics flowed in such disagreements, they had real strategic content to the considerations of the CCP faced with the first problem of survival in the heat of encirclement and suppression.

What I propose to discuss presently then is the revisionist-classicist dispute over the strategy prevailing in the Red Army's attempt to find a solution to the KMT innovation of block-house warfare of the Fifth KMT Encirclement Campaign. This is to illustrate the origins of revisionist thinking lodged in the real practice of war, and beyond this, the rather important fact that this new vision of strategy only blossomed out of a growing reaction against classical impedimenta.   Again, I find it necessary to emphasize that there remain many issues surrounding the KMT successes in the Fifth Campaign and the collapse of the Central Soviet Area which are excluded from my present discussion.   Not the least of

these is, perhaps, the extent to which Mao Tse-tung was fully
justified in attributing the responsibility for this insurgent
débâcle especially to the principles of strategy of the classical strategist Hua Fu. This matter is a fruitless quibble
simply because it is, in the final analysis, largely unanswer-
able. What is of sole importance here is that Mao, however
justified, employs an increasingly articulate revisionist
critique to purge what was essentially a classical formulation
devised and imposed on the Red Army by Hua Fu known as the
theory of 'short, swift thrusts'. It is this single issue
which is of very special interest, being one of the most controversial if not critical phases in the origins of strategic
revisionism. I draw here the first substantive view[1] for
Western strategists into the disagreement which so vividly
illustrates in the real practice of war the very points about
general theory to which I draw attention.

It is important to recall that Mao, at the time of the
Fifth KMT Encirclement Campaign, had already been ousted by
Chou En-lai, probably as early as the Ningtu Conference of
August 1932, from his position in the army and, as a result,
simply lost his influence over military matters.[2] Certainly
by 8 May 1933, Chou En-lai, by becoming political commissar
of the Red Army, had gained control of the Red Army in general and the First Front Army in particular.[3] Presumably,
Mao's main preoccupation just prior to, and for the first
month or so of the Fifth KMT Encirclement Campaign was the
previously discussed land investigation drive. This not unimportant circumstance enabled Mao to escape responsibility
for the general collapse of the Central Soviet Area as the
dénouement of this campaign. Moreover, it is coupled with
the strong suspicion that the German military agent Li T'e
(Otto Braun) sent by the Comintern to the Central Soviet Area

in August 1933,[4] actually pulled the wires behind the scenes,
especially as regards the Fifth Campaign.[5]   All of this is of
some interest since the identity of Hua Fu serving as a *nom de
guerre* for either Otto Braun[6] or Chou En-lai[7] appears to have
been until recently open to question.   Whatever the reality
of the matter is, it is not of vital importance for our purposes.   However, if the former is correct (the alternative I
prefer, if only because Chou En-lai's signed articles[8] published during the Fifth Campaign differ, quite distinctly, in
style, temperament and content from those published under the
pseudonym of Hua Fu), then it can be said that the character
of the Fifth Campaign was influenced by German classical
advisers on both sides, General von Seeckt being Otto Braun's
counterpart in the KMT camp.[9]   This being the case, the
flavour of strategic thinking which prevailed in this campaign
should not be unexpected.   Nor should one find unusual the
scathing dismissal of Hua Fu's strategic and tactical formulations first laid out by Mao in the Tsunyi Resolutions adopted
by the Conference of the Politburo little more than two months
after the collapse of the Central Soviet Area and the com-
mencement of the Long March, October 1934.   It is in these
Resolutions that we find a partially articulated scheme of the
general form, time and spatial distinctions in which the
organization and application of armed power is conceptualized,
later given in the theory of protracted war.

It is, or should be, at once obvious that block-house warfare is a poor solution to the social phenomenon posed by
strategic revisionism, simply because it fails to grasp the
essential point.   Chou En-lai quite correctly understood the
strategic object of block-house warfare to be a classical one.
That is to say, its *essential* purpose is gradually to flush
out the armed forces of the opponent who remain blind to the

convention of 'decisive battle': 'By building block-houses
everywhere and creating a blockade line of several thousand *li*
around the Soviet region, the enemy tries to conduct a final
decisive battle with the Red Army'.[10]   In the view of the
Tsunyi Resolutions, the KMT decision to adopt block-house warfare was a consequence of its failure to find 'decisive
battle' solutions in the first four Encirclement Campaigns:

> After the failure of the 4th 'Encirclement', the KMT,
> Chiang Kai-shek, and his imperialist military advisers knew
> the disadvantages of fighting with us in the soviet by
> using the strategy and tactics of 'deep penetration'.
> Therefore, in the 5th 'Encirclement', [they] adopted the
> strategy and tactics of a protracted war and the principle
> of block-houses.   Their attempt was to wear out our human
> and material resources, to reduce the size of our soviet
> and finally to destroy us by engaging our main forces.[11]

According to KMT sources reviewing a captured publication
by Hua Fu, the shift to block-house strategy forced upon the
Red Army a drastic alteration in its guerrilla warfare method
of the past in favour of building Red block-houses, in front
of which operations of 'short, swift thrusts' were unleashed
by the regular forces of the Red Army:

> The tactics adopted by the National Army in suppressing the
> bandits before the 5th Encirclement and Suppression were
> mainly that of resolute assaults [into their base areas]
> which caused the National Army to suffer some defeats.
> When starting its 5th Encirclement and Suppression Cam-
> paign, the National Army, based on its previous battle
> experiences, changed its policy.   They set up many block-
> houses and adopted a strategy of advancing gradually and
> steadily and entrenching themselves at every step in order
> to eliminate the bandit army's power, destroy its resour-

ces, and also systematically to have the various technical troops co-ordinate with the infantry.   The bandits called this tactic 'block-house warfare'.   The bandits admitted that they could not cope with this tactic by using the guerrilla warfare methods of the past, and they were forced to search for new tactics.   Thus we have the so-called defence tactic of 'building strong-points' and 'short, swift thrusts' tactic.[12]

KMT sources list eleven items which constitute a résumé of the guerrilla tactics of the Red Army largely discarded prior to the Fifth Campaign: (1) breaking up the whole into parts, (2) assembling the parts into a whole, (3) harass the strong and destroy the weak, (4) avoid the strong and attack the weak, (5) strengthen our defence works and clear the field (of the population and grain with the Red Army in retreat), (6) fighting in circles, (7) 'sparrow' warfare (employing rapid movement of small guerrilla bands to give the impression of large formations), (8) penetrate-deep-into-the-mountains policy, (9) break out of the encirclement, (10) threaten the enemy (morale operations), and (11) look at the far distance from high mountains (luring the opponent into mountainous and unfamiliar terrain).[13]

Mao Tse-tung having been consistently edged out of positions of real influence, especially over military matters, to the probable point of semi-exile and probation just prior to the Long March,[14] the Tsunyi Resolutions provided the first opportunity for him effectively to criticize the military line prevailing in the Red Army during the Fifth Campaign.   The Tsunyi Resolutions constitute an indictment especially against two men, Comrades XX and Hua Fu, the former, it is generally presumed, being Po Ku[15] as the representative of the Party centre who led the Military Commission.   According to the

text of the Resolutions, 'the enlarged Conference of the
Politburo specially names Comrade XX for his serious mistakes
in this respect, for he, as the representative of the Centre,
led the Military Commission'.[16] Since in this capacity 'he
did not correct Comrade Hua Fu's mistaken way of conducting
the war; nor did he rectify the abnormalities in the Military Commission in good time - on the contrary he actively
encouraged the development of the mistakes',[17] the entire
matter, then is essentially redirected towards Hua Fu.

In those circumstances, which led to the collapse of the
Central Soviet Area, 'Comrade Hua Fu monopolized all the work
of the Military Commission', and thus 'all different views on
military matters were not only unheeded but also suppressed
by all available means'.[18] As a consequence, the inevitable
was that 'in the 5th campaign, because the policy of pure
defence resulted from a fear of the block-houses and the
theory of "short, swift thrusts" put forward by Comrade Hua
Fu, we switched from mobile to positional warfare'.[19] The
former is, of course, the cornerstone of the first stage in
protracted war; the opponent, seeking 'decisive battle', is
lured through mobile operations into the appropriate expanse
of base areas in which his armed forces are bled by a hostile
mass of people and the foreign social order through which
they conduct mass guerrilla war, by the extension of which
(in the 1938 version) the cancerous guerrilla zones spring to
life in his rear areas during the first two stages. In the
eyes of the Resolutions, Hua Fu's disdain for this strategy
is made quite clear: 'In consequence, past experience of
mobile warfare was discarded, the method of luring the enemy
to come in and destroying him was discarded'.[20] Apart from
their elusive existence having only recently appeared in
translation, the essential interest of the Tsunyi Resolutions

is, then, that we see for the first time a partially articulated conception of the form, time and spatial distinctions
later developed into the theory of protracted war.   Of even
more interest is the conclusion that this first real instance
of insurgent reasoning was further motivated by a general reaction against the thin convention on which classicalism
rests.   This is shown in the following excerpts:

> The enlarged conference of the Politburo agrees that on the
> strength of all available evidence, our failure to defeat
> the enemy's 5th 'Encirclement' was mainly due to the mili-
> tary line of pure defence.   All efforts to use the Party's
> correct line to defend the mistaken line of the military
> leadership (e.g., Comrade XX's report and Comrade Hua Fu's
> statement) are in vain.[21]

> The leaders of the pure defence policy misunderstood the
> problems of a protracted war and *blitzkrieg*.   It must be
> realized that the civil war in China is not a short, but a
> long, protracted war.[22]

> The leaders of the pure defence policy assigned to the Red
> Army the central tasks of halting the enemy's advance and
> destroying parts of the enemy forces by 'short, swift
> thrusts'.[23]

> The pure defence line which voluntarily put ourselves in a
> passive position did not and could not in one blow defeat
> the enemy along the entire front;   it endeavoured to halt
> the enemy there.   Comrade XX had in the past issued the
> slogan: 'Attack along the entire front'.   This was
> changed to 'Defend the entire front'.   Strategically,
> both were wrong.[24]

The pure defence strategy in the 5th campaign was fundamentally wrong;   under its guidance, the 'dare-to-die' battles (e.g., the battles of Maosanting, Sanhsifang, P'ingliao and Kuangch'ang) were equally wrong.   The Red Army should have avoided all these battles in which [it] had no confidence of victory.[25]

To the leaders of the policy of pure defence and short, swift thrusts, all this was perfectly natural and logical.[26]

[The block-houses] make the enemy's units tired, disperse his strength, and nurse his reliance on them - a loss of confidence in victory once he leaves them.   He must come out of them when he advances towards us;   he cannot build them all over the country in order to restrict our operations.   All these are in our favour to defeat the principle of block-houses.   And our method of defeating it is still mobile warfare - by relying on the development of guerrilla wars around the block-houses to give support to the operations of the Red Army and relying on the penetration of [our] agitators working among the white armies.[27]

Only by developing from defence to counter-offensive (both in campaigns and strategically) and then to offence, by winning decisive engagements and by whittling down the enemy's strength, can we pulverize the enemy, defend our soviets and develop the soviet revolutionary movement.
    In accordance with this strategic line, we must not engage the enemy in a decisive battle in which we have no confidence to win because we have neither discovered nor created the enemy's weakness.   We should use our secon-

dary forces (e.g., guerrilla units, armed masses, independent battalions and regiments, and a part of the main
forces of the Red Army) to confuse or bait the enemy.
[We] must check the enemy with mobile warfare while our
main forces should retreat to a suitable distance or transfer themselves to the enemy's flank or rear.   [They
should] be secretly assembled, awaiting a favourable opportunity to strike at the enemy.   Fighting on interior
lines, the Red Army's retreat and hiding can tire the
enemy out and cause him to feel conceited and relaxed,
thereby inducing him to make mistakes and expose his weaknesses.   This is to pave the way to a transformation into
counter-offensive and decisive victories.[28]

The soviet revolution has been developed and consolidated
by continuously defeating the enemy 'Encirclements'.
Therefore, under favourable conditions, we absolutely must
shift from defence to counter-attack or offence so as to
destroy the enemy and his 'Encirclement' (e.g., the first
four campaigns and the 5th campaign before the battle of
Kuangch'ang).   Under unfavourable conditions, we may temporarily retreat in order to preserve our strength.   When
favourable conditions present themselves again, [we] should
transfer to counter-attack or offence (e.g., the 5th campaign after the battle of Kuangch'ang).   This is the first
basic principle.[29]

However, in the 5th campaign, *all* these principles were
violated.[30]

The Tsunyi Resolutions indicate, without reserve, that the
origins of the theory of protracted war are quite deeply
rooted in the Kiangsi Soviet period, the last portion of

which, Mao insists, consisted of a classical *débâcle*.   Of
special interest in the dispute over whether a mass of people
and the foreign social order through which they conduct mass
guerrilla war should be used to bleed the war capacity of the
opponent or, on the other hand, if his armed forces should be
met at the extremities of the Central Soviet Area by Red
block-houses in front of which prevail short, swift thrusts by
regular forces, is the appearance of the three stages of protracted war.   The pattern of stages of defence, counter-
attack and offence coupled with the insistence that these constitute 'the first basic principle' in which the organization
and application of armed power is determined was further elab-
orated in a December 1936 résumé by Mao of the five Encirclement Campaigns:

> In defensive warfare the retreat to the prescribed terminal
> point belongs basically to the passive, or 'defence',
> stage.   The counter-offensive belongs to the active, or
> 'attack', stage.   Although the strategic defensive retains
> its defensive character, throughout its duration, still as
> compared with the retreat the counter-offensive is transi-
> tional between the strategic defensive and the strategic
> offensive, and in the nature of a prelude to the strategic
> offensive;   it is precisely for the purpose of the counter-
> offensive that troops are concentrated.[31]

The similarities between this and the three stages found in
the essay 'On Protracted War' (May 1938) are more than
obvious.[32]

This is not to say that the Tsunyi Resolutions set out what
is essentially a fully matured revisionist theory of strategy.
To my knowledge, there is no evidence of this period that suggests a highly integrated theory in which distinctions in
space (insurgent base areas, guerrilla zones and counter-

insurgent strongholds) and form (mobile, guerrilla and positional warfare) were fully worked into these three stages in
time, as I have previously discussed.   The Kiangsi Soviet
period gave birth to the nine general distinctions, which only
later went into the theory of protracted war, as they seem to
drift largely without substantive connection throughout the
documents of this period.   The reason for this is that these
nine distinctions and their interplay in a maturing strategic
situation in which the organization and application of armed
power is conceived only make sense if they are seen in the
larger context of an invasion of social order in the first
place.   Thus, for these to be fully worked out requires the
understanding that their common basis is a social one resting
on mass resocialization in the field (as previously discussed).   This provides the vital connection between the use of
armed power and the general invasion of social order in which
the former is an offspring and servant of the latter.   As I
shall further elaborate in the next chapter, this vital connection balances on the one key to the entire strategy, that
is, *the social content of the guerrilla phase of operations*
throughout which occurs the principal thrust of the invasion
of social order, and around which all these distinctions
revolve.   Suffice it to conclude here that, in contrast to
this, we recall in the strategy and tactics of land revolution
the varied phases of operations which structure the invasion
of social order, their distribution being fitted into a tri-
partite pattern in space.   *But this was largely abandoned*
here without any substantive connection to the organization
and application of armed power.   The revisionist state of
affairs in which the obsession with social order and thus with
a scheme of social strategy and tactics such as land revolution acts as the conceptual basis for the organization and

application of armed power as its offspring and servant, is
then cut short. As a consequence, the three stages in time
in which the organization and application of armed power is
now conceived seem to merit only some social content and an
indication of the mobile nature of the first, coupled with a
distaste for positional warfare and, most importantly, the
addendum of guerrilla operations somewhat lacking clear social
content or position in time.[33] In essence, the vital connections between a scheme of social strategy and tactics through
which the invasion of social order is consummated principally
in the guerrilla phase and the organization and application of
armed power as its real offspring and servant were, as of the
Tsunyi Conference, simply left in a shambles. Armed power is
not yet fully integrated into the picture as an instrument of
revisionist strategy.

What is more startling about these Resolutions is that the
above distinctions in time, space and form (which ultimately
make sense in terms of an invasion of social order) only began
to blossom out of a growing reaction against classical impedimenta in the real practice of war. Precisely for this
reason, the Tsunyi Resolutions are difficult, if not impossible to understand without being read in conjunction with
Hua Fu's rather infrequent, but highly important articles.
These, to my knowledge, have remained untranslated and certainly have not received a percentage of the attention they
merit because they so perfectly illustrate in the real practice of war the very points about general theory to which I
draw attention. As a consequence, I find it necessary to
take the unusual course in quoting from them *in extenso* as the
classical midwife, according to Mao Tse-tung, assisting the
birth of insurgent reasoning:

In its battles with the KMT army in the past, the Red Army

of the Central Soviet Region has gained many great victories. These victories were gained by attacking the
enemy on the move through mobile warfare and, in co-ordination with it, the expansion of guerrilla warfare behind the
enemy lines. This clearly shows the basic characteristics
of the revolutionary army; a high degree of flexibility,
resolute in actions and brave in attack.

The enemy has received many bitter lessons in the past,
and therefore the present 5th 'encirclement and suppression' launched by the enemy totally differs from the previous campaigns. In strategy, the enemy abandons the
resolute thrusts adopted in the past and is now trying
gradually to exhaust our manpower and material, for which
they have adopted a special tactic. The main characteristic of this tactic is the principle of block-houses, and
with this, gradually to reduce the size of our Soviet
regions and deprive us of the possibility of carrying out
mobile warfare. They also want to isolate our guerrilla
forces in their rear lines so as to cut off these forces
from our main force. And at the end [they hope to] create
a tight network of block-houses around our Soviet regions
and Red Army. The enemy also systematically employs
technical warfare - adequate ground firepower (machine
guns, mortars and artillery units) and the Air Force rein-
forcing and supporting its weak infantry.

Clearly, using our simple guerrilla warfare method of
the past is insufficient to face such a tactic of the
enemy. In order to win decisive victories in the face of
the enemy's new tactics, the Red Army must, therefore, have
recourse to new military tactics. Besides maintaining our
main virtues of the past, we must adopt new fighting
methods. The new tactics under the present conditions

must mainly be based on the following three principles:

A With the object of carrying out guerrilla actions,
send small units which, in co-ordination with local forces,
should carry out guerrilla warfare in the enemy's rear
lines, its flanks and sometimes in its front, in order to
detain, weaken and disintegrate the enemy.   [These units]
can carry through this important mission only with the
support of the local people and only if they demonstrate a
high degree of initiative, flexibility and resoluteness in
all their battle actions.   Guerrilla warfare includes
missions such as destroying roads and fortifications,
strengthening our defence positions and clearing the field.

B In the most vital sectors, deploy a system of defence
to protect directly the Soviet region, and with a minimum
of men and material (also ammunition) pin down the enemy's
main forces.   Only this is a true defence.   For this purpose, fortified posts must be built or block-house areas
capable of withstanding enemy artillery and bombardments.
Or in the mountain regions, carry out continuing mobile
defensive warfare.

Under any condition, we must evaluate our army's spec-
ialities, especially its fearless vigour.   In defensive
operations we must adopt a strategy of active defence -
defending the block-houses with a small number of men and
arms, while using the main force to launch short, swift
thrusts and assaults to wipe out the enemy in front of the
block-houses.   A passive defence is bound to fail.

C Concentrate the main force in a certain direction to
launch resolute and swift thrusts and destroy the enemy's
effective force outside his block-houses.   *Although guerrilla warfare and defensive actions are indispensable in a
revolutionary war, they are only auxiliary forms of battle*

- while the mobility and swift thrusts of the main [i.e. regular armed] force have a decisive significance.   Only through this way can we win victories in the 5th 'encircle- ment and suppression' and in the enemy attacks in the future, and again switch to a strategic offensive.

But in this respect, the tactical method also changes. Regularly the enemy scarcely ever ventures over ten to twenty *li* [one *li* = one-third English mile] from its block- houses (often less), therefore it became impossible to lure the enemy deep inside our territory.   We must look for the enemy while keeping ourselves under cover, and when the enemy attacks, we must hit them fiercely in a well-planned way or through ambush.   We must mainly hit the enemy's rear units from the flank or strike at its vanguard units, and cut off the enemy's communications with his basic block-houses in order to guarantee to wipe out the enemy's effective force and capture its equipment.   When engaged in battle, we must fight with all our energy in order to settle rapidly, with one blow, the fate of the battle.[34]

Judging from recent battle experiences, [we] find it neces- sary to further relate and more specifically explain the various tactical problems mentioned in [our] previous articles:

1   It is not very often that the enemy refuses to fight a decisive battle with our main force.   Sometimes [the enemy] concentrates a large force on a narrow face-to-face front (e.g., concentrating 10 divisions or more in an area of 20 to 30 *li*, or having an assault force consisting of three to four divisions in an area of less than 10 *li*). And sometimes they are even searching for a decisive battle.

2 Under such circumstances the enemy doesn't stop
making daring advances, i.e., advancing 10 to 15 *li*, even
20 *li*, away from their basic block-houses. Concentrating
several columns, with each column consisting of two to
three divisions, the enemy would employ its special manoeuvre - mainly that of alternate attacks (e.g., first one
or both flank columns advance, after which the centre main
column rapidly advances; when one of its columns encoun-
ters our main force, this column will temporarily stop
advancing, build fortifications and deploy its firepower
in order to form a face-to-face battlefront, while the
other columns will try to break through the resistance of
our detain forces and advance to the designated area to
build block-houses). This way, in campaigns, [the enemy]
creates a fan-shape attack throughout the entire front
line. By penetrating in columns, [the enemy] could easily
shift to the direction where our main force is located and
could rapidly and surely create a face-to-face battlefront.

3 The enemy's attacking tactics are based on the fact
that our firepower is relatively weak. Also, they try to
overcome the weakness of their troops in the political
aspect by attacking in large concentrated forces, which
results in a Napoleon-type tactic : in the lead are the
most reliable troops who form a broad and rather dispersed
firepower force to carry out a firepower battle. Under
their cover, a concentrated assault force will advance in
concentrated columns, followed by Fascist troops (armed
with swords and pistols or machine guns) who will, without
mercy, force the soldiers to attack and not have them
retreat (those who retreat will either be beheaded or
shot).

Such an assault method often inflicted heavy casualties

among the enemy.   On the other hand, bayonet combat has a
nature of being an unyielding and protracted battle (often
assault and counter-assaults or seven to eight assaults are
launched throughout the day).

4 The use of technics also conforms with this tactical
method.   But the enemy seldom carried out systematic air
raids and preparations to adjust the fire-range of their
artillery before a battle.   As soon as they launch their
attack, they use the infantry (the infantry's firepower and
its assault force), while [their] cannons and mortars are
mainly used to give direct support to the infantry.
Planes will continuously observe the battlefield in order
to hinder our mobility on the battlefield, while bombardments - the same as with the artillery - are carried out
mainly to directly support their infantry.

5 In co-ordinating our firepower, we must seriously
take such tactics of the enemy into account.   Before a
bayonet combat by the infantry, it is not necessary to distinguish time and terrain in the purpose of launching long-
range firing and to make preparations to arrange continuous
firepower.   Firepower battles and bayonet battles must be
integrated and turned into well-planned mobile actions.

When moving out from [our] hidden starting point,
machine guns must take the lead and occupy positions.   The
machine guns are not used to suppress the enemy's firepower
(this can't be achieved since the enemy has more weapons
and ammunition), but to open fire in surprise at the
enemy's concentrated assault columns.   Rifle fire has the
same task at the time the battle starts and during the time
[the enemy] is still beyond the distance for launching an
assault (when the enemy's effective force is still 200 to
500 metres away).   The enemy's machine-gunners, artillery-

men and officers are the special targets of [our] sharpshooters. When [the enemy] is within the range for
launching an assault, the machine guns and part of the
sharpshooters must continue their close-range firing while
the assault troops must use hand grenades and engage in
bayonet combat. As for the firepower of [our] mortars and
artillery (considering our shortage), it must only be concentrated in one direction (towards a certain assault
division) and mainly firing at the subsequent forces of
the enemy's assault column, that is, firing at the effective force of the enemy's concentrated columns.

Such firepower arrangement could most effectively create
casualties among the assault force of the enemy's entire
column, and is the most effective way to directly support
the assault of our infantry.

6 Mobility at the battlefield: (A) Before the enemy
ceases to advance and starts to build fortifications
(building such fortifications requires only half an hour to
one hour), and before its following troops could come in
support, [we] must rapidly approach the enemy's effective
force and settle the battle through bayonet combat.   (See
part on 'Short, Swift Thrusts' related in another article
in this issue.)[35]

Correct understanding: Short, swift thrusts mean that [we]
should advance towards the starting point of [our] attack
under cover and closely approach the routes to be taken by
the enemy so that when [we] launch a sudden attack and
assault, [we] will be able to cross the space separating us
from the enemy within the shortest time and engage in a
bayonet fight at once before the enemy has time to build
fortifications and employ its firepower.

Such a short, swift thrust assumes the character of a
surprise attack or an ambush. At the appropriate time
choose and study the terrain for engaging the enemy, reduce
the time and distance of movements at the battlefield (to
prevent from being spotted by the enemy and prevent air
attacks), and quickly settle the battle through hand-to-
hand combat before the arrival of the enemy's main force -
these are the special characteristics of such short, swift
thrusts.

Most advantageous is a short flank attack, but this too
must not be applied mechanically, for sometimes frontal
thrusts must also be launched. Assaults must often be
launched in two directions - assault on the enemy's vanguard units as support and a main assault directed to the
enemy's rear units (launched by the detain units and
assault units).[36]

One searches in vain through this obsession with armed
power as an instrument of strategy for the slightest hint of a
revisionist conception of strategy. There seems to be no
evidence of an assumption of the relative insecurity of social
resources leading to a pattern of strategy formulated on the
condition of the continuing invasion of social order principally through the dispersal of armed power in the guerrilla
form. Indeed, guerrilla warfare is entirely reduced to the
classical notion of being 'only an auxiliary form of battle'.
The range of strategic thinking is then cleared for the usual
classical bias for the 'strategic centre of gravity', being,
in essence, the armed forces of the opponent as the prime
seat of his will and capacity to wage war, the compromise of
which is, almost inevitably, therefore realized through the
contest of battle. It is here that the distinctions in time,
space and form set out by Hua Fu entirely reside. Thus any

trace of interest in the invasion of social order and therefore in a scheme of social strategy and tactics is entirely
lacking, rendering this an unlikely conceptual basis for the
organization and application of armed power.   In this event,
it is not possible that the general distinctions in time,
space and form in which this organization and application is
conceived have, in a more fundamental sense, degenerated into
socially based distinctions resting on mass resocialization
in the field or the invasion of social order.   The principles
governing the organization and application of armed power have
thus retained their independence from the sovereign linkages
to the general invasion of social order from which they
neither derive nor serve and therefore, cannot be identified
by any one of the six revisionist propositions.   In essence,
Hua Fu's conception of strategy is, quite obviously, a
straight classical proposition almost entirely dedicated to
armed power to the exclusion of social order in which, therefore, strategy defined as the formulation and distribution of
social order is a special *bête noire*, if not utterly foreign.
What we are left with is not only a view into the radical differences separating the revisionist and classical conceptions
of strategy but also the important conclusion that, in the
real practice of war, the origins of the former culminated in
a general reaction against the thin convention inherent in the
latter.

   The way is now cleared for the last remaining issue which
closes the final pages of the empirical observations made
through the writings of Chinese strategists in their experiment with revisionism.   This concerns the vital social content of guerrilla warfare unifying the instrument of armed
power with the alteration of the fabric of land and social
relations through land revolution.   It is here one finds the

key which joins all of the threads I have thus far woven into
the fabric of demonstration of strategy defined as the formulation and distribution of social order.   The entire proposal
of strategic revisionism as a general theory of strategy,
which employs these observations made through the writings of
Chinese strategists on strategy defined as the formulation and
distribution of social order, now flows straight into this one
issue around which all other strategic connections revolve.
The state in which this critical link was abandoned in the
Fifth Campaign (apart from Hua Fu's essential disinterest and
classical bias which reduced guerrilla warfare to being 'only
an auxiliary form of battle', thus effectively severing the
use of armed power from the general invasion of social order)
is summed up as follows just prior to the collapse of the
Central Soviet Area:

> The Central Committee has more than once issued a directive
> on the tasks of the Party in the guerrilla zones and on the
> possibility of launching a widespread guerrilla warfare;
> but up until now, in many regions occupied by the enemy, a
> mass guerrilla warfare has not yet been actually carried
> out.   Many guerrilla forces who went to the guerrilla
> zones were not only reduced in size, but also often re-
> treated back to the Soviet regions, while the guerrilla
> forces who persisted in carrying out activities in the
> guerrilla zones didn't mobilize the local masses and turn
> their activities into a mass guerrilla warfare.... Both
> the local Party departments in the Soviet region and the
> Party organizations in the battle zones and guerrilla zones
> lack understanding about the *political* importance of guer-
> rilla warfare.   In general, they still do not regard the
> launching of a mass guerrilla warfare as the Party's prime
> task.[37]

This fatal blunder, according to a revisionist eye not yet entirely matured, was of the utmost strategic and tactical importance, principally perpetrated by a *blitzkrieg* mentality - and one which was thrown into considerable disrepute thereafter.   Chou En-lai's eleventh hour regret of 20 August 1934, that 'the movement to develop guerrilla warfare deep behind the enemy lines was the weakest link in the Fifth Campaign'[38] was one regret in which the Chinese strategists would never so sorely languish again.

7   The Cinderella of classical theory

Social life is a moral state in the fullest sense under the conditions of violence. If a natural condition of the former is war, the guerrilla form is the means by which its instruments approach the very nearest to their primal social origins. In the degree to which the conception of war is *free* from those fatal assumptions which have contaminated, and may further contaminate it, then this conception should always pursue its social roots. It is the tension between these two that lay at the root of so much error in classical theory. Liddell Hart is here the perfect victim. The problems which his work can be seen to confront were silently bequeathed to him by the unspoken assumptions supporting earlier generations of strategists. Having envisaged the strategy of indirect approach in reaction to central obsessions embodied in the 'decisive battle' mentality, he then languished in the dilemma of how far to pursue this into a full denial of the notion of the will to resist being a function of armed forces - by altogether failing to grasp its silent convention which sustains everything. Had he only discovered the revisionist solution in which war finds its natural social basis where the will to resist is seen as a true function of moral and social order, he could have suc-

cessfully dispatched classical obsession, and achieved so
much more.   But as a thinker of his time he could not share
the advantages we do today.

This is so simply because all of the general considerations
I have been discussing could have remained less well recognized had it not been for the one fatal insight into the moral
and social roots of insurgent reasoning first unlocked by the
Chinese strategists, later imitated in South-east Asia, and,
one fears, now engulfing southern Africa.   Strategists are
increasingly likely to be pressed into a serious consideration
of the larger and foreign questions raised by a free drift of
war towards the insurgent and guerrilla model lodged firmly in
the poorly researched social dimensions of strategy.   The
real danger is our being caught in a deeper crisis in strategic theory by the comforts of tradition which draw on normally scarce resources for research, development and testing of
the usual strategic embellishments of classical theory that
may less and less serve reality - and yet in which we are
still asked to find and entrust our security.   What is
equally, if not more important from the structural side, such
deliberations for strategists may never again be quite the
same.   It is surely futile to hope to organize effectively
the daily concerns of our area of study without a secure
grasp *of the philosophical and theoretical groundwork which
informs this area of study in the first place.*   As strategists, we are set apart from all else because the root everywhere present in our deliberations is the phenomenon of violence as an articulate social activity, the endemic and unique
fact of social life; and if not the actual event itself, at
least (in the peripheral avenues of general theory) there lies
at the root of events its expectation as the prime ingredient.
But here must always remain its real use as the well-spring

from which all other considerations in general theory issue.
Otherwise, strategists simply lose the one real *raison d'être*
they may rightly call their own.   We follow from here, since
this social fact can come from nowhere else, into the principles on which social life is founded to arrive at the vision
of this life that explains, through the conception of social
order, all of the primal elements which are necessary for the
theoretical groundwork that informs our area of study and
delivers into our hands our very credentials.   It is our firm
conclusion that we must thrive on our debt to the Chinese
strategists, who had no idea of the larger philosophical and
theoretical considerations which would sooner or later be
drawn from their one extraordinary insight into the almost
too obvious impedimenta of classical theory and everything we
may still hold to be true in one degree or another.   It is
difficult to imagine how those beliefs, so full with denial of
their own roots, can survive the free drift towards general
theory that dwells on the very contractual device by which
they were so firmly sustained.   The more we grasp the real
dimensions of our subject, the deeper we flow into its inalienable social roots, the further behind we leave this
classical impedimenta.

   Classical obsession, driven onward by its latent assumption of the inviolability of social order, naturally is forced
along those avenues of reasoning by which guerrilla warfare
'is never chosen in preference to regular warfare;   it is
employed only when and where the possibilities of regular warfare have been foreclosed'.[1]   Whether the former is regarded
only as 'an auxiliary form of battle' or simply the poor substitute for the latter it is, in the classical realm, denied
real social and strategic purpose of its own.   Central to
the following reassurance is the process of reasoning which
constitutes the classical act of faith:

In any future general or limited war, guerrilla warfare
undoubtedly will be a significant supplement to regular
operations.[2]

The guerrilla can destroy but he cannot conquer. God remains on the side of the bigger battalions - and guerrilla
battalions are always small. Guerrilla warfare makes the
most of small battalions, but guerrilla troops are no more
a substitute for superior conventional forces....[3]

If general theory shares this 'faith' in the future of the
guerrilla form, it does so for entirely different reasons.
Once we knock away the thin convention on which the roots of
a good part of tradition thrive, this 'Cinderella' of classical theory is brutally transformed, now everywhere dominating
in full majesty as the purest and most forceful expression of
the same social phenomena of which war is the natural extension. Only then do the instruments of war freely approach
the very nearest to the social womb in which they are born.
When, therefore, the conception of war is free to depart from
tradition, then the great hand of moral and social order that
ultimately wields the instruments of strategy should seek out
its natural guerrilla form. If the origins of war are as I
have judged them, so should theory proceed on the basis that
it is in the very essence of things to pursue their purest
forms of expression. Only the uncertainties of reality and
those hindrances given in the first chapter remain concealed
in the real practice of war, trapping those strategists foolish enough to swallow its revisionist metamorphosis as pure
religion. But we can never hope to grasp the reality of war
unless we grasp hold of the pure forms of expression which, in
the very nature of things, this reality pursues. That the
conception of war may never attain real purity is important;

what is more important is the discovery of those principles by which it works.   If my theoretical judgment is correct about the social basis that war seeks then this conception should be drifting towards the insurgent and guerrilla form;   and if not this, at least a state of affairs in which the organization and application of armed power, in whatever form, issues from and serves the invasion of the foreign social order through which the enemy conducts war.

Careful attention to the method by which I have illuminated the poorly lighted avenues of general theory will suggest the one remaining thread binding together its empirical observations (and through these leading into the larger theoretical insights and philosophical assumptions).   It is this over which I so quickly passed in chapter 2 so as not to overload my initial purpose with the more developed analysis of the very social key by which the theory of protracted war is rendered intelligible.   I return here to a final consideration, now facilitated by the work of earlier chapters, of these observations made through the more explicit writings of Chinese strategists to tie up this thread in the remaining subject of the armed invasion of social order and capacity to wage war through, in the Chinese case, directing the guerrilla phase of operations to serve the social design of land revolution.   The guerrilla form may embrace many differing social combinations depending on, among other considerations, the nature of social relations constituting the fabric of social order to which this form is directed.   These social relations in the Chinese case were mainly cast in the form of land relations, making it natural that the Chinese strategists should set the guerrilla warfare on this basis.   The very instant one makes this strategic judgment around which protracted war revolves, then the theory of strategy can be seen turning

towards a state of affairs (the larger roots and consequences
of which have been discussed) in which the overall organization and application of armed power is nothing more than an
offspring and servant of the general invasion of social order.
This is true for the theory of protracted war since all the
distinctions in time, space and form with which this organization and application is conceived ultimately come to rest on
the pace, distribution and depth of such invasion in the
guerrilla phase.   This is even more true of a fully revisionist state of affairs, because there is lacking entirely on all
sides the eleventh-hour temptation to switch into the classical and regular form.

The avenue by which I observe land revolution, guerrilla
warfare and the armed invasion of social order, on which all
else turns, is to shift our attention away from the classical
débâcle of the Fifth and final KMT Encirclement Campaign of
the Second Civil War (ending in 1934) to a collection of internal Party reports on guerrilla warfare published in June
1947, by the Hopeh-Shantung-Honan Committee of the CCP.   This
special issue dedicated to the nature of guerrilla warfare,
although to my knowledge it remains untranslated and entirely
unconsidered by Western strategists, is nicely placed for our
purposes because it came out of the experience and real practice of such warfare within the crucial Shansi-Hopeh-Shantung-
Honan Border Region.   Not only was this region of prime
strategic importance in the Third and final Civil War (July
1946-October 1949) as one of the main insurgent base areas,
but its Hopeh-Shantung-Honan portion, with which these primary
observations are concerned, lay in the heavily populated and
fertile plains of North China, here providing, within some
variation, the necessary raw materials for land revolution.
Moreover, this internal Party document is made up from reports

that concern the period of the Third Civil War starting with
the insurgent stage of strategic retreat (beginning July 1946)
to the stage of strategic counter-offensive (beginning July
1947) in which, according to Maoist thinking,[4] guerrilla warfare is primary, with emphasis on the mobile form in the very
early stages.   Finally, the initial strategic counter-offensive of the Third Civil War did originate from this same base
area and surrounding guerrilla zones.   This collection of
primary observations on guerrilla warfare, to which I shall
turn shortly, could not be better placed in time, space and
form, by the calculations of which the organization and application of armed power is conceived.

Before I reflect on this last remaining thread which holds
together the theory of protracted war, it is necessary to
pause for a number of ancillary considerations which (requirements of space prevailing) barely touch on the near impossible
conditions of real war - especially in the dispersed guerrilla
situation.   The select empirical observations which issue
from such conditions were not made by Chinese strategists in a
vacuum but in the complex, rarely uniform and sometimes contradictory mainstream of real war, little of which I have the
occasion to discuss.   The method of theoretical generalization, which traces the connections lodged in the heart of
general theory by fishing the relevant observations out of
this fearful mainstream, would simply drown if it dared open
the door too wide to the flood of complexity and confusion of
real war.   This is even more true of the Chinese case for
reasons already discussed.   The ideal picture and the real
practice of war ought never to be divorced, as it is in the
very nature of war, the articulate moral and social activity
in which social order is everywhere crucial, that these two
constantly play on each other.   Our interests cannot stray

too far from the theoretical side in the one hope of filling
the classical vacuum in our unsettled area of study.   I
pause, however, momentarily to delve into only those ancillary
considerations that flow in prime connection to such observations in this same mainstream I have consistently employed in
the role of means fashioned here for our immediate purpose.

The first is to explain why I have shifted attention from
the Kiangsi Soviet period to the Third Civil War.   The reason
is simply that I am forced to do so.   No other than this
latter war in the history of the Chinese Communist Party
offers sufficient documentary analysis of the role of land
revolution in the relevant guerrilla zones during the vital
period preceding and leading into the strategic counter-offensive.   In its fully matured version, the whole reasoning of
protracted war comes down to this single point in time (stages
one and two), space (guerrilla zones, especially out of those,
as only in this case, from which the initial counter-offensives later spread) and form (the guerrilla form supporting
widely dispersed land revolution) for which there is no other
sufficient evidence available.   The theory of protracted war
was pieced together here and there as experience was gained.
The fact that the best documentary evidence for the theory of
land revolution is given in the earlier Kiangsi period, some
of which was later reprinted as rural surveys, theoretical
essays and class analysis documents for the Third Civil War,
plus the very pertinent disagreements about the use of classical or revisionist patterns of strategy make the consultation
of this earlier period essential.   Unhappily, the Kiangsi
Soviet fell before these issues were resolved, forcing us now
to search elsewhere, which brings us to the later and only
other sufficiently documented example illustrating the single
point in time, space and form this study urgently requires.

Moreover, I should warn that, whatever the interest to students of China, our special purpose must not stray into the
larger considerations of the state of social order (including
the differentials in land tenancy patterns that need not
detain us) and land policy in general just prior to, and
during, the Third Civil War.   Rather, our theoretical concern
is *strictly focused on the relationship expressed in the
writings of Chinese strategists* between the guerrilla invasion
of social order in land revolution and the relevant guerrilla
zones leading up to and later supporting the initial strategic
counter-offensive; because for insurgent theory it is around
here precisely that the larger organization and application of
armed power should wholly and ideally revolve.   In short, I
am forced to rely on a case in which the documentation,
although the best available, may well not support a definitive
study of the socio-military significance of the land-based invasion of social order; this need not obstruct the purely
illustrative use I make of such documentation.

The next ancillary consideration is simply to remind that
in the substantial stretch of CCP history flowing from the
classical *débâcle* of the Fifth KMT Encirclement Campaign as
the turning-point in the Second Civil War and continuing up
to our present area of interest in the Third Civil War, land
revolution formally ceased during the intervening War of
Resistance against Japan (1937-45).   It was then generally
referred to as 'land reform' as formally reinstated just in
time for the first stage of strategic retreat in the Third
Civil War by the following 4 May 1946, CCP Central Committee
'Directive on Liquidations, Rent Reductions, and Land Problems':

This refers to the 'Directive on the Land Question' issued
by the Central Committee of the Communist Party of China on

4 May 1946. After Japan's surrender, in view of the
peasants' eager demand for land, the Central Committee
decided to change the land policy of the period of the War
of Resistance, that is, to change from the reduction of
rent and interest to confiscation of the land of the landlords and its distribution among the peasants. The 'May
4th Directive' marked this change.[5]

What came to be known as the 'May 4th Directive' simply
recognized as a *fait accompli* that the various mass mobilization campaigns based on the land policy of the reduction of
rent and interest (or double reduction) had indeed, in some
measure, amounted to a policy of 'land to the tiller', that
is, a real alteration in the fabric of land and social relations for the prosecution of war. The directive confirmed,
in part, that:

In the struggles of opposing traitors, settling accounts,
reducing rent and interest, the peasants have been acquiring land directly from the hands of the landlords and have
thus been carrying out the system of 'Land to the Tiller'.
...

Under these circumstances our Party must of necessity
have a consistent policy: we must resolutely support the
direct action adopted by the masses to carry out land
reform and assume a planned leadership so that in every
Liberated Area land reform may be quickly accomplished in
accordance with the scale and intensity of the development
of the mass movement.[6]

Western observers visiting the just-mentioned Shansi-Hopeh-
Shantung-Honan Border Region confirm that the conditions there
pursued the frequently radical alteration of land and social
relations prior to the formal reinstatement of land reform 4
May 1946.[7] The comments from one such observer I briefly
record here:

The land revolution in Long Bow [village, Lucheng County in Shansi] began with the retreat and surrender of the Japanese Army and its Chinese puppet forces in 1945.[8]

The Anti-Traitor Movement in the whole Fifth District was brought to a close in December 1945.   In the course of the struggle, important gains were made, but serious shortcomings also marred the record.   The gains, as seen by a leading district cadre who made a report to the County Committee of the Communist Party, included the complete rout of the gentry-Kuomintang attempt to set up a regime based on the old political machine and the wartime collaborators.   In the course of this rout, half the landlords and rich peasants in the district were attacked and punished with the confiscation of some or all of their property, thus cutting back considerably the holdings on which the old system was based.   Many people were mobilized, organized, and educated by these events and learned to see some connection between collaboration and the dominant feudal class.[9]

Conventional grievances concerning lower rents and lower interest rates were made retroactive to cover the war years in villages where the occupation had given the landlords a free hand not only to continue the collection of rent and interest but to increase the rate of both.   Now the peasants demanded not only the correction of abuses but also the repayment of overcharges and the restoration of lands and property seized in default of debts which were, by 'double reduction' standards, illegal.   In practice, when the grievances were totalled up, the charges almost always mounted up to more than most gentry families could

pay, and everything they owned was expropriated for distribution.   The peasants even matched the excesses of the
1930s by a policy of *sao ti ch'u men*, or 'sweep the floor
out the door', which meant to clean the family out of house
and home and drive them from the area.   They called this
whole movement 'settling accounts'.[10]

The campaign to 'settle accounts', launched in January
1946, lasted about four weeks.   The destruction of the
feudal land system, well begun by the Anti-Traitor Movement [Fall, 1945], was almost completed in this one month
of drastic action.   As a result of these two movements
together, 211 acres were seized from exploiters, large and
small, and 55 acres from various institutions.   This
amounted to more than a quarter of the village's 931
acres.[11]

By the middle of March [1946], when all the 'fruits' had
been distributed, the landless and land-poor found themselves living in an entirely new world.   Two hundred and
forty-two acres of land had been allocated to the families
in this group, thereby doubling the acreage in their possession.   Their holdings had jumped from an average of
.44 acres per capita, to an average of .83 acres per
capita.[12]

In order to insure that the full potential of the people
for victorious defence against the impending Nationalist
offensive was aroused in good time, the Central Committee
of the Chinese Communist Party had already issued a directive which reversed the wartime policy of 'Double Reduction' and called once more for 'Land to the Tiller' inside

the Liberated Areas.   This policy declaration, issued on
4 May 1946, came to be known as the May 4th Directive....

This [offensive] was but another encirclement similar to
the five that Chiang Kai-shek had mounted in the 1930s and
to countless others carried out by the Japanese during
eight long years of occupation.   With many years of
experience to draw on and a vastly stronger position than
they had ever held before, the members of the Central Committee were confident that the encirclement could and would
be smashed.

Such an outcome depended, in the last analysis, on the
kind of support which millions of peasants were willing to
give to the Revolution.   The crux of the matter lay in the
land question.   With land in their own hands the peasants
could be counted on to volunteer for service in the regular
armed forces by the hundreds of thousands, to support the
front with transport columns and stretcher brigades, and to
organize irregular fighting units in every corner of the
Liberated Areas.   Land ownership was capable of inspiring
both at the front and in the rear the kind of determination
among the rank and file that no terror could shake and no
reverses deter.   Land ownership could also release among
the people that infinite capacity for concealment, harass-
ment, ambush, and surprise attack that is the despair of
enemy commanders.   It could serve as the foundation for a
wall of silence capable of sealing the ears and stopping
the eyes of the enemy's offensive intelligence so that
both the regular and irregular forces of the Revolution
could concentrate and disperse, attack and retreat with
relative freedom.[13]

The May 4th Directive reached Lucheng County after the

Civil War had already reached flood tide.   In the heat of
a defensive campaign, with a large Nationalist army advancing to within 50 miles of the county seat, its moderate
proposals were honoured more in the breach than in the
observance.   The struggle that actually developed became
even sharper and more violent than that which had gone
before.[14]

The notion that the social consequences issuing from the
land policy of the reduction of rent and interest did not show
an entirely dissimilar design to that of land reform as
regards the fabric of land and social relations must be left
here without further comment.   What is necessary for the purposes of concluding our present interest is the understanding
that land reform was formally reinstated just in time for the
first stage of strategic retreat of the Third and final Civil
War, where our concern rests.   It is not difficult to see why
the theory of protracted war approaches the ideal the more its
operational basis is driven into the full-scale invasion of
social order by means of land revolution (or reform) in dispersed guerrilla warfare, initially in the Kiangsi origins and
especially the later application of this theory, if not consistently in between.   This is entirely sufficient to serve
the present method through which I illuminate the cardinal
relationship between social order and the organization and
application of armed power in the theory of strategy by
tracing this relationship through the more explicit writings
of Chinese strategists.   We thereby avoid the burden of a
distended body of primary sources and observations that would
fail the limited service it is intended to perform.

The next ancillary consideration of prime connection to the
impending observations of Chinese strategists on guerrilla
warfare is that Communist historians generally divide the

strategy of the Third and final Civil War into the two familiar insurgent stages of strategic retreat (July 1946-June
1947) and strategic counter-offensive (July 1947-October
1949),[15] beginning with the first advances into the Central
Plains.   Separate mention is frequently made of the all-out
strategic offensive within the latter stage consisting of the
four decisive and large-scale campaigns of the war starting
with the Tsinan campaign in September 1948 and following with
the Liaohsi-Shenyang, Huai-Hai and the Peking-Tientsin campaigns.   What is lacking in this analysis is the usual
emphasis on the second stage of strategic stalemate.   We are
reminded by Mao Tse-tung that in this second stage the invasion of the social order through which the enemy conducts war
is carried forward by the guerrilla warfare initiated in the
stage of strategic retreat:

> [The] war as a whole is being fought on interior lines;
> but as far as the relation between the main forces and the
> guerrilla units is concerned, the former are on the inter-
> ior lines while the latter are on the exterior lines, pre-
> senting a remarkable spectacle of pincers around the
> enemy.... In the first stage of the war, the regular army
> operating strategically on interior lines is withdrawing,
> but the guerrilla units operating strategically on exterior
> lines will advance with great strides over wide areas to
> the rear of the enemy - they will advance even more fierce-
> ly in the second stage - thereby presenting a remarkable
> picture of both withdrawal and advance.[16]

A Western observer who visited the guerrilla zones of
Anyang in the Shansi-Hopeh-Shantung-Honan Border Region,
Spring 1947, and whom I shall consult shortly in more detail,
quotes Communist sources explaining: 'The Japanese war had
three stages, but this war will have only two stages.   There

will be no long period of stalemate'.[17]   What is required
throughout is the precise appreciation of the pace, depth and
distribution of the invasion of social order through which a
mass of people conducts war, the relative weight of which is
pitched against the opponent's armed forces, of which his will
to wage war is a function in the classical fashion.   The
dimensions and especially depth of a sea of hostile people in
insurgent base areas and guerrilla zones are served up to
balance the armed power of the opponent throughout the continuum of shifting distinctions in time, space and form intended to serve the invasion of social order, in the collapse of
which the enemy sooner or later finds himself in serious difficulty.   This continues right up until the instant the
insurgent is tempted by a failing enemy to cast aside the very
strategy by which he survives (and wins) and, in the irony of
it all, pursues the same classical illusions at the root of
the latter's defeat.   Here, it is the hand of classical error
that signs for the guerrilla form both its birth and death
certificates (the latter being this insurgent transformation
into the regular form).   We are reminded by Mao Tse-tung that
the life span of this guerrilla form is as short or long
(hence *protracted* war) throughout the first and second stages
as this precise appreciation demands: 'The duration of this
[second] stage [of strategic stalemate] will depend on the
degree of change in the balance of forces between us and the
enemy'.[18]   If the initial balance is overweight in the insurgent disfavour and the social scales in which the goods are
measured too stiff, then the second stage comes to dominate
everywhere; if this balance is further in the opposite favour
and the same social scales well oiled, then this second stage
almost vanishes.

Following from this it is also necessary to recognize that

a shift in land policy was initiated during the strategic
counter-offensive in the directives of the CCP Central Committee, on 22 February 1948[19] and 25 May 1948.[20]   This concerned
the separation and then the temporary suspension of land
reform in new liberated areas, including those which still had
guerrilla activity or were guerrilla in nature.   By means of
explanation of a shift in land policy that, on first sight,
would appear to derive from the utter failure of the very
strategy through the analysis of which I conclude with a set
of propositions on general theory, I seek refuge in Appendix
B[21] found translated *in toto* from the Chinese original.   This
vital assistance is provided by an editorial of the 'West
Honan Daily News', 24 August 1948, intended as a follow-up
with the reasons for the shift in land policy prescribed in
the just-mentioned CCP Central Committee directive of 25 May
1948.[22]   This editorial particularly refers to the Central
Plains liberated areas where the initial counter-offensives
had first taken place (Summer, 1947) in part by the armed
forces flowing from the same Hopeh-Shantung-Honan guerrilla
zones to be examined shortly.   What has, in fact, happened is
made abundantly clear.   Land reform is temporarily suspended
in the new liberated areas, including those which are still
guerrilla in nature or have guerrilla activity, not because it
was a failure (or as some argue unsustainable in the insecure
conditions of the guerrilla zone), but precisely as a result
of its strategic success in the earlier guerrilla phase.   The
key to the entire matter is a simple one - again resting on
the first strategic appreciation of the continually shifting
distinctions in time, space and form with which the organization and application of armed power is conceived, all, of
course, with a critical eye on the pace, depth and distribution of the invasion of social order.   It is, in short, a

question of nice timing whereby the insurgent is tempted into
throwing aside the strategy by which he survives, that is, the
guerrilla warfare and its twin - land reform - in the guerrilla zones, all of which is redirected into the regular form
as it comes to dominate in the counter-offensive.

The essence of the editorial's explanation is found in the
central distinction made between two types of area.   The
first consists of 'new liberated areas occupied during the
great advance [strategic counter-offensive] of last year
[1947]' in which, we are informed, the complex and lengthy
preparations for land reform were not made, nor possible; all
of which is thus suspended and laid to rest in its less
arduous and preparatory phase of rent and interest reduction.
The remaining regions are those old liberated areas occupied
prior to this crucial date (this is, including the guerrilla
phase of our impending interest) which were to continue land
reform on the firm base of social order already established.
As for grey regions falling in between these two, that is to
say, new liberated areas occupied since the insurgent counter-
offensive (July 1947) in which land reform had already com-
menced, the situation was frozen into no return to prior land
and social relations, again laying the land policy to rest in
rent and interest reduction.

It is not difficult to find the source of the lack of
preparations and resulting disorders and confusion in land
reform arising *only* in the new liberated areas which the
editorial explains is the reason for the shift in land policy.
Excluded here entirely are those areas in which land reform
met its strategic object in guerrilla warfare and the key dispersal of armed power into the fabric of the opponent's social
order in the cancerous guerrilla zones before July 1947,
during the stage of strategic retreat.   Once, however, this

guerrilla form begins to fulfil its strategic task of trans-
forming itself into regular warfare as the insurgent is drawn
towards the very same classical reasoning through which the
enemy is, by now, quickly failing, then he is not only induced
to cast aside the guerrilla form but also its twin, land
reform.   If the insurgent cannot see this at first (which
indeed seems to have been the case with the Chinese strategists whose land policy of the strategic retreat dragged on
for up to at least six months into the strategic counter-
offensive), he will sooner or later be compelled to do so by
the very same intestine disorders shown here in a land policy
struggling against, and disrupting, the flow of resources from
guerrilla to regular warfare.   Within the transformation into
the concentrated regular form in which widely dispersed land
reform has no place, and the rapid acquisition of overwhelming
expanses of territory conducted through the offensive of
large regular forces in the mobile and positional forms,
little surprise can be had out of the despair of the above
editorial at the lack of preparations and resulting disorders.
Land reform sooner or later follows the general design:
having fulfilled its strategic task it is laid to rest quietly
in its less demanding and preparatory phase of rent and interest reduction in all newly occupied areas while resources flow
into the foreign grasp of classical *savoir faire*.   The relative security of social resources, the last remaining joker
hidden in the pack of all strategic playing cards, is shuffled
out and the contest proceeds on the classical plane, one
player having, for all real purpose, lost.   Otherwise, the
continuum in which the instruments of insurgent strategy
embrace new form and movement at precise points in time and
space - at once rooted in a new insight into general theory
and in its Siamese twin the classical obsessions of the enemy

- would all be abandoned to the intestine disorders witnessed
above.   In his own manner, not always the easiest to follow,
Mao Tse-tung made this same point 24 May 1948 in a discussion
of tactical problems of rural work in the new liberated areas,
and in a later analysis of the Civil War, 10 October 1948:

> It is necessary to give overall consideration to the tacti-
> cal problems of rural work in the new Liberated Areas.   In
> these areas we must make full use of the experience gained
> in the period of the War of Resistance Against Japan;   for
> a considerable period after their liberation we should
> apply the social policy of reducing rent and interest....
> In this way, social wealth will not be dispersed and public
> order will be comparatively stable, and this will help us
> concentrate all our forces on destroying the Kuomintang
> reactionaries.[23]

> The present situation demands that our Party should do its
> utmost to overcome these phenomena of indiscipline and
> anarchy, localism and guerrilla-ism and centralize all the
> powers that can and must be concentrated in the hands of
> the Central Committee and its agencies, so as to bring
> about the transition in the form of the war from guerrilla
> to regular warfare.[24]

Finally for our purposes, the remaining consideration
underlying the empirical observations by which I conclude with
a set of propositions on general theory is the understanding
that the scheme of social strategy and tactics in land revolution of the Kiangsi Soviet period (1929-34), as previously
discussed, naturally would change to meet differing social
conditions in our present area of interest.   Western observers visiting the Shansi-Hopeh-Shantung-Honan Border Region
confirm, however, that the principles of class analysis at the

basis of CCP land policy remained essentially the same:

The theory and practice of classification had been worked
out by the Chinese Communist Party as far back as the
period of the rural soviets, during the civil war of 1927-
36.   At that time definitions of each class had been ham-
mered out so that it could be clearly understood what made
a man a landlord, a rich peasant, a middle or poor peasant
or farm-labourer and so on.

Though minor modifications were made from time to time
in accordance with changing conditions, the basic principles underlying these definitions remained the same.[25]

The standards they introduced were roughly the same as
those adopted by the Communist Party of China in 1933 when
the first 'Land to the Tiller' policy was carried out in
the old revolutionary base at Juichin, Kiangsi.   Most of
the poor peasants, after two years of campaigning, understood the standards fairly well, but as they applied them
the deficiencies of the relatively simple concepts of 1933
became more and more apparent.

The Juichin standards, it turned out, were strong in
defining the center of gravity of each rural class, that
pole which determined the special nature of its typical
members and their special relationship to the means of production.   The standards were weak, however, in defining
exact boundary lines between the classes.   They lacked the
precision necessary to distinguish between the many border-
line, atypical cases that showed up so frequently in real
life.

By far the most important dividing line was that between
the middle peasants and the rich peasants.   The Draft
Agrarian Law of 1947 had made this the great divide between

friend and enemy, between the people and their oppressors, between revolution and counter-revolution.   It was absolutely essential that this line be clear and unequivocal. Yet here the Juichin documents were most ambiguous....

As classification progressed, both the cadres and the peasants in Long Bow [village, Shansi] keenly felt the need for something more precise.   This need was met, in part at least, by a set of supplementary regulations issued by the Central Committee in the fall of 1947.[26]

We must explain, discuss, report, evaluate, classify, post results; explain, discuss, and report - again and again. This is very troublesome, very difficult, very time-consuming.   But the people do not find it troublesome because it fixes their fate.   This is the most important work of the whole movement.   He who leads the classification holds the knife in his hand.   If you class a middle peasant as a rich peasant, it is as serious as killing him.   You push the family into the enemy camp.   You violate the policy of uniting with the middle peasants to isolate the enemy. If, on the other hand, you classify a landlord as a middle peasant, you protect a landlord.   You clasp a viper to your bosom.   You violate the policy of destroying feudalism.   [Observer quoting CCP official][27]

Moreover, the same broad distinctions which shaped the strategy of land revolution of the Kiangsi Soviet period (the stage of land confiscation and redistribution in newly developed areas, the stage of land investigation in comparatively retarded struggle areas and the stage of land reconstruction in intensified struggle areas) reappear in land reform intact along with, of course, some tactical variation.   To return and consult the Central Committee directive of the CCP of 22

February 1948[28] will reveal these same broad distinctions
rooted in the pace, depth and distribution of the alteration
of land and social relations.   The directive is careful to
qualify all of this by the addendum:

> As for border areas, if they are still guerrilla in nature
> these should be regarded as new liberated areas.   The Cen-
> tral Committee has [other] regulations on the land reform
> applicable in new liberated areas which should not be con-
> sidered as falling under this document.[29]

Three familiar types of area are here identified: regions in
which land reform has been thoroughly carried out, where, on
a general basis feudal remnants were more or less destroyed,
solid regimes have been instituted and the land correctly redistributed; regions in which land reform, in comparison, has
not been thoroughly carried out, where the land redistribution
was not satisfactorily advanced and feudal remnants remain
here requiring widespread adjustments in land, that is, land
investigation; and finally, those regions where land reform
was so poorly carried out, if at all, that 'class and land
relations are only slightly altered', thus requiring a clean
slate and full land confiscation and redistribution.[30]   With
this rather oversimplified comparison I should remind, in
turning to our last area of prime interest, that I have had to
sweep *extra muros* many issues in the history of the CCP, including the endless problem of to what extent the just concluded ancillary considerations and impending observations I pluck
from the mainstream of war are truly representative of all
areas (over time) under insurgent control.

As an entrée into the remaining volley of observations made
through the writings of Chinese strategists, I first relate
here the comments of a Western observer who had the rare
opportunity of visiting the guerrilla zones of Anyang in

Spring, 1947, in the same Border Region from which these observations are drawn:

This Border Region covers an area of two million square kilometres in the heart of North China. If you will look at a map you will see that it has a good strategic unity. It is shaped something like a four-sided box, the bottom of which is the Yellow River, the top of which is the Chengtai Railway and the Shihchiachuang-Techow highway, the left side of which is the Tungpu Railway and the right side, the Tientsin-Pukow Railway....

Half of this area contains the biggest plain in China; namely, the North China or Yellow River Plain. The other half - the Taihang and Taiyueh area - is all mountains....

Because of all these things - strategic location, self-sufficient economy and thirty million tough people - what happens to our Border Region and to the one on our flank in eastern Shantung will probably determine the fate of the whole civil war.

If we can stop Chiang from getting through here, then we can build up bases in Inner Mongolia and Manchuria and thus have a great and safe rear area. But even if Chiang breaks through here, as did the Japanese, we can still maintain the independence of the Shansi-Hopei-Shantung-Honan Border Region by retiring into the impenetrable mountains of the Taiyueh and Taihang ranges. [Observer quoting CCP official][31]

While I was in the Taihang Mountains I was continually hearing stories that the farmers in Anyang County in Honan Province, angered by the depredations of Chiang Kai-shek's troops and raiding landlords, were carrying on a vengeful guerrilla warfare behind the Kuomintang lines. This news

greatly interested me because I had never seen that kind of
warfare.   So I determined to go to Anyang to have a look
for myself.

A small unroofed cart, with solid wooden wheels, having
been obtained for the first stage of the journey, I set out
on a cool spring day in 1947.[32]

At the time of my arrival, the city of Anyang on the plains
below and about four-fifths of the whole county were occupied by Kuomintang troops and numerous Home Returning Corps
organized by the landlords.   We were pressed into a very
small area of the county between the towns of Kwangtai and
Suiyeh, which were held by good-sized Kuomintang garrisons.
Between these two towns, from which they sometimes emerged
on raids, the Kuomintang had tried to set up a blockade
line, but we were continually penetrating through this line
into the Kuomintang rear.[33]

It is a very instructive fact that when the Eighth Route
Army evacuated most of Anyang, the few cadres huddled up in
the western corner of the county were unable to start
guerrilla warfare.   Yet within a few months of the arrival
of the Kuomintang, that guerrilla warfare was being waged
on a scale that dwarfed anything seen in the Japanese
war.[34]

Now, on my arrival in Anyang, the [guerrilla] raids were
spreading deeper and wider into Kuomintang territory....
Most often, however, the raids were intimately connected
with the land reform.   Their purpose was to protect the
results of the land division, to force the landlords to
return what they had taken from the people and generally to

encourage the poor.   Such operations went under the
sinister-sounding name of Counter-Counter Settlement.
Although there was often much shooting, the raids did not
seem to me to be essentially military.   Rather did this
kind of warfare seem to be a political and a social combat
carried on by armed means.   The targets of the raids were
not so often strongpoints or even lines of communications
as they were social institutions, government organs and
private individuals....

I do not mean that propaganda replaced combat, but
rather that the guerrilla war was carried on in an entirely
different emotional environment than regular war.[35]

I emerged from the guerrilla areas of Anyang in a disturbed
and confused frame of mind.   Many of the things that I had
heard and seen in that dark medieval world just would not
fit into the usual Westerner's conception of war.[36]

The chief contribution of the Chinese Communists to the
arts of war and revolution was that they combined both
politics and combat to a degree never before observed in
so complete a form, wielding both almost as a single
instrument.[37]

With this in mind, the following observations are such
eloquent expression of the central and remaining thread leading into the general considerations to which I have drawn
attention that I shall simply reproduce here, from the Chinese
original, excerpts from the various guerrilla reports which
best persuade the reader to pull together the philosophical
assumptions, theoretical insights and empirical observations
through which we have passed:

1 [The guerrilla warfare] has preserved the [Border]

Region, protected the masses and has consolidated our positions.   Except for the sixth sub-region, guerrilla warfare
was launched throughout the entire region.   At present, of
the thirty-nine counties in the five sub-regions south of
the Yellow River alone, thirty have been persisting in
guerrilla warfare; in the remaining nine, guerrilla warfare has not been [consistently] carried out.   But here
there are five counties where guerrilla warfare was stopped
only for a short time.   Basically, the enemy occupies the
points while we occupy the surface, the enemy occupies a
small part while we occupy the major part.   We control
over seventy per cent of the vast countryside.   In the
process of the guerrilla warfare, fifteen counties have
carried out a *preliminary* land reform movement and constructed tunnels, while fifteen other counties are in the
process of carrying out land reform and digging tunnels.
Because of the distribution of land and grain which has
been carried out, and because of the construction of tunnels, our rural bases have been greatly consolidated and
improved.   Also, due to the distribution of land and
grain, the masses took direct participation in the guerrilla warfare....

Our armed forces participated in the mass land reform
movement, and the ranks of our troops became consolidated
(e.g., troops in the first and seventh sub-regions).

3 [The guerrilla war] has trained the cadres - taught
them the art of guerrilla warfare, and has improved the
relations between the Party and the masses.   [The cadres]
have learned how to combine guerrilla warfare with land
reform....

All regions and counties have gained rich experiences,
of which the prominent ones were: the prefectural Party

Committees, sub-regions and independent brigades took the
lead in persisting in the guerrilla warfare position; the
[example of the] Li Ju-t'ai armed work team and the Ch'i-kac
region persisting in stepping up the anti-mop-up campaign
can be regarded as a typical experience and a banner for our
region's armed work teams in carrying out activities and
persisting in struggle in the interior; the experience of
controlling the landlords in Ch'ing-ch'eng, Yun-ch'eng and
Liu-tse in the second sub-region is even more mature; the
experiences of Chü-nan, Ch'eng-wu, Chü-yeh, Ting-t'ao and
Fu-ch'eng counties in carrying out a large-scale land
reform movement during the guerrilla war; the experience
of Ch'ang-ch'ing and T'ai-an where, under the pressure of a
large enemy force, the bulk of the armed forces moved away
leaving behind a small crack force to persist in struggle;
the experience of the armed work team of Chi-ning which,
within a small area on the one hand persisted in guerrilla
warfare, while on the other, carried out land reform.[38]

Land reform must be directly combined with guerrilla warfare, and guerrilla warfare must directly *serve* land
reform. The fan-shen [socially transformed] peasants
joined the war.[39]

In areas in the central region where land reform has not
yet been carried out, the land reform must be carried out
at once; while in areas where the land reform has not
been thoroughly carried out, we must make it up by carrying out a land investigation drive without any delay.[40]

The county and district guerrilla forces must resolutely
fight the enemy when they attack; if not, then these

guerrilla forces must either organize a defence system in
the perimeter areas in order to protect the land distribution, or disperse and take part in the land distribution.[41]

Experience has proved that without a rural base it is impossible to persist in a protracted guerrilla warfare and,
moreover, impossible to persist in a highly dispersed and
concealed guerrilla warfare.... The main tasks in consoli-
dating the rural base are to control the landlords, to distribute land and grain, to construct tunnels, to set up a
militia defence and to establish the leadership of the
Party branch. Of these five tasks, the distribution of
the land and grain forms the centre link.[42]

In guerrilla warfare, we are not only able to maintain our
present bases but also able to develop new bases. The
vital link in developing new bases is land reform. In
areas where [the enemy] has staged a comeback and settled
accounts, [land reform] must be carried out in combination
with the struggle to re-settle accounts. Versions such
as 'the masses do not dare to accept', 'it is too early',
'don't offend the landlords again', are all wrong.[43]

Carry out land reform and [land] reinvestigation work,
totally eliminate the feudal force of the landlords,
mobilize the masses to the fullest extent, vigorously per-
sist in guerrilla warfare and energetically prepare for
the counter-offensive.
As for policy, we fully adhere to the summary of Comrade
Lin Chih at the Land Reform Conference. In this aspect
there is no difference between Honan and Hopeh. As to our

methods, we must absorb the experiences of the various
places in the guerrilla zones in carrying out land reform.
The general policy is: totally eliminate the landlords and
mobilize the masses to the fullest extent. We must oppose
the concept of guerrilla zones being 'exceptional'. Some
wrong ideas such as land reform cannot be carried out thoroughly in the guerrilla zones and that in the guerrilla
zones the landlord cannot be eliminated, must be corrected.
But, we must start from the present level of consciousness
of the masses, which will be raised gradually so that our
policy can be combined with the masses. In short, a
thorough land reform must be carried out in the guerrilla
zones, and under no circumstances must the construction and
consolidation of rural bases be neglected.

As for the method, continue to expand the armed forces
in the guerrilla zones, and the administration must give
powerful support. In the past, we didn't pay enough
attention to the consciousness and initiative of the
masses. From now on, we must emphasize the combining of
giving support with arousing the consciousness and initiative of the masses; emphasize the point that the peasants
should solve the problems themselves. Work must now be
done in a more deep-going and meticulous way, and let the
masses do more. We must change the situation where the
government suppresses the landlords into one where the
masses themselves suppress the landlords; little by little
change the situation where cadres personally give a hand
into one where the masses themselves carry out large-scale
mass movements with activists taking the lead. (See the
experience of land reform in Hopeh.)

The specific experience of the guerrilla zone is: land
reform must be carried out in conjunction with a defensive

war (tunnel warfare, militia defence). We must avoid a
situation of throwing aside land reform when taking up
guerrilla warfare, or throwing aside guerrilla warfare when
taking up land reform.[44]

Besides confirming the experiences put forth in the 'Summary of the Guerrilla Warfare for the Past Five Months',
this two-month summary further proves that we must persist
in guerrilla warfare and raise the level of guerrilla warfare mainly to solve the two questions of an armed fist and
a rural base. If we don't have an armed fist or have an
armed fist but don't know how to use it, we shall be weak
and defenceless in face of the enemy's suppression, and in
the course of a period of time we shall lose our rural
bases. If we don't have rural bases, or if we have rural
bases but are unable to control and consolidate them, we
will be alone - the armed forces and cadres shall be danc-
ing *strip-tease* and the enemy could hear and see everything
while we will be deaf and blind. We would always be in a
passive position and receive blows every time. Our armed
forces could only enter and leave, and shall be unable to
take root and gain a foothold (for instance in Tung-yuen
and Tung-ming). In the course of a period of time, our
armed forces will become weak and thus forced to retreat.
If we have an armed fist, we can control the rural bases
(e.g., in Chi and Kao) - and if we have a consolidated
rural base, we are able to further expand our rural bases
and armed forces (e.g., in Yun-Ch'eng county). If we
combine our armed fist with the rural base, we are able to
concentrate our forces to destroy the enemy, and also able
to disperse our forces and go underground, to carry out
mobile and flexible actions and to hold out in the interior

areas. We will always have the initiative in our hands
and be able to attack everywhere.[45]

The purpose of the enemy in launching their 'mop-up' campaigns was to directly support the reactionary feudal
forces. They expanded the war to the countryside, thus
turning the war into an undisguised class war. Once the
reactionary forces gain the upper hand, they will fero-
ciously suppress the peasants and establish their own reactionary pao-chia system. A handful of landlords are
able to suppress the masses who form the majority because
they receive the backing of the enemy's armed forces.
But, the enemy's armed forces alone cannot change the
[social] order in the countryside. *The collapse of a
rural base is not caused by an attack of the enemy, but by
the restoration of the landlords.* Only a combination of
the enemy's armed force and the reactionary landlords could
destroy our rural base. Therefore, the very first step to
be taken in controlling the rural base is to control the
landlords and wage a tit-for-tat struggle against the
enemy. We have a foundation of several years' work and
basically the masses are on our side. And if we wage a
guerrilla war and if we keep the landlords under control,
we can maintain the superiority of the masses and maintain
our rural bases. Thus, the basic struggle in the countryside is a struggle where the enemy suppresses the peasants
in order to assist the restoration of the landlords, while
we keep the landlords under control in order to protect the
peasants and the [strategic] positions we have gained.

The general method in controlling the landlords is:
exert, to the fullest extent, the strength of the political
power in the guerrilla zone.[46]

The character of the land reform carried out in the guerrilla zones during the past nine months is: support by
the government until the landlords were brought to their
knees - high pressure and control. Let us first begin
with the landlords - press the landlords if the peasants do
not want to hold meetings, press the landlords if the
peasants do not want land, and suppress the most vicious
landlords by killing them.[47]

We must, under the leadership of the Party branch, carry
out a mass struggle in every village. When the enemy
attacks, we must carry out guerrilla warfare, and when the
enemy leaves, we must continue the land distribution. We
must persist in guerrilla warfare, persist in carrying out
the land reform to the very end, and lead the masses from
taking part in the land distribution movement into taking
part in the guerrilla warfare.[48]

By way of a final word, for all its difficulties the
Chinese experiment with the rejection of classical impedimenta, however halting and stumbling, was the first of real significance and, of course, is only one in a potential mosaic of
revisionist combinations in strategy which flow towards the
social womb of general theory. Whatever fresh combinations
may arise in the theory of strategy, these are to be taken as
revisionist in so far as they remain true to the six general
propositions with which they are identified. If my judgment
proves correct, no thread in the theory of strategy, and in
the larger conception of war itself, can now be left untouched by the real obsession with moral and social order, of
which the will to wage war is the true function. We are now
free to return to the larger theoretical considerations that
these experiences inform while remembering that the details of

the Chinese case, such as land reform as a means of invasion of social order, may never reappear in any future cases, and in our pursuit of these larger considerations these same details can now be put aside.

8   Clausewitz and silent contract

The contractual notion of the inviolability of social order
inherent in classical theory remained the one silent hurdle
which this reasoning had generally to negotiate. By this unspoken device such theory, until the Chinese experience, had
been rather lured away from *full* access to its natural sociological foundation. This hidden act of theft has secretly
robbed theory of a good rooting in its *freely* acknowledged
philosophical and theoretical basis.

In the nuclear age, wars conducted on paper look substantive so long as no reasonable alternative is seen to obtain,
safely locked away into 'the widespread impression that the
costs of using national military power have risen strikingly,
and that the political utility of employing military force has
suffered a corresponding decline'.[1] Nuclear wars conducted
on paper, because they are too horrific to be conducted any-
where else, may very well serve as expository aids in the
problems of how to deploy nuclear weapons, but they can never
satisfy the inherent and everywhere present social roots of
violence that demand real expression. This expression is
delineated by revisionist theory that places at the disposal
of the pursuit of moral and social objectives the instruments
to obtain, by real violence, the results which this pursuit is

otherwise unable to attain through the conduct of paper wars
or the 'skilful non-use' of nuclear weapons.   Nor can the
failing convention inherited from classicalism and still influential in conventional and limited wars provide any joy,
for the reasons already examined.   Neither can such expression seek a muted satisfaction in the attempts to rescue out
of the moral poverty of nuclear weapons, the risks in the use
of which appear to have little conceivable political content,
some semblance of reason along the other avenues of arms control, disarmament and crisis management.   Nuclear weapons, to
exhibit any veneer of reason that is the minimal property of
an instrument, must be 'controlled', 'deployed' and 'skilfully
non-used', and the events that may lead to their involvement
'managed'.   Here again the real use of violence as an instrument of policy finds little substantive expression along the
avenues of tactical nuclear weapons and limited nuclear war
that, as yet, dare not slip through the 'line of demarcation
[that] is at once so clear, ... so easily defined, and understood as the line between not using and using nuclear
weapons'.[2]   The fantasy that 'it is becoming clear that war
is not a continuation of policy but a failure of policy',[3] and
that 'there is no strategy any more - only crisis management'[4]
simply serves to sever theory further from the resort to violence which had since Clausewitz, if not consistently before,
been its prime distinction.   War, as an expression of real
violence, is being driven down further into its last and
primal unit, social order and its guerrilla invasion or security, because it is increasingly on this basis alone that, in
the nuclear age, the pursuit of moral and social objectives by
real violence can obtain the results which this pursuit is
otherwise unable to attain.   Theory has been rather corrupted
by the burlesque that the nuclear age is 'a novel situation in

the face of which all past experience with military operations
fades into insignificance'.[5]   Instead theory should be working towards readmitting into the heart of strategy, in a
greatly revised form, the old classical notion of violence as
an instrument of policy, the place of which in the nuclear age
is so well put in the following:

> For all these reasons, and in spite of the growing compli-
> cation of war in three elements, one can still trace in the
> Second World War the basic characteristics of the conflicts
> waged by Napoleon, by Ulysses S. Grant, by Moltke, and by
> Ludendorff and Haig.   There was the mobilisation of the
> resources of the nation, involving a transformation of the
> peacetime pattern of the national economy.   There was the
> conversion of those resources into effective military
> power;   and there was the deployment of that power by mili-
> tary specialists, according to classical principles of
> strategy, for the defeat of the enemy armed forces.

> It is of course an over-simplification to talk of the
> age of mass-warfare as 'beginning' in 1792.   Eighteenth-
> century habits of military thought and organisation ling-
> ered long into the nineteenth and twentieth centuries -
> perhaps longer in this sheltered country than anywhere
> else.   Very few of Goethe's contemporaries could have
> understood what he meant by observing that a new age had
> opened when the French volunteers stood firm under the
> Prussian cannonade at Valmy on 20 September 1792.   But
> there was no lack of would-be Goethes to proclaim the
> beginning of a new era on 6 August 1945, when the first
> atomic bomb was dropped on Hiroshima....

> We should not, therefore, overestimate the change
> brought about in international relations through the intro-
> duction of nuclear weapons.   The reluctance to contem-

plate the use of such weapons, which is fortunately so
characteristic of the Powers which at present possess them,
is a continuation, although vastly intensified, of the
reluctance to use the older techniques of mass war.   Even
as the statesmen of the 1930s found it difficult to conceive of a cause urgent enough to justify the use of the
massive weapons of which they potentially disposed, so, a
fortiori, is it still more difficult for us to foresee the
political problem to which the destruction of a score of
millions of civilians will provide the appropriate military
solution.   It is for this reason that political influence
does not necessarily increase in direct proportion to the
acquisition of nuclear power.   Similarly, there is no
cause to suppose that the capacity to use nuclear weapons
will be any more effective as a deterrent to, or even as an
agent of, disturbances of the international order than was,
in the 1930s, the ability, given the will, to wage mass
war.   Those who wish to use violence as an instrument of
policy - and since 1945 they have not been rare - can find,
as did Hitler, more limited and effective forms;   and those
who hope to counter it need equally effective instruments
for doing so.[6]

If the theory of strategy is to preserve, in the nuclear
age, this one real distinction - violence as an instrument of
policy which delivers into the hands of strategists their one
firm credential - it must return into its classical origins
and re-examine how it lost sight of its inalienable sociological foundation.   It is here in the poorly researched social
dimensions of strategy - in which are found the very roots of
violence, the last sanctuary of the decisive pursuit of power
and thus the prime basis for the pursuit of the latter by
means of the former - that strategic considerations should

start, otherwise they become prey to all manner of current
fashions. By its own reasoning classical theory ought to have
launched into a full analysis of the sociological roots underlying its central political insight into the nature of war.
But it could not do so without pulling down the whole edifice
covertly founded in a silent contract about the isolation of
war from the political and social world that swept out these
roots in the first place.   If theory is now to explain how
war is drifting into its natural social state, it must first
reach back into its classical heritage and grasp hold of this
notion of violence found to be endemic throughout the realm of
the political and social world first and most expertly seen
through the lens of unspoken contract by Clausewitz - and let
it lead theory where it will.   We simply cast away the lens
that, in one manner or another, came to influence all classical theory as a partly hidden structure of reasoning that
still infests theory today.   But before we are able to do so
we must first understand its nature and theoretical function,
and only then can theory free itself from the original sin of
contract underlying, in one fashion or another, all classical
theory, of which Clausewitz is the first and most eloquent
expression.   This is why I shall use what may appear to be an
excessive volume of quotations from his theoretical writings
to show directly from the original how Clausewitz lost sight
of the contractual-like assumptions on which he was working,
simply as a way of representing this fatal weakness influencing all classical theory in our continuing discussion of paradigm opposites in which these writings have an illustrative
role to play.   By this route in the development of general
theory intended to persuade theorists to take on board a host
of sociological considerations as the more elemental ones,
they may come to appreciate better where now politically moti-

vated violence seems more than ever headed in the nuclear age.

Whether any of us - or indeed the classical theorists of the past - had ever read or accepted Clausewitz is not at issue. It may well be that our heritage looks disjointed, misread and fratricidal; some present-day theorists may well accept that there are other ways of striking at the total power and will of the enemy than *ultimately* through his armed forces, they may not even have read, understood or accepted any of Clausewitz's theories. At real issue here is that whatever the confusion, disagreement and lack of identity that plagues contemporary strategic studies, we all share in varying degrees of intimacy with the classical theorists of the past in Clausewitz's original sin, which involves a contractual arrangement about the isolation of war from the political and social world that came somehow to influence theory. *This is so because no one was, or is willing to grasp this idea of violence as a real instrument, tear down the remainder and bulk of the classical edifice founded by one route and in one fashion or another on this notion of isolation, and start over once again with the fundamentals lodged in the political and social world.* This subconscious unwillingness, and the partly hidden structure of reasoning that leads into this unwillingness, is what binds classicalism into a tradition that is still very powerful today, however much theorists may consciously believe otherwise. Classical theorists are a polite society that may disagree on almost anything, but it survives because things were so constructed that one question is never asked.

I pause here briefly to clarify the intentions and methods behind the impending discussion of Clausewitz and contract that will close our deliberations on the relevance of social order to the theory of strategy. We now leave the empirical

observations made through the writings of Chinese strategists
as a rehabilitated invalid would throw away his crutches.
What we should be left with is the freedom to run along the
classical avenues of reasoning as a classicist could never
do.   We gain this new freedom (as indeed the reality of war
and the theory of strategy has already started to win) by
virtue of the general conclusions drawn from the Chinese case.
These should never be confused with their underlying minutiae
without which the general conclusions could not have been
found in the first place.   But having now skimmed the cream
from the top, this being the six revisionist propositions and
their concomitant theory, we can return to the heart of classical theory and exorcise the contractual influences that
still infest theory today which is thus unable to break out of
the contractual notion that literally blinds us to the present
and continuing drift of war into its natural social state.
The intention of this final chapter is to release theory from
the unspoken contract that has held back theory, in one degree
or another, since Clausewitz, as no theorist has taken the
theoretical lengths described here.   It is by this route that
I seek to persuade theorists further of the proper concerns of
theory, its inalienable sociological foundation and the return
to violence as its first credential.

    Since it is my intention to release theory from the con-
straints left us by classicalism into the free flow of revisionist theory, the method is directed to serve only this
object.   As I deal in paradigm opposites that are not to be
taken as historical contradistinctions, no comment is intended
as such on the history of classical theory and its constituent
theorists, their influence, if any, on one another or on the
general development of classical theory.   Nor will the historical background in which these theorists worked be consid-

ered.   There are always risks in approaching the very select
and more explicit writings of one orthodox theorist, as the
most eloquent expression of the contractual arrangement that
came by one route or another to influence our heritage, without detailed reference to the historical conditions through
which this heritage spans.   Purpose must rule method.   So
long as the latter faithfully serves the former in the final
balance of all risks, the present purpose cannot allow its
method to wander off into ancillary corridors that have
already been illuminated, some more clearly than others.[7]
Theory today may possess little, if any recollection of the
detailed historical conditions in which its own heritage was
born, but what it does suffer is the system of reasoning that
this same heritage still insists on forcing into our way of
thinking, and holding us back from the leap into the political
and social world on which the recent and profound develcpments
in contemporary strategy are based.

Rather, I move to pluck out of the classical spectrum one
theorist whose theoretical writings express most expertly and
fundamentally the contractual device that not only struck down
theory before it could firmly sink its roots into its own and
proper sociological foundation, but makes it unnatural and
even painful for theorists to accept the direction in which
events around them seem more than ever to be drifting.   Employed simply as expository aids, these are the theoretical
writings of Carl von Clausewitz, that most closely serve the
present purpose because they form the first and most eloquent
expression of contract at the heart of all classical theory.
This is why I choose these to represent those elements in our
heritage the after-effects of which still grip theory today.
Although Clausewitz may be taken as firmly lodged in the classical tradition since his reasoning, like much of tradition,

was held back by the contractual arrangement of the isolation
of war from the political and social world that kept diverting
theory into the 'decisive battle' paradigm, there are, at the
same time, many elements in his reasoning that go well beyond,
indeed criticize, simple classical obsession with this paradigm.   He is at once the most forceful, and yet most critical, of the classical theorists.   Here, there are really two
Clausewitzes, between them engaging in a kind of broken-backed
reasoning; it was both who surprisingly, as we shall see
later, rather stumbled their separate ways towards the very
same revisionist critique developed here over a century and a
half later.   There, in the first keystone of one's theory lay
the model of war in the abstract, constructed on the notion of
its isolation from the political and social world that came to
haunt everywhere the other's growing dedication to the view of
war as a political act.   Pushing aside the nuclear strategists who remain beyond the scope of this discussion, as they
have little to contribute to the full readmission of real violence as an instrument of the pursuit of social and moral
objectives that this same pursuit is otherwise unable to
attain, of all the classical theorists it is he alone who
stands out in the light of revisionist theory, for reasons
more fully explained shortly.

Before I discuss the nature and function of contract in
Clausewitz's theoretical writings, some brief preliminary comments will help to introduce the substance of our singular and
distinctive interests.   I shall concentrate on the major
theoretical work 'On War'[8] because this not only is the most
mature and comprehensive collection of Clausewitz's theoretical writings, but most of the main analytic devices developed
in earlier periods reappear here expanded and placed in a
larger theoretical whole.   This is to the extent that these

analytic devices and 'many similar repetitions exist that may
be said to stitch together the writings of Clausewitz's youth
and maturity'.[9]   Clausewitz's reply to two strategic exercises received by him six months after his plans for revision
of 'On War' had been proposed will also be consulted.[10]   This
reply (the main theoretical part of which is found translated
from the German original in Appendix D), although less well
known, is an important supplement to 'On War' not only for its
timing, but primarily for its pursuit of the interplay of
politics and strategy - the very revisions intended but never
completed.

Moreover, I should pause to explain why I choose the writings of a theorist who, on first sight, may not appear to be
the best available device for the illustrations I am attempting to make about classical theory.   As regards the preliminary point that Clausewitz dealt with the social and political
aspects of war more than any other classical theorist, it is
precisely because he did so at such length against the flow of
reasoning the bulk of his theory had come to embrace by force
of contract, that serves him up as the very best means of
illustration.   The traps hidden in classical theory only come
to light the further one pursues the more elemental social and
political roots this theory was built to ignore.   Few, if
any, of the classical theorists ever reached this point in
reasoning, at which new considerations challenge strategy
today.

The more fundamental basis for supposing Clausewitz to be a
poor device involves the problem of the social and political
content of some of his historical writings.   In one of these
particularly,[11] where there is nothing like it in the history
of the literature of that period, Clausewitz discusses war as
invaded by a host of social and political concerns - the whole

conduct of war as based on the social make-up of the nations
involved.   It may seem as though I risk falsifying the texts
of the broader writings of Clausewitz and the mind behind
those texts.   Now, the point here is that although Clausewitz
was concerned with the integration of social and political
elements with the element of violence in certain of his his-
tories, essays and letters, *he did not integrate this into a
systematic analysis in his theoretical work*.   Here is precisely the point of this chapter to show how, through the mishandling of contractual assumptions, he found it very difficult to do so.   For the purposes of discussion of paradigm
opposites in which Clausewitz's theoretical writings have an
illustrative role to play, I may well have to concede the
position of having to forget about Clausewitz as the historical man - and, in this, perhaps a good part of Clausewitz
altogether - and think of the methodological snags crippling
his theoretical attempt in 'On War' to integrate social and
political elements with the element of violence in systematic analysis.   This attempt best illustrates the same snags
lurking in all classical theory, however likewise or poorly
developed into the political principle.

It is not my present task to discuss how far I do, if at
all, falsify the mind behind the whole range of Clausewitz's
writings.   But surely it is as dangerous to swallow the
methodological problems I shall attempt to expose shortly as
being central to Clausewitz as though they represent the whole
rather than a part, as it is to disassociate the impending
discussion from the whole of Clausewitz altogether.   The correct balance here is to appreciate that I shall now proceed to
analyse the central thread (the mishandling of assumptions) in
Clausewitz's theory construction, and that this is not to be
taken as a broader interpretation of Clausewitz's writings as

such.   Whatever the merits of the balance I hope to maintain
in my approach to Clausewitz for the purpose of illustration,
it must be appreciated that however much he elsewhere attempted to integrate social and political elements with the element of violence, Clausewitz never pushed considerations far
enough to arrive at the definition of strategy as the formulation and distribution of social order.   This (and all else
that goes along with this definition) is what separates general theory from all others.   Here is found the complete integration of violence with its social and political milieu; but
first the problem of silent contract lurking in the background
of too much of our strategic heritage must be solved.

Finally, for those concerned about the dissimilarities
between my interpretation of Clausewitz from within a twentieth-century perspective and an early nineteenth-century and
somewhat different way of looking at things as represented in
Clausewitz's theoretical writings, these dissimilarities are
not to be regarded, for present purposes, as significant.
The reasons for this are the following.   My interpretation of
Clausewitz is for present-day theorists, who are more likely
to share with me the former rather than the latter with
Clausewitz.   And yet, although some may not have actually
read Clausewitz, many theorists still see a number of
Clausewitz's ideas, particularly those concerning the political aspects of war, and without knowing it, as I have argued
throughout, the one silent assumption that still haunts theory
today, as being prevalent in twentieth-century strategic
thinking.   I employ the impending interpretation of Clausewitz as a way of illustrating the traps hidden in the reasoning that theorists today have somehow inherited, whether or
not directly from Clausewitz or via subsequent generations of
theorists.   The object in this is to free present-day impasse

from the chains of the past so that theorists may come to
recognize and more fully appreciate those more elemental considerations which they have been unable to see in the past
which are the mortal challenge to theory at present. For
these reasons Clausewitz's ideas, especially those which are
contractually based along with his views on the political
aspects of war, can be made accountable to the rigours of
twentieth-century methodology.

Now, in turning to 'On War' one should not seek understanding in the theoretical writings without first taking brief
note of the relationship between these and their accompanying
historical references, along with Clausewitz's view of the
nature of theory. The study of war is seen before all else
rooted in military history since 'the critic must naturally
frequently refer to military history, for in the art of war
experience counts more than any amount of abstract truths'.[12]
Only through experience, whether first-hand or second-hand in
the form of military history which transcends the narrow
limits of personal observation, is derived the knowledge basic
to the art of war that is practical. It is the pursuit of
this experience that, in the first instance, accounts for the
format Clausewitz adopted, as so well described in a recent
interpretation of 'the psychological and historical genesis'
of his theories:

> Not only did Clausewitz shift back and forth between his-
> tory and theory; his historical writings contain theoreti-
> cal discussions, and his essays and chapters on theory are
> filled with historical material. Their interaction was
> determined by the concepts of the two disciplines that he
> began to develop in his early twenties, and which by 1812
> he had brought to completion in all essential aspects....
>
> We should note that the dominance of history over his

theories is more comprehensive than the influence which
theory exerted on his historical analyses.[13]

In the light of Clausewitz's greater reverence for military
history it is ironic that his major theoretical work 'On War'
should have so thoroughly outshone everything else he wrote
(particularly the severe neglect his historical writings suffered, the greater part of which appeared in 'Werke', published posthumously).[14]   This reverence may have helped to
suppress any concern that the assumptions, distortions and
errors hidden in theory can come to dominate the reality of
war, in which it is largely the consequence of the shared
'theory', vision or system of reasoning of its conduct that
men carry into it, and which the theorist may employ to analyse it.   Here, theory is not merely the poor sister of
practical concerns and their record in the form of military
history.   It may well be that the conduct of war can come to
be dominated by new weapons, freak accidents of geography or
circumstance, but always the last court of appeal in war is
lodged in the social conditions that give it life, including
the minds of men and the 'theory' or system of reasoning
that shapes its conduct.

I shall return and pick up this important thread shortly,
because it is partly Clausewitz's reverence for military history as the best representation of reality beyond personal
observation that lay at the root of his apparent disinterest in
and real mishandling of the contractual assumptions on which
he was working.   It is obvious where the weight of his reverence lies, simply because he suggests the application of
theory, as a litmus paper, to seek out the properties of the
real world.   The danger is that the abstract form of war and
its theory of strategy is far more than some dead litmus paper
and his ungenerous claims for it.   The phenomenon of war does

not present a hard choice between empirical or abstract
knowledge.   Rather, the two can become one and the same, that
is, to the extent that the assumptions, distortions and errors
hidden in theory, namely, about the isolation of war from the
political and social world, can determine how we come to recognize and formulate the former knowledge.   Reality, and particularly the social reality that is war, is, in large part,
fashioned by the ideal or abstract models through which we
come to acknowledge it and act in it.   And this is what
Clausewitz forgot in his reverence for military history, which
it was hoped would put any analytic errors right.   In doing
so, he became his first and own victim of the lens of contract
so subtly built into the abstract form of war, his central
theoretical concept, that helped to determine what he grasped
as reality, what he saw as strategic facts and what he threw
away as non-essentials.   Clausewitz stated formally only once
then promptly forgot in his preference for history that he was
a contract theorist, someone whose bulk of reasoning rested on
a contractual arrangement about the isolation of war from the
political and social world and the notion of the inviolability
of social order contained therein.   More than most classical
theorists, who by one route or another fell victim to this
same contract and the way it fashioned how they came to see
reality, Clausewitz attempted, especially in his later theoretical writings, to escape the grip of this contract by pushing
theory further towards the notion of power, 'the hand of politics', moving always closer towards the political world and
sociological roots from which this notion springs.   Any non-
contractual or *free* theory of strategy and concept of war that
is moved by 'the hand of politics' embraces fully the concept
of social order out of which it rises.   It is natural for
free theory to pursue the notion of power into its inalienable

social roots. This is precisely what many armed and guerrilla groups are doing today, at whatever level of reasoning
and however haphazardly and instinctively. They are working
their way down into the last unit of power found lodged in
the fabric of social relations common to all social order.
Clausewitz did move around the concept of social order, at
times making direct mention of it; but in each instance he
could not logically pursue it without virtually starting from
the beginning again. As we shall see, he could only pursue
the political nature of war by letting drift into the recesses of theory the formally and only once stated conditions
underlying the absolute form of war, all of which came down
to the assumption that war was an act wholly isolated from
the political world, this is, another way of assuming the inviolability of social order. By way of this drifting away
of a so obviously offensive assumption that was, at first,
needed to build his model of war in the abstract, he was more
comfortably able to plant the political flower further into
the hard soil of the abstract form of war and its theory of
strategy that was already built on the contractual notion
expelling social order and making theory now *silently* hostile
to any substantive analysis of power. Here is expressed so
eloquently the century-old dilemma, the everywhere present
tension between military facts and political facts, between
strategy and policy that has harassed theory since Clausewitz.

But I leave this for later, where the discussion of his
mishandling of assumptions will be made clearer, and return
to conclude our brief note of Clausewitz's greater reverence
for military history - now armed with our special interest.
This interest is that the way he came to recognize and formulate historical facts was, in large part, fashioned, in the
first place, by his central theoretical concept, the abstract

form of war, particularly its suppressed conditions without
which its logic cannot stand (regardless of how this form was
then moderated to meet a reality already so fashioned).   What
slipped his attention is that he started theory construction
with a formally stated contract holding together the abstract
form of war as he needed its services to build this abstract
model, and ended up in silent contract now dropped out of
theory so he could pursue the relations between war and the
political world the very isolation of which the bulk of theory
had come to grasp in the absolute form.   Wash theory as he
may of its vital premises, they lurked in every corner of
theory holding all back from a real plunge into the very intimacies of the political world, on which revisionism now
feeds.   As other classical theorists, for all their differences, Clausewitz reasons within a kind of a circle set up by
the inviolability of social order.   The main thread of this
chapter must here firmly resist the temptation of sliding down
an ancillary line towards a survey of Clausewitz's historical
writings to demonstrate the recognition and formulation of historical facts by, in large part, the device of contract embedded in the abstract form of war.   Except for abandoning this
in the hands of the opinion quoted below, in any case our
singular purpose can properly ignore, for reasons I have
already discussed, the overall chronology of the matter, and
need only make its claims on the methodological level as regards the major theoretical work, 'On War':

> Even a decade earlier Clausewitz was in no doubt about the
> consequences for methodology as well as for the selection
> of topics to be studied that resulted from the rigorous
> concern for naive reality, proper to a 'practical art'
> such as war.   Much remained to be done before he was ready
> to formulate a comprehensive theory; but his notes and

brief essays already identified major elements of an integrated system that existed in his mind long before it was
openly stated or fully developed.[15]

In contrast to what free theory will reveal about his
method of enquiry, in the first instance Clausewitz insisted
that as for 'abstract reasoning, we wish to add that experience, far from leading to a different conclusion, is the very
source of our conviction, and lies at the root of this train
of thought'.[16]   Military history served as the starting-point
for theoretical speculation that went beyond the limits
imposed on personal observation:

> We therefore turn to experience and study those sequences
> of events related in military history.   The result will,
> of course, be a limited theory, based only on facts recor-
> ded by military historians.   But that is inevitable, since
> theoretical results must have been derived from military
> history or at least checked against it.   Such a limitation
> is in any case more theoretical than real.
>
>   A great advantage offered by this method is that theory
> will have to remain realistic.   It cannot allow itself to
> get lost in futile speculation, hairsplitting, and flights
> of fancy.[17]

In the relationship between history and theory it is the
former that is seen exercising the greater influence over the
latter, rather than the reverse: 'Just as some plants bear
fruit only if they don't shoot up too high, so in the practical arts the leaves and flowers of theory must be pruned and
the plant kept close to its proper soil - experience'.[18]   In
the balance of all influences, because 'historical examples
clarify everything and also provide the best kind of proof in
the empirical sciences - this is particularly true of the art
of war',[19] the method of enquiry must proceed as if 'military

history in all its aspects is itself a *source of instruction*
for the critic, and it is only natural that he should look at
all particular events in the light of the whole'.[20]   Since
this method of enquiry insists that 'the influence of theoretical truths on practical life is always exerted more through
critical analysis than through doctrine',[21] military history
is subjected to the *critical approach*:

> We distinguish between the *critical approach* and the plain
> narrative of a historical event, which merely arranges
> facts one after another, and at most touches on their
> immediate causal links.
>
> Three different intellectual activities may be contained
> in the critical approach.
>
> First, the discovery and interpretation of equivocal
> facts.   This is historical research proper, and has
> nothing in common with theory.
>
> Second, the tracing of effects back to their causes.
> This is *critical analysis proper*.   It is essential for
> theory; for whatever in theory is to be defined, suppor-
> ted, or simply described by reference to experience can
> only be dealt with in this manner.
>
> Third, the investigation and evaluation of means em-
> ployed.   This last is criticism proper, involving praise
> and censure.   Here theory serves history, or rather the
> lessons to be drawn from history.
>
> In the last two activities which are the truly critical
> parts of historical inquiry, it is vital to analyse every-
> thing down to its basic elements, to incontrovertible
> truth.   One must not stop half-way, as is so often done,
> at some arbitrary assumption or hypothesis.[22]

Theory is primarily concerned with the 'task of investigating the relation of cause and effect and the appropriateness

of means to ends [that] will be easy when cause and effect, means and ends, are closely linked'.[23] The manner in which 'critical investigation gets us into theory proper is the analysis of normally concurrent causes and the deduction of their effects'.[24] On the other hand, the examination of the means 'poses the question as to what are the peculiar effects of the means employed, and whether these effects conform to the intention with which they were used'.[25] These same effects lead to the investigation of the nature of means in which critical enquiry once more moves into the realm of theory.

The methodological problems spring to life the instant one insists that 'the influence of theoretical truths on practical life is always exerted more through critical analysis than through doctrine'.[26] If theory were simply to be cast off into the realm of doctrine with provision for the usual acknowledgments of a changing reality that demands periodical amendments, then a host of other methodological difficulties may apply - but not the one which concerns us at present. This is simply: how does one actually go about discovering and interpreting equivocal facts, on what basis does one trace effects back to their causes, and how does one proceed in the investigation and evaluation of means employed? The answer Clausewitz gives is that critical analysis not only yields theory, that is, 'gets us into theory proper', but it can only do so by the application in the first place of theoretical truths to actual events: 'critical analysis being the application of theoretical truths to actual events, not only reduces the gap between the two but also accustoms the mind to these truths through their repeated application'.[27] Critical analysis can remain a prisoner of its own theoretical truths and their underlying assumptions by which it proceeds

through the real world and to which (truths) it is meant to
contribute.   It does little good to expect of a polite
reality already 'house-trained' by theory, particularly its
universally held assumptions, any lively check on bogus
theory, certainly the more subtle of theories that feed on
silent contract.   This can amount to continually recirculat-
ing unspoken and contractual assumptions.   The danger here is
found in Clausewitz's 'rigorous concern for naive reality'[28]
which led him to ignore the possibility of methodological
errors that can threaten theory and which may have already
violated a reality in the form of military history that was
intended to provide the best kind of proof and, in itself, a
source of instruction.[29]   This is to suggest that in the
mutual interplay between history and theory, that is to say:
in 'the study of the past and the searching out of the time-
less aspects of war [that] fulfilled the same need of cogni-
tion; both were allied in the same emotional and intellectual quest',[30] Clausewitz's rigorous concern for the former
blinded him to the possibility of assumptions, distortions
and errors built into the latter by which he came to recognize and formulate reality in the first place.   In one form,
and by one route or another, this same methodological error
has infested classical theory ever since.

In the formulation and application of theory, one must
never have too much blind faith in reality or experience,
that is, discount the mirages built into theory in determining
that reality in the first place, how we all perceive and think
about it.   Here the observer comes to believe that what he
sees and formulates is real, or at least an approximation of
reality with the usual qualifications, when in fact all this
may be born in the womb of *how* he, and the participants in
war, perceive and reason.   All the theorist can do is to

throw away the false gods in whose qualities he may seek undue
comfort and make certain, as best his talents permit, to keep
his own house in order.   In particular, in this case it is
important to ensure that the assumptions one uses to build
models are reasonably valid, and that they are not thrown away
during the development of the theory in the hope that a continued deference to reality and its historical representation
will put all right.

I pass briefly into Clausewitz's view on the nature of
theory which would provide no strict doctrine or magic formulas because reality, in fact, frequently fell short of the
logical extreme, the pure abstraction that alone stood as the
standard of all measurement and analysis:

> Theory must concede all this [in terms of the modifications
> and imperfections lodged in reality]; but it has the duty
> to give priority to the absolute form of war and to make
> that form a general point of reference, so that he who
> wants to learn from theory becomes accustomed to keeping
> that point in view constantly, to measuring all his hopes
> and fears by it, and to approximating it *when he can* or
> *when he must*.[31]

The absolute form of war or 'the pure concept of war',
which I shall later argue (and as Clausewitz did admit only
once) is founded on the assumption that war is regarded as an
wholly isolated act from the political world that itself embraces the contractual notion of the inviolability of social
order, is not given the free licence of doctrine.   This is
because reality could fall short of pure abstraction that may
not always account for real modifications to and diversions
from the logical extreme, and also the realms of thinking and
action are taken to be voluntaristic (free will and genius),
not crudely deterministic:

The function of theory is to put all this in systematic
order, clearly and comprehensively, and to trace each
action to an adequate, compelling cause....

Theory should cast a steady light on all phenomena so
that we can more easily recognize and eliminate the weeds
that always spring from ignorance; it should show how one
thing is related to another, and keep the important and the
unimportant separate. If concepts combine of their own
accord to form that nucleus of truth we call a principle,
if they spontaneously compose a pattern that becomes a
rule, it is the task of the theorist to make this clear.

Any insights gained and garnered by the mind in its
wanderings among basic concepts are the benefits that
theory can provide. Theory cannot equip the mind with the
formulas for solving problems, nor can it mark the narrow
path on which the sole solution is supposed to lie by
planting a hedge of principles on either side. But it can
give the mind insight into the great mass of phenomena and
of their relationships, then leave it free to rise into the
higher realms of action. There the mind can use its
innate talents to capacity, combining them all so as to
seize on what is *right* and *true* as though this were a
single idea formed by their concentrated pressure - as
though it were a response to the immediate challenge
rather than a product of thought.[32]

Theory can deliver to the mind an insight into the great
mass of phenomena and their relationships because critical
analysis that employs and contributes to the body of theory
has worked its way through the chains, upward and downward, of
causes and effects, of means and ends: 'One can go on tracing the effects that a cause produces so long as it seems
worth while. In the same way, a means may be evaluated, not

merely with respect to its immediate end: that end itself
should be appraised as a means for the next and highest one;
and thus we can follow a chain of sequential objectives'.[33]
In this 'theory will have fulfilled its main task when it is
used to analyse the constituent elements of war, to distinguish precisely what at first sight seems fused, to explain in
full the properties of the means employed and to show their
probable effects, to define clearly the nature of the ends in
view, and to illuminate all phases of warfare in a thorough
critical inquiry'.[34] Theory is seen in a resistant medium
to be striving for universality and absolute truth: 'All the
positive results of theoretical investigation - all the principles, rules, and methods - will increasingly lack universality and absolute truth the closer they come to being positive
doctrine'.[35] In the attempt to investigate the essence of
the phenomena of war and to indicate the links between these
phenomena and the nature of their component parts, 'only a
theory that will follow the simple thread of internal cohesion as we have tried to make ours do, can get back to the
essence of things';[36] that is to say, 'we are concerned with
examining the essential content of what has long existed, and
to trace it back to its basic elements'.[37] With the new
light that revisionist theory sheds on the primal concerns of
strategy, particularly in the direction of its sociological
roots, we are in a position to move on and judge for ourselves
how far Clausewitz's theoretical work satisfied its own objectives.

If one seeks too much from history in the final arbitration
that it cannot give because this arbitration is already
stained by a circular or self-fulfilling application of the
very theoretical truths (and their underlying assumptions to
which insufficient attention has been paid) now up for judg-

ment, then theory gains an even greater and serpentine power
if the critic now feels secure enough in the hands of history
to rush forward by use of gross and silent assumptions into
the realm of extreme abstraction and philosophic ideal: 'Thus
in the field of abstract thought the inquiring mind can never
rest until it reaches the extreme, for here it is dealing with
an extreme: a clash of forces freely operating and obedient
to no law but their own'.[38]   This is, in part, why the absolute form of war, to which we now turn, is such a powerful
source of surreptitious reasoning in the central relationship
between absolute and real war (regardless to what extent, if
any, past strategists in the classical tradition may or may
not have misread this relationship).   If the critic is to
conduct his investigation of history in the manner Clausewitz
says he ought to, then it could yield no more than the bounds
of generosity of a methodology that asks no *real* questions.
It may appear that this same methodology need not even bother
asking such questions, in that the absolute form and the real
world are, at times, one and the same:

> This is its usual appearance, and one might wonder whether
> there is any truth at all in our concept of the absolute
> character of war were it not for the fact that with our own
> eyes we have seen warfare achieve this state of absolute
> perfection.   After the short prelude of the French Revolu-
> tion, Bonaparte brought it swiftly and ruthlessly to that
> point.   War, in his hands, was waged without respite until
> the enemy succumbed, and the counter-blows were struck with
> almost equal energy.   Surely it is both natural and ines-
> capable that this phenomenon should cause us to turn again
> to the pure concept of war with all its rigorous implica-
> tions.[39]

Here it is not so much the real issue that the extreme

abstraction has become reality and thus properly valid.
Rather, it is that this reality is little more substantive
than the participants' unconscious agreement to honour the
contract embedded in the absolute form.   As Clausewitz admitted only once in the first chapter as we shall see, the absolute form can be the case in reality only as long as all
accept this contractual assumption on which everything hangs.
The instant one party in the real practice of war reaches down
and grasps its more fundamental threads, then the silent contract and its concomitant 'reality' vanishes for what it
always was.   The reality of classical theory stretches only
so far as everyone's willingness to play out the contract,
and we shall see shortly Clausewitz's half-conscious recognition of this single weakness in classical theory.   And so we
have come to the heart of the matter: because of Clausewitz's
methodology which basically comes down to the inattention to
and mishandling of assumptions, these came to dominate everywhere, rendering the conception of war hostile to its own and
freely acknowledged philosophical and theoretical basis which
would otherwise have revealed instantly the primal concerns of
strategy.   Moreover, not only did he pass over the possibility that the contractual assumptions first needed to build the
logical extreme can dominate theory, but he actually helped
this along by later suppressing these assumptions, that
together came down to the notion that war be thought of as a
wholly isolated act from the political world, into the recesses of theory after only giving them formal statement once.
This vital condition simply vanished, but the body of reasoning to which it gave life silently carried its poor influence
into every corner of theory, holding back all considerations
from a free plunge into their natural sociological basis.

I pause here briefly to remind that once seen in their

deeper, natural and social whole unsevered by the sharp edge
of silent contract, strategic considerations emerge as a
specific reality *sui generis*.   It is dominated by the deeper
social conditions which gave them life in the first place.
It ought never to be dominated by the use of contractual
assumptions that arbitrarily expel from the heart of theory
those primal considerations that would have, by their own
right, been otherwise recognized as such.   Mixed into the
underlying social roots that bring war to life must be, as in
any social and moral phenomenon, the real influence of the
abstract or general vision of its nature that its constituents
carry into it.   If reality comes to be dominated by poor
assumptions and twisted reasoning then it will rarely give up
a greater judgment on the validity of theory than the power of
theory to shape this reality in the first place.   This is
especially so in the wholly integrated social activity that is
war when all constituents share the same general vision of its
nature and conduct.   Here, what has been overwhelmed and saturated by shared reasoning simply appears as a neutral and
pure reality into which one must never seek too much.   This
is so because such reality is rarely, if ever, pure, but
stained by the faulty assumptions and procedures by which we
come to recognize and act in it.   In the social world not all
is concrete, but flesh and blood that perceives and acts by
some manner or structures of reasoning.   If left on its own,
liberated from the foreign stain of poor assumptions and
twisted reasoning that men carry into its nature and conduct,
then war would have an opportunity to seek out its freely
acknowledged social basis: no conditions, conventions or
ceremony - just a near free-for-all in which the baser social
considerations that classical convention could avoid prevail
everywhere.   There is no other more primal state that war can

find.   It can be propped up into contractual or fleeting
forms by all manner of convention, hindrances or unusual circumstances that may prevail at any one time, or may come to
rest in its natural and revisionist state.

Clausewitz was in error to debase theory as some sort of
dead litmus paper and so heavily rely on an experience already
stained by his own methodology and the faulty assumptions and
twisted reasoning that its constituents had carried into it.
Here his interest had little hope of revealing its more elementary nature.   He might have been able sooner and more
forcefully to push into the social roots of power behind the
'hand of politics', for which he is most remembered, had he
given theory more chance to seek out its natural philosophical
basis.   Instead, his efforts turned on not only relying on
the good offices of a 'neutral' experience that, by his own
procedure, could not be there to serve, but also on the pursuit of the logical extreme in abstract thought stretched
along the avenue of unspoken contract that only paved over
more of the elementary considerations into which a proper
regard for theory, in particular its underlying and contractual assumptions, may have led.   Theory should never formulate
its assumptions around simple contract but in its own and inalienable social roots.

It was the use of the contractual notion of the inviolability of social order that made the pursuit of the ideal possible only because the absolute form of war is not, in itself,
a viable logical proposition without this one grand assumption.   Once made, the flood of proposition after proposition
sets up a stream of obsessions that, in some degree, still run
throughout contemporary strategy today.   In the face of this
torrent, unlike many classical theorists who found the current
of theory so swift they let themselves be swept past the more

elementary social and political considerations that today
threaten more and more, Clausewitz did try and grasp 'the
hand of politics'.   But by then, especially in the later
writings, his grasp had become so infected by the arthritis
of unspoken contract, which had swept out these considerations
and on which the bulk of theory rested, that it was a hopeless
task: he was pushing against a whole system of reasoning
that was driving silently in the opposite way.   He was not
free to pursue theory into its more elementary social origins
because the better part of theory secretly rested on the
notion of the isolation of war from the political and social
world along with the inviolability of social order that this
notion embraces.   Clausewitz may have thought that his deliberations were driving into the essential content of war, following the simple threads of internal cohesion; in fact, the
larger portion was quietly pursuing an opposite direction.
This is the most persuasive example or representation of how
theory has been adrift from its proper and social moorings
ever since.   Particularly here this is so because Clausewitz
did increasingly recognize these moorings, but his deliberations never came to embrace fully the political and social
beacon towards which they had so belatedly struggled.   Unlike
armed groups today whose instinct or learning of the various
insurgent models have given, in the nuclear age, new life to
violence as an instrument of policy and war as 'a true political instrument, a continuation of political activity by other
means',[40] Clausewitz could not drive the problem of power central to all social life right down to the last unit of the
decisive pursuit of power endemic in the fabric of all social
relations.   Nor then could he *fully* visualize war as a wholly
articulate social and moral activity, an extension of the
social pursuit of power by other means of which social moral-

ity is the principal author.   Had he done so, there waiting
at the apex of theory would have been the conception of social
order around which all other elements in war fall straight
into place.

This is not to say that Clausewitzian theory did or did not
truly represent, within the stated qualifications, the reality
of war at the time of writing or at later periods.   Whatever
the interest here for historians or strategists with an eye
for the past, my singular purpose must remain firm because
contemporary theory is not left with the burden of the conditions of the last century but with the contractual system of
reasoning that grew out of these conditions.   Naturally
Clausewitz could not be expected to pursue the political insight into the nature of war, for which he is most warmly remembered, any further than the conditions of his reality
would permit.   Therefore, it is simply for the purpose of
illustration when I suggest that had he freed himself from the
tyranny of his own assumptions and driven his own insight down
to its elementary units of power, this is, the fabric of
social relations, he would have arrived at the natural and
most elementary state of war free from conventions foreign to
its real nature: the sovereignty of social order and the revisionist theory that describes its reign.   This illustration
seeks only to expose a scheme of reasoning that, regardless of
the conditions from whence it sprang, in its own right, by its
own methodology and structure, blinds theory to its natural
and social state.   That is what went wrong in classical
theory, this is what still haunts theory today;   and that is
why I take the trouble to consult directly Clausewitz's theoretical writings in some detail.

It is this violent and more elementary pursuit of power
through the fabric of social life that our classical heritage

blots out of our view because it was built that way.   Too
much of classical theory since Clausewitz has rested on
sweeping away its natural foundations into which war is now
dissolving, where violence as an instrument of policy is, in
the nuclear age, free to pursue ends of a moral and social
nature.   In war's more natural and unfettered state the ten-
sions inherent in classical theory are similarly dissolved;
the most arbitrary of these is the separation of political
and strategic facts spun out by the serpentine hand of silent
contract.   If strategists are to appreciate this present-day
dissolution of war into its more elementary social state in
which our highly contractual tradition is hastily discarded
and the primal concerns of war that this contract could safely
ignore now emerge as the sole test, then they must not fail to
return to analyse the best illustration of where theory went
wrong.   The conception of war can find few deeper roots than
those traced by revisionist theory - so much so that the elementary and foreign considerations that strategists could pass
over before have suddenly become everything.   If contemporary
strategy is to regard the primitive nature of guerrilla and
insurgent war (and the first social imperatives it suggests)
as beneath the deliberations of the modern world, its superior
technology and weaponry, it could not be more right.   Once
tradition starts to dissolve, this elementary rot eats more
and more away at the very roots of contemporary theory.
Those who do not have access to this modern world see a new
way in the poorly researched social dimensions of strategy of
pursuing their objectives by violence with some hope of success, where before they had little; and those who have access
to the technology and weaponry of the nuclear age may see an
alternative way of avoiding the risks inherent therein, and
obtain by violence (including it seems through so-called

'proxy wars') the objectives that they could not otherwise
attain.

How extraordinary the reasoning in Clausewitzian theory by
which war was burdened with a split personality: 'Its gram-
mar, indeed, may be its own, but not its logic'![41]   This
twisted scheme through which the conception of war was robbed
of its essential content leads our deliberations into the central relationship throughout this theory between real war and
its abstract representation in the absolute form - because it
is here precisely that the contractual assumptions used in
theory construction are left to sink away into the recesses of
theory.   What is our special interest, that carefully de-
limits the following discussion, is the wholly contractual
basis of the absolute form, without which it cannot stand.
Clausewitz, only at one point, gave the formal conditions
underlying the absolute form as a viable and logical proposition.   But he elsewhere, for reasons described later, let
these crucial conditions drift into the recesses of theory
where they remained unnoticed.   To drop out of the development of theory the assumptions that were first needed in its
construction cannot wash theory clean of the hidden temptation
to reason on the basis by which it was built, particularly if
this involves the isolation of war from the political and
social world.   So I now turn to how this theory came to work
against its own and proper theoretical and philosophical foundations by examining the wholly contractual nature of the
absolute form and its relations to real war, particularly
those politically determined relations.   The intent for
posing the notions of abstract or absolute war and real war,
that is to say what can be two rather different notions of war
simultaneously in the same theory (among a number of other
similarly posed concepts that are not embraced by our special

interest), is explained in the following passage referring to
the attack in relation to defence, but equally applies here:

> Where two ideas form a true logical antithesis, each com-
> plementary to the other, then fundamentally each is implied
> in the other. The limitations of our mind may not allow
> us to comprehend both simultaneously, and to discover by
> antithesis the whole of one in the whole of the other.
> Nevertheless each will shed enough reciprocal light to
> clarify many of the details.[42]

The way Clausewitz handled the philosophic ideal and logical extreme of the absolute form of war taken as the 'general
point of reference', a basis for measurement and ultimate
analytic standard lies at the heart of the problem of a theory
rendered hostile to any substantive analysis of its own roots,
and that is why I exclude from this discussion a whole range
of issues treated elsewhere[43] and concentrate our interest
here.

Revisionism shares with tradition - indeed tries to persuade contemporary strategy of its continued necessity - the
fundamental proposition that 'war is thus an act of force to
compel our enemy to do our will'. The parting of ways
begins the instant theory insists that:

> Force - that is, physical force, for moral force has no
> existence save as expressed in the state and the law - is
> thus the *means* of war; to impose our will on the enemy is
> its object. To secure that object we must render the
> enemy powerless; and that, in theory, is the true aim of
> warfare. That aim takes the place of the object, discard-
> ing it as something not actually part of war itself.[44]

By one firm sweep, a simple stroke of a pen, the whole mass
of considerations that give life to the conception of war, and
nowadays find their way into the heart of strategy, here find

themselves banished from the arena of theory. Social morality, as its principal author, has no existence in this conception, and the higher political and thus socially rooted
object is usurped and discarded beyond the domain of war by
the subordinate and more immediate aim of rendering the enemy
militarily powerless to act. There is no innate reason why
such sentences of banishment should be passed except, in the
first instance, that which is expelled somehow offends the
logic of the matter:

> If wars between civilized nations are far less cruel and
> destructive than wars between savages, the reason lies in
> the social conditions of the states themselves and in their
> relationships to one another. These are the forces that
> give rise to war; the same forces circumscribe and
> moderate it. They themselves however are not part of war;
> they already exist before fighting starts. To introduce
> the principle of moderation into the theory of war itself
> would always lead to logical absurdity.[45]

It is this obsessive and extreme logic of the matter that
dominates the absolute form of war, and which is described
here along with its underlying conditions that, in effect,
embrace the inviolability of social order because they expel
the conception of social order central to the political world
from any consideration whatsoever:

> Thus in the field of abstract thought the inquiring mind
> can never rest until it reaches the extreme, for here it
> is dealing with an extreme: a clash of forces freely
> operating and obedient to no law but their own. From a
> pure concept of war you might try to deduce absolute terms
> for the objective you should aim at and for the means of
> achieving it; but if you did so the continuous inter-
> action would land you in extremes that represented nothing

but a play of the imagination issuing from an almost in-
visible sequence of logical subtleties. If we were to
think purely in absolute terms, we could avoid every difficulty by a stroke of the pen and proclaim with inflexible
logic that, since the extreme must always be the goal, the
greatest effort must always be exerted. Any such pro-
nouncement would be an abstraction and would leave the
real world quite unaffected....

   But move from the abstract to the real world, and the
whole thing looks quite different. In the abstract world,
optimism was all-powerful and forced us to assume that both
parties to the conflict not only sought perfection but
attained it. Would this ever be the case in practice?
Yes, it would if: (a) war were a wholly isolated act,
occurring suddenly and not produced by previous events in
the political world; (b) it consisted of a single decisive
act or a set of simultaneous ones; (c) the decision
achieved was complete and perfect in itself, uninfluenced
by any previous estimate of the political situation it
would bring about.[46]

This conception of war, well taken to be simple abstraction, the conditions for which are only here formally stated
once, but which nevertheless is pleaded as 'a general point of
reference', is so cleanly stripped of its social and political
flesh that all which remains is the skeleton of its own necessary logic, where nothing is left behind to offend. One of
the principal offenders (and the one our interest singles out)
is the place of policy and the political world, which is
simply driven out by the 'complete, untrammeled, absolute
manifestation of violence (as the pure concept would require),
[in which] war would of its own independent will usurp the
place of policy the moment policy had brought it into being;

it would then drive policy out of office and rule by the laws
of its own nature'.[47]   These laws constitute a torrent of
necessary causes that are indivisible, all threads leading to
and reducing all interaction in war to final decisive victory,
and which 'derives its validity from the nature of the
subject':

> In the absolute form of war, where everything results from
> necessary causes and one action rapidly affects another,
> there is, if we may use the phrase, no intervening neutral
> void. Since war contains a host of interactions, since
> the whole series of engagements is, strictly speaking,
> linked together, since in every victory there is a culmi-
> nating point beyond which lies the realm of losses and
> defeats - in view of all these intrinsic characteristics
> of war, we say there is only one result that counts: *final
> victory.* Until then, nothing is decided, nothing won,
> and nothing lost. In this form of war we must always keep
> in mind that it is the end that crowns the work. Within
> the concept of absolute war, then, war is indivisible, and
> its component parts (the individual victories) are of value
> only in their relation to the whole.[48]

Once the flow of obsessive logic of absolute war washes
away, through gross assumption, the political, hence social
foundations of war, it has no other avenue left but the central proposition that the will to wage war is to be taken primarily and, in the case of secondary or intervening factors,
ultimately a function of the armed forces. In this state the
absolute form is simply reduced wholly to 'the aim of *disarming the enemy* (the object of war in the *abstract*, the ultimate
means of accomplishing the war's political purpose, which
should incorporate all the rest)'.[49] This process of logical
reductionism of a spectrum of varied means into one only works

if the large mass of political and social considerations are
deemed to possess no connection with the conception of war
itself:

> If for the moment we consider the pure concept of war, we
> should have to say that the political purpose of war had no
> connection with war itself; for if war is an act of vio-
> lence meant to force the enemy to do our will its aim would
> have *always* and *solely* to be to overcome the enemy and
> disarm him. That aim is derived from the theoretical
> concept of war; but since many wars do actually come very
> close to fulfilling it, let us examine this kind of war
> first of all....
>
> The fighting forces must be *destroyed*: that is, they
> must be *put in such a condition that they can no longer
> carry on the fight*. Whenever we use the phrase 'destruc-
> tion of the enemy's forces' this alone is what we mean.[50]

This method of reasoning guarantees by means of a strict
law of inherent necessity 'the principle that the destruction
of enemy forces must be regarded as the main objective; not
just in the war generally, but in each individual engagement
and within all the different conditions necessitated by the
circumstances out of which the war has arisen'.[51]   This
principle is intended to embrace, by logical extension, those
circumstances in which such destruction does not even take
place:

> Combat is the only effective force in war; its aim is to
> destroy the enemy's forces as a means to a further end.
> That holds good even if no actual fighting occurs, because
> the outcome rests on the assumption that if it came to
> fighting, the enemy would be destroyed. It follows that
> the destruction of the enemy's force underlies all military
> actions; all plans are ultimately based on it, resting on

it like an arch on its abutment. Consequently, all action
is undertaken in the belief that if the ultimate test of
arms should actually occur, the outcome would be favorable.
The decision by arms is for all major and minor operations
in war what cash payment is in commerce. Regardless how
complex the relationship between the two parties, regardless how rarely settlements actually occur, they can never
be entirely absent.

If a decision by fighting is the basis of all plans and
operations, it follows that the enemy *can frustrate everything through a successful battle*. This occurs not only
when the encounter affects an essential factor in our
plans, but when any victory that is won is of sufficient
scope. For every important victory - that is, destruction
of opposing forces - reacts on all other possibilities.
Like liquid, they will settle at a new level.

Thus it is evident that destruction of the enemy forces
is always the superior, more effective means, with which
others cannot compete.

But, of course, we can only say destruction of the
enemy is more effective if we can assume that all other
conditions are equal.[52]
What is required throughout is that no act escape this
singular obsession in war, that is to say, 'while a battle is
the principal means, it is not the only one'.[53]   Other means
such as the capture of fortresses or occupation of territory
all amount to the destruction of enemy forces; this is their
real value: 'So the occupation of an undefended strip of
territory may, aside from its direct value in achieving an
aim, also have value in terms of destruction of enemy
forces'.[54]   Moreover, not only do these ancillary means in
themselves amount to direct destruction of enemy forces, but

they also 'may lead to further destruction, and thereby
become an indirect means as well'.[55]

This process of logical reductionism first grasps everything not already assumed out of the absolute form of war, and
then is able to pursue the logic through a flood of inter-
related propositions into its elementary level. This boils
down to the 'task of reducing the sources of enemy strength to
a single centre of gravity',[56] since 'the first task, then, in
planning for a war is to identify the enemy's centers of
gravity, and if possible trace them back to a single one'.[57]
As all political and social phenomena of which the conception
of war is the natural extension are dismissed from a *free* consideration that lies at the genesis of revisionist theory,
there is only one avenue of reasoning left along which theory
is strictly rampant:

> After everything we have so far said on the subject, we can
> identify two basic principles that underlie all strategic
> planning and serve to guide all other considerations.
>
> The first principle is that the ultimate substance of
> enemy strength must be traced back to the fewest possible
> sources, and ideally to one alone. The attack on these
> sources must be compressed into the fewest possible actions
> - again, ideally, into one. Finally, all minor actions
> must be subordinated as much as possible. In short the
> first principle is: act with the utmost concentration.
>
> The second principle is: act with the utmost speed.
> No halt or detour must be permitted without good cause.[58]

This typical obsession with concentration and speed (to
which I shall return shortly) takes hold of a whole mass of
varied social action that a free consideration of war would
equally embrace and refines it down into its pure state -
decisive battle - directed at 'a certain center of gravity

[which] develops, the hub of all power and movement, on which everything depends'.[59] Since 'there are very few cases where this conception is not applicable - where it would not be realistic to reduce several centers of gravity to one',[60] in the absolute form all is reduced to the central proposition that the will to resist is a function of armed forces. Moreover, this abstract obsession, founded, as Clausewitz only once admitted,[61] on the assumption that war is an isolated act having no relations with the political and social world, is further driven into the heart of the armed forces known as the decisive point:

> A center of gravity is always found where the mass is concentrated most densely. It presents the most effective target for a blow; furthermore, the heaviest blow is that struck by the center of gravity. The same holds true in war. The fighting forces of each belligerent - whether a single state or an alliance of states - have a certain unity and therefore some cohesion. Where there is cohesion, the analogy of the center of gravity can be applied. Thus these forces will possess certain centers of gravity, which, by their movement and direction, govern the rest; and those centers of gravity will be found wherever the forces are most concentrated....
>
> It is therefore a major act of strategic judgment to distinguish these centers of gravity in the enemy's forces and to identify their spheres of effectiveness. One will constantly be called upon to estimate the effect that an advance or a retreat by part of the forces on either side will have upon the rest....
>
> Our position, then, is that a theater of war, be it large or small, and the forces stationed there, no matter what their size, represent the sort of unity in which a

single center of gravity can be identified.   That is the
place where the decision should be reached;   a victory at
that point is in its fullest sense identical with the
defense of the theater of operations.[62]

To come down to the central proposition in the absolute
form of war, as the ultimate analytic authority, that the will
to resist is taken everywhere as a function of armed forces is
really a fabrication resting entirely on the equally fabricated notions that: '(a) war were a wholly isolated act, occurring suddenly and not produced by previous events in the political world; ... (c) the decision achieved was complete and
perfect in itself, uninfluenced by any previous estimate of
the political situation it would bring about'.[63]   These
assumptions through which the absolute form is wholly sustained, and for which there is otherwise no innate reason,
incorporate the inviolability of social order - the banning
of the decisive and violent pursuit of power throughout its
most elementary level followed down (many armed groups have
done so today) into the fabric of social relations out of
which it springs.   By this route the conception of war is
upheld from a free and quick dissolution into its more effective and natural social state.

This conception is further led from its free state by the
next flood of necessary propositions flowing from this reduction of the sources of the will to resist by gross contract.
Once all such varied sources are reduced to the single notion
of armed forces in which all the threads come to rest, the
absolute form tends to be lured straight into the 'decisive
battle' solution.   With regard to 'the progress of military
interaction as a whole' it follows quite strictly that 'if
every action in war is allowed its appropriate duration, we
would agree that, at least at first sight, any additional

expenditure of time - any suspension of military action -
seems absurd'.[64]   The drive to, or obsession with 'decisive
battle' is the product of this sort of reasoning, only valid,
of course, as supported by previously stated assumptions:

> Seen in this light, suspension of action in war is a con-
> tradiction in terms.   Like two incompatible elements,
> armies must continually destroy one another.   Like fire
> and water they never find themselves in a state of equili-
> brium, but must keep on interacting until one of them has
> completely disappeared.   Imagine a pair of wrestlers dead-
> locked and inert for hours on end!   In other words, mili-
> tary action ought to run its course steadily like a wound-
> up clock.[65]

In a free state, the conception of war simply discards this
notion and finds itself plunged into a state of affairs in
which prevails a rarely decisive and never ending series of
guerrilla wars where action is frequently suspended.

Once again the absolute form consists of extreme reductionism, this time of all military activity, this is to say,
while 'every battle or engagement has a special purpose that
gives it its peculiar characteristics',[66] none the less: 'The
concept of the engagement lies at the root of all strategic
action, since strategy is the use of force, the heart of
which, in turn, is the engagement.   So in the field of
strategy we can reduce all military activity to the unitary
concept of the single engagement, and concern ourselves
exclusively with its purposes.'[67]   As all concepts of the
will to resist have been reduced into being a function of the
armed forces and all military activity to the unitary concept
of the single engagement, this logic leads swiftly into a dual
law: 'These facts lead to a dual law whose principles support
each other: destruction of the enemy's forces is generally

accomplished by means of great battles and their results;
and, the primary object of great battles must be the destruction of the enemy's forces'.[68]   This state of affairs is seen
to be 'less inconsistent, more in concert with its own nature,
more objective, and more obedient to the law of inherent
necessity'[69] - wholly applicable only under the previously
stated conditions of contract.   If this necessity is properly
to dominate everywhere through which all military activity is
reduced to the unitary concept of the single engagement, then
the decision derived from this activity in which battle or
engagement is not obvious must rest on the notion of possible
engagements:

> Such a decision may be made up of a single battle or a
> series of major engagements; it may also consist, however,
> of the mere effect of the relationships that arise from the
> disposition of both forces - in other words, from *possible
> engagements.*[70]

POSSIBLE ENGAGEMENTS ARE TO BE REGARDED AS
REAL ONES BECAUSE OF THEIR CONSEQUENCES

If troops are sent to cut off a retreating enemy and he
thereupon surrenders without further fight, his decision
is caused solely by the threat of a fight posed by those
troops.

If part of our army occupies an undefended enemy province and thus denies the enemy substantial increments to
his strength, the factor making it possible for our force
to hold the province is the engagement that the enemy must
expect to fight if he endeavors to retake it.

In both cases results have been produced by the mere
possibility of an engagement; the possibility has acquired
reality....

This shows that the destruction of the enemy's forces
and the overthrow of the enemy's power can be accomplished
only as the result of an engagement, no matter whether it
really took place or was merely offered but not accepted. [71]

The notion of possible engagements is simply a device to
press all military activity further into its unitary concept,
that is, a catch-all notion by which no military activity is
meant to escape reduction however remote from the thrust of
logic that comes to rest on direct engagement:

But having stripped the engagement of all other objects, we
must also exclude that of using it to effect indirectly a
greater destruction of the enemy forces.   Consequently,
only the direct profit gained in the process of mutual destruction may be considered as having been the object.
This profit is absolute: it remains fixed throughout the
entire balance sheet of the campaign and in the end will
always prove pure gain. [72]

As Clausewitz admits 'if combat or the engagement is
defined as the only directly effective activity, the threads
of all other activities will be included because they all lead
to combat', [73] then theory has little choice but to define tactics and strategy thus: 'According to our classification,
then, tactics teaches *the use of armed forces in the engagement;* strategy, *the use of engagements for the object of the
war*'. [74] Since it is partly the task of theory to study the
nature of ends and means, its prime obsession rests on 'the
outcome of the battle as a whole [that] is made up of the
results of its constituent engagements'. [75] In this, 'the
fact that only one means exists constitutes a strand that runs
through the entire web of military activity and really holds
it together'. [76] This single means dominates throughout military activity by which the purpose assigned to each engagement
by strategy is achieved:

If all threads of military activity lead to the engagement,
then if we control the engagement, we comprehend them all.
Their results are produced by our orders and by the execu-
tion of these orders, never directly by other conditions.
Since in the engagement everything is concentrated on the
destruction of the enemy, or rather of *his armed forces*,
which is inherent in its very concept, it follows that the
destruction of the enemy's forces is always the means by
which the purpose of the engagement is achieved.[77]

Strategy, in connecting these factors with the outcome of
an engagement, confers a special significance on that outcome and thereby on the engagement: *it assigns a particular aim to it*. Yet insofar as that aim is not the one
that will lead directly to peace, it remains subsidiary
and is also to be thought of as a means. Successful
engagements or victories in all stages of importance may
therefore be considered as strategic means. The capture
of a position is a successful engagement in terms of terrain. Not only individual engagements with particular
aims are to be classified as means: any greater unity
formed in a combination of engagements by being directed
toward a common aim can also be considered as a *means*.[78]
Given the reduction of all military activity to its unitary concept, of the sources of the will to resist into one,
and of the notion of means into one that holds all together,
'decisive battle' is now rendered inevitable: 'Everything is
governed by a supreme law, the *decision by force of arms*.
If the opponent does seek battle, this recourse can never be
denied him.'[79] Any deviation in the realm of real war (to
which we come shortly) from this supreme form of solution is
taken, from this most extreme view, simply as a result of

special circumstances foreign to its innate concept:

> At a later stage and by degrees we shall see what other
> kinds of strategies can achieve in war. All we need to do
> for the moment is to admit the general *possibility of their
> existence*, the possibility of deviating from the basic con-
> cept of war under the pressure of special circumstances.
> But even at this point we must not fail to emphasize that
> the *violent resolution of the crisis*, the wish to annihi-
> late the enemy's forces, is the first-born son of war.[80]

This paradigm of the 'pure concept of war' is so brutally
reduced and narrow that the flood of necessary propositions,
free from any offending or mitigating circumstance, forms a
torrent along the few remaining and overloaded avenues of
reasoning. It is here that one finds unreserved expression
of the many obsessions so familiar in classical theory. Of
course, the most notorious are the obsessions with 'decisive
battle' itself, armed power as the principal instrument, and
thus the destruction of the enemy's armed forces as the centre
of the will to resist, from which no corner of theory is
allowed to escape. Clausewitz came close to seeing this
fabrication as a contractual form of war when he gave the conditions for this abstraction to become the case in reality.
These came down to war being a wholly isolated act not produced by previous events in the political world.[81] This
single assumption, by which the absolute form of war survives
as a set of logical propositions intended as the ultimate
analytic authority, locks away theory even before it has a
chance to sink its roots into its proper social soil. Revisionist theory springs from the fact that the 'decisive
battle' paradigm so typical in classical theory is founded on
simple contract that, in the first instance, signs away its
political and social birthright, in particular, the driving of

theory right down into the last and most elementary unit of
the decisive pursuit of power as endemic in the fabric of
social relations common to all social order. Armed groups
in the world today who have already taken this step through
intuition, example or training would, if given the opportunity, look at the absolute form of war as some ancient ritual
wholly contracted out of the political and social world.
Since no one can any longer rely on the good offices of tradition to enforce such contract, theory, and those who wish to
survive in the field, must consider a whole host of new considerations that tradition could largely skim over, so long as
no one thought to swim against the tide of classical obsessions and reach down to grasp the more fundamental threads of
war concealed in the poorly researched social dimensions of
strategy.

This tide can be necessary and overwhelming, and obsessions
which start out as fabrication can start to look like reality.
A classicist would take the obsession with tactical successes,
this is, 'by direct destruction we mean tactical success', [92] as
a proposition firmly lodged in the reality of war only to be
ignored at one's peril: 'We maintain therefore that only
great tactical successes can lead to great strategic ones;
or, as we have already said more specifically, *tactical* successes are of *paramount importance* in war'. [83] This is symp-
tomatic of a theory that has nowhere else to go. Likewise,
'the kind of war that is completely governed and saturated by
the urge for a decision - of true war, or absolute war', [84]
where the decision is the keystone of an arch upon which all
the lines of strategy converge hence 'the unbridled violence
that lies at its core, the craving and need for battle and
decision' [85] is all further thrust into the notions of simultaneous action, time, concentration and mass. Reasoning is

pressed inevitably into 'elementary laws' that are little more
than fragile products of the assumptions and logic from which
they derive: 'This would seem not to allow a protracted, con-
secutive, employment of forces: instead, the simultaneous use
of all means intended for a given action appears as an elementary law of war'.[86] Here there is a vital difference between
strategy and tactics in 'that in the tactical realm force can
be used successively, while strategy knows only the simultaneous use of force':[87]

> If in a tactical situation initial success does not lead to
> a conclusive victory, we have reason to fear the immediate
> future. It follows that for the first phase we should use
> only the amount of force that seems absolutely necessary.
> The rest should be kept out of range of fire and out of
> hand-to-hand fighting, so that we can oppose the enemy's
> reserves with fresh troops of our own or defeat his weak-
> ened forces with them. In a strategic situation this does
> not hold true. For one thing, as has been shown, once a
> strategic success is achieved, a reaction is less likely to
> set in, because the crisis has passed; for another, not
> all strategic forces have necessarily been *weakened*. The
> only troops that have suffered losses are those that have
> been *tactically* engaged - those, in other words, that have
> fought. Provided they have not been wasted, only the
> irreducible minimum will have been in action, far from the
> total that has been strategically committed.[88]

This curious dilemma, founded on the craving for battle and
quick decision and yet on the obsession with tactical successes
down into which theory has been driven and that can only be
successive in nature, is summed up as follows:

> While the successive use of force in a tactical situation
> always postpones the main decision to the end of the

action, in strategy the law of the simultaneous use of
forces nearly always advances the main decision, which need
not necessarily be the ultimate one, to the beginning.[89]

Not only is this simply discarded in revisionist theory,
but with it the related notion of time that follows: 'It
cannot be the intent of the strategist to make an ally of time
for its own sake, by committing force gradually, step by
step'.[90]   The anathema in this logic is that 'any unnecessary
expenditure of time, every unnecessary detour, is a waste of
strength and thus abhorrent to strategic thought'.[91]   What is
vital to remember throughout is that which is defined as unnecessary, and thus necessary, had already been given by the
qualifications upholding the absolute form.   To forget this
is to fall into the classic mentality flowing in a good part
of tradition: 'The decision can never be reached too soon to
suit the winner or delayed long enough to suit the loser'.[92]
This commonplace notion that the victor would prefer victory
now rather than later, and that one would prefer a defeat
postponed, is founded on the misconception that such a preference obtains in war in the first place.   Revisionist
theory rejects this mentality entirely because it dismembers
the chain of argument by which it is supported:

That chain of argument was designed to show that no conquest can be carried out too quickly, and that to spread it
over a *longer period* than the minimum needed to complete it
makes it not less difficult, but more.   If that assertion
is correct, it follows equally that if one's strength in
general is great enough to make a certain conquest one must
also have the strength to do so in a single operation, not
by stages.   By 'stages' naturally we do not mean to exclude the minor halts that are needed for reassembling
one's forces or for administrative reasons.

We hope to have made it clear that in our view an offensive war requires above all a quick, irresistible decision.[93]

If this is to be retired from revisionist theory, so are its sister notions of concentration, mass and superior numbers. In marked contrast to the guerrilla dispersal of armed forces throughout the fabric of social relations, classical tradition is best exemplified by the horror of anything less than concentration generally, and in particular, at the decisive point:

> The best strategy is always to *be very strong*; first in general, and then at the decisive point. Apart from the effort needed to create military strength, which does not always emanate from the general, there is no higher and simpler law of strategy than that of *keeping one's forces concentrated*. No force should ever be detached from the main body unless the need is definite and *urgent*. We hold fast to this principle, and regard it as a reliable guide.[94]

> [One should] call for the *utmost possible concentration of strength* permissible under the circumstances. A major battle in a theater of operations is a collision between two centers of gravity; the more forces we can concentrate in our center of gravity, the more certain and massive the effect will be. Consequently, any partial use of force not directed toward an objective that either cannot be attained by the victory itself or that does not bring about the victory should be *condemned*.[95]

In the flow of necessary logic that floods the absolute form, any action that does not conform can have no other basis save that of error or confusion: 'An attacker bent on a major

decision has no reason whatever to divide his forces.   If in
fact he does so, it may usually be ascribed to a state of confusion.   His columns should advance on no wider a front than
will allow them to be brought into action simultaneously'.[96]
The idea is, 'here all action is compressed into a *single
point* in time and space'.[97]   Where general or absolute
superiority is not possible, then theory can fall back on the
notion of relative superiority at the decisive point: 'To
achieve this, the calculation of space and time appears as
the most essential factor, and this has given rise to the
belief that in strategy space and time cover practically
everything concerning the use of the forces'.[98]   Distinctions
and calculations in time and space in revisionist theory are
always socially, never contractually, based.   This logical
reductionism, if carried into its last corner of reasoning,
pulls theory down into only one remaining distinguishing
factor (unless it returns to the assumptions on which it was
built - there is nowhere else to proceed):

> If we thus strip the engagement of all the variables aris-
> ing from its purpose and circumstances, and disregard the
> fighting value of the troops involved (which is a given
> quantity), we are left with the bare concept of the engage-
> ment, a shapeless battle in which the only distinguishing
> factor is the number of troops on either side.
>
>   These numbers, therefore, will determine victory.   It
> is, of course, evident from the mass of abstractions I
> have made to reach this point that superiority of numbers
> in a given engagement is only one of the factors that
> determines victory.[99]

The unitary concept of the single engagement is so thoroughly reduced by the flood of necessary propositions that it
is refined down into a single point in time and space around

which smaller engagements appear as necessary by-products,
like woodshavings: 'Since war is nothing but mutual destruction, it would seem most natural to conceive and it is possibly also most natural in fact, that all the forces on each
side should unite in one great mass, and all successes should
consist of one great thrust of these forces'.[100] *In a more
fundamental sense what contemporary strategy is left with are
the blinding effects of the hidden basis and structures that
allowed this kind of system of reasoning to flourish in the
past.*

Although the review of the absolute form ends here and
concludes this phase of our discussion of its wholly contractual nature, the methodological problems are only just coming
to light. Clausewitz was quite right to suggest the absolute form of war as wholly contractual in nature, although he
did not grasp the depth of this contract reaching down into
the political world towards its most elementary problem of
power endemic in the fabric of all social relations. This
is, of course, the inviolability of social order and its configuration of power alienation on which present-day insurgency
feeds. So central is this to the argument at hand that I
find it helpful to return to those conditions outlined by
Clausewitz for the absolute form to be rendered into practice:

But move from the abstract to the real world, and the whole
thing looks quite different. In the abstract world,
optimism was all-powerful and forced us to assume that both
parties to the conflict not only sought perfection but
attained it. Would this ever be the case in practice?
Yes, it would if: (a) war were a wholly isolated act,
occurring suddenly and not produced by previous events in
the political world; (b) it consisted of a single decisive
act or a set of simultaneous ones; (c) the decision

achieved was complete and perfect in itself, uninfluenced by any previous estimate of the political situation it would bring about.[101]

Had Clausewitz left the absolute form at this point he may well have had difficulties in defending it on other grounds, particularly the gross nature of these assumptions, without which the excessive and reductionist logic to which they gave life could otherwise never stand as a set of logical proposi- tions; but his most serious methodological error did not leave matters here. At this point the sin of gross contract underlying the logic of the absolute form leads only into simple abstraction, although a vital one as the ultimate analytic authority. To make matters worse, Clausewitz did not maintain these crucial qualifications to the absolute form of war throughout, thus lending a fatal impression of reality, minus qualifications, to what should always remain an abstrac- tion upheld by clearly stated assumptions, particularly the inviolability of social order concealed therein. Now this contractual assumption was ready to poison all theory. Clausewitz sadly failed to maintain the fabricated essence of the absolute form intended as 'a general point of reference' and it came to acquire a veneer of reality without its so obviously unreal qualifications:

Its validity was demonstrated and its necessity was proved only too plainly by the revolutionary wars. In these wars, and even more in the campaigns of Bonaparte, warfare attained the unlimited degree of energy that we consider to be its elementary law. We see it is possible to reach this degree of energy; and if it is possible, it is neces- sary.[102]

Moreover, Clausewitz admits that he had actually observed this abstraction in reality and wholly intact: 'One might

wonder whether there is any truth at all in our concept of the
absolute character of war were it not for the fact that with
our own eyes we have seen warfare achieve this state of absolute perfection'.[103]   But the last straw by which the integ-
rity of the abstraction is broken, and its now unspoken
assumption slips into the domain of reality and silently into
the remainder of theory that deals with real war,is given in
what started out to be the case in practice 'if war were a
wholly isolated act ... not produced by previous events in the
political world' suddenly becoming a consequence of this same
political world:

> The military art on which the politicians relied was part
> of a world they thought was real - a branch of current
> statecraft, a familiar tool that had been in use for many
> years.   But *that* form of war naturally shared in the
> errors of policy, and therefore could provide no correc-
> tive.   It is true that war itself has undergone signifi-
> cant changes in character and methods, changes that have
> brought it closer to its absolute form.   But these
> changes did not come about because the French government
> freed itself, so to speak, from the harness of policy;
> they were caused by the new political conditions which the
> French Revolution created both in France and in Europe as
> a whole, conditions that set in motion new means and new
> forces, and have thus made possible a degree of energy in
> war that otherwise would have been inconceivable.
>
> It follows that the transformation of the art of war
> resulted from the transformation of politics.   So far from
> suggesting that the two could be disassociated from each
> other, these changes are a strong proof of their indissol-
> uble connection.[104]

It is hard to imagine how the absolute form only stands as

a working proposition and can only be the case in reality if
it were wholly isolated from the political world (which is
another way of restating the heart of the entire revisionist
critique of classical theory) and yet, at once, taken entirely
to be a real product of this same political world.   It is one
thing to build an abstraction by assuming away a large mass of
the reality it is supposed to represent (otherwise abstrac-
tions could rarely function as logical propositions, having to
be founded on far too many contrary variables in the complex
and real world).   Even more so, it is barely acceptable in
the pursuit of the logical extreme to assume *so much* out of
the heart of reality that what remains is highly reductionist,
narrow and obsessive, those few remaining avenues of logic now
cleared of any contradictory or intervening considerations.
But what is unforgivable is to turn the entire fabrication (a
fabrication because the logic only works if all accept the
underlying assumptions as Clausewitz rightly stated and as
the Chinese case rather stumbled into over a century later)
into something real by discarding the important assumptions
by which it stands in the first place.   What happens, of
course, is that, that which was once a clearly defined
abstraction, however representative of reality and thus
useful, slips into the realm of reality intact but without
its offending and obviously fabricated assumptions clearly
stated.   In effect, they go underground.   This is at the
heart of Clausewitz's original sin, and it has infested, by
one route or another, too much of classical theory ever since.
What greater proof could any strategist ask for than the
everywhere constant (and indeed fabricated) antinomy between
strategy and politics rampant throughout the greater part of
classical tradition.

Accept the reasoning that constitutes the absolute form of

war, or embrace this 'decisive battle' paradigm, even with
some qualifications and reservations, and one swallows its
built-in assumption (of which, as far as I can see, Clausewitz only made formal mention once) and the inviolability of
social order that it contains. That is why classical theory,
working on an unspoken assumption (or at least only once formally stated) has too often found it painful to embrace its
proper philosophical and theoretical roots in the political
and social world, which, in contrast, revisionist theory has
embraced entirely. I repeat, in order to make the 'decisive
battle' paradigm real, one has to sweep its contractual
assumptions under the rug, otherwise it so obviously locks the
fabrication it always is. Warfare can only approach its
classical abstraction in reality if all parties, by silent
contract, accept its underlying condition to render it, in one
measure or another, isolated from the intervening considerations of the political world, particularly its most elementary
one at the root of all warfare. This is the decisive pursuit
of power throughout the fabric of social relations endemic in
all social order, of which war is the natural extension.
This really comes down to the manner in which the absolute
form of war is applied to reality 'as a general point of reference'. Instead of the proper manner of application in
which its important assumptions are maintained or later relaxed in a clear and orderly way that would require changing
the model itself entirely, Clausewitz simply made this
abstraction a wholly intact point in reality by dropping away
the offending assumptions that were forced to seek a silent
existence in the remaining logic they had once brought to
life. This silent existence has remained the one great and
hidden trap in all classical theory, and still exerts a
powerful and serpentine influence today.

The notion that war is a wholly isolated act not produced
by previous events in the political world was obviously offensive to Clausewitz. Although he needed its services to build
the absolute form of war as the ultimate analytic authority,
he was no doubt relieved to see the end of it by losing it
underground into the recesses of theory as the only way of
giving the absolute form any substantive and intact office in
reality. We have now arrived at the point in the present
analysis where the absolute form of war is really two things.
In the first instance it is clearly an abstraction, a general
point of reference with its assumptions and conditions formally stated; and second, it is an unchanged point in
reality, an indissoluble consequence of 'the transformation of
politics' in which its life-giving assumptions (in terms of
its logical structure that cannot stand otherwise) are lost
into the recesses of theory where they can no longer offend.
Classical theory since Clausewitz has, by one route or
another, been too often influenced by the latter. This is
one important reason why armed groups today in the insurgent
mould are so successfully able to take advantage of those who
are blinded by tradition.

Moreover (and we now come to the issue that concludes our
interest in Clausewitz), this single assumption on which
everything hangs in classical theory must not only be lost
into the recesses of theory to slip, without immediate and
drastic modifications, what is so obviously an abstraction
into the domain of reality, but this must be even further
lost from sight if one is to maintain and persuade that war
is 'a true political instrument, a continuation of political
activity by other means'.[105] Launder as one may the offending assumptions out of the absolute form, its reductionist and
necessary logic still carries everywhere with it their silent

influence as this logic cannot stand otherwise. So one is
always, unconsciously or not, tempted by the hidden suggestions in every corner of theory, regardless of how much one
may join the reality of the absolute form with the alternative of possible modification in the real world. It is this
serpentine power of assumption that held Clausewitz back from
the pursuit of theory into its inalienable social and political roots that he only managed to start, particularly in his
later writings - and so eloquently expresses how theory was
held back far too frequently ever since.

More than any other classical theorist, Clausewitz
approached the doorstep of general theory, but he could not
enter with the burden of logic that pinned him down. And
yet, he still managed to fight the weight of theory, the
great bulk of which was held together by the suppressed notion
of war as a wholly isolated act, into 'the final correction of
the regulative idea on which his theories of war were based -
the theoretical acceptance of gradations of violence - [which]
is perhaps Clausewitz's most impressive intellectual and psychological achievement'.[106] Our interest with Clausewitz's
theoretical writings not only focuses on the relations between
absolute and real war but, in particular, the role of the
political world in these relations, as it is here precisely
that the contractual assumptions used in theory construction
are left to slide off sideways even further into the recesses
of reasoning. Our singular purpose then must drive straight
into the heart of misconception and pass over factors inherent
in the war-machine itself that can interrupt and modify, in
the real world, the necessary and reductionist logic of the
absolute form. These are given as the fear and indecision
native to the human mind, the imperfection of human perception and judgment, and the greater strength of the defensive.

But these alone are not adequate 'to span the gap between the
pure concept of war and the concrete shape that, as a general
rule, war assumes'.[107]   In the real world the other possible
'barrier in question [to the absolute form] is the vast array
of factors, forces and conditions in national affairs that
are affected by war',[108] in which:

> No logical sequence could progress through their innumer-
> able twists and turns as though it were a simple thread
> that linked two deductions. Logic comes to a stop in this
> labyrinth; and those men who habitually act, both in great
> and minor affairs, on particular dominating impressions or
> feelings rather than according to strict logic, are hardly
> aware of the confused, inconsistent, and ambiguous situa-
> tion in which they find themselves.[109]

[For this reason] we must, therefore, be prepared to
develop our concept of war as it ought to be fought, not on
the basis of its pure definition, but by leaving room for
every sort of extraneous matter. We must allow for natural inertia, for all the friction of its parts, for all the
inconsistency, imprecision, and timidity of man; and
finally we must face the fact that war and its forms result
from ideas, emotions, and conditions prevailing at the
time - and to be quite honest we must admit that this was
the case even when war assumed its absolute state under
Bonaparte.

If this is the case, if we must admit that the origin
and the form taken by a war are not the result of any ultimate resolution of the vast array of circumstances involved, but only of those features that happen to be dominant,
it follows that war is dependent on the interplay of possibilities and probabilities, of good and bad luck, condi-

tions in which strictly logical reasoning often plays no
part at all and is always apt to be a most unsuitable and
awkward intellectual tool.   It follows, too, that war can
be a matter of degree.[110]

Our interest must abandon these considerations in the hands
of outside discussions[111] and move on straight into the politically determined relations between absolute and real war.
The problem facing theory, whose 'purpose is to demonstrate
what war is in practice, not what its ideal nature ought to
be', is simply that 'a theory, then, that dealt exclusively
with absolute war would either have to ignore any case in
which the nature of war had been deformed by outside influence, or else it would have to dismiss them all as miscon-
strued'.[112]   This is so because in the real world, for
another vital reason, war did not always approach 'its true
character, its absolute perfection' that in any event remained the 'general point of reference' and the ultimate
analytic authority:

> The manner in which war in practice deviates in varying
> degrees from its basic, rigorous concept, taking this form
> or that, but always remaining subject to that basic con-
> cept, as to a supreme law: all these points must be kept
> in mind in our subsequent analyses if we are to perceive
> the real connections between all aspects of war, and the
> true significance of each; and if we wish to avoid con-
> stantly falling into the wildest inconsistencies with
> reality and even with our own arguments.[113]

If 'the abstract world is ousted by the real one and the
trend to the extreme is thereby moderated'[114] and thus 'war,
if taken as a whole, is bound to move from the strict law of
inherent necessity towards probabilities',[115] then one essential factor in the equation is given as follows:

THE PROBABILITIES OF REAL LIFE REPLACE THE
EXTREME AND THE ABSOLUTE REQUIRED BY THEORY

Warfare thus eludes the strict theoretical requirement that
extremes of force be applied.   Once the extreme is no
longer feared or aimed at, it becomes a matter of judgment
what degree of effort should be made; and this can only be
based on the phenomena of the real world and the *laws of
probability*.   Once the antagonists have ceased to be mere
figments of a theory and become actual states and governments, when war is no longer a theoretical affair but a
series of actions obeying its own peculiar laws, reality
supplies the data from which we can deduce the unknown that
lies ahead.

From the enemy's character, from his institutions, the
state of his affairs and his general situation, each side,
using the *laws of probability*, forms an estimate of its
opponent's likely course and acts accordingly.

THE POLITICAL OBJECT NOW COMES TO THE FORE AGAIN

A subject which we last considered in Section 2 now forces
itself on us again; namely, the *political object of the
war*.   Hitherto it had been rather overshadowed by the law
of extremes, the will to overcome the enemy and make him
powerless.   But as this law begins to lose its force and
as this determination wanes, the political aim will re-
assert itself.   If it is all a calculation of probabilities based on given individuals and conditions, the *political object*, which was the *original motive*, must become an
essential factor in the equation.   The smaller the penalty
you demand from your opponent, the less you can expect him
to try and deny it to you; the smaller the effort he

makes, the less you need make yourself. Moreover, the
more modest your own political aim, the less importance
you attach to it and the less reluctantly you will abandon
it if you must. *This is another reason why your effort
will be modified.*[116]

Indeed, 'the counterweights that weaken the elemental
force of war, and particularly the attack, are primarily
located in the political relations and intentions of the government'.[117] At this point in reality war may leave the
necessary logic inherent in its nature, cease to be absolute
perfection, and 'becomes an art in the broadest meaning of
the term - the faculty of using judgment to detect the most
important and decisive elements in the vast array of facts
and situations':[118]

The degree of force that must be used against the enemy
depends on the scale of political demands on either side.
These demands, so far as they are known, would show what
efforts each must make; but they seldom are fully known -
which may be one reason why both sides do not exert themselves to the same degree.

Nor are the situation and conditions of the belliger-
ents alike. This can be a second factor.

Just as disparate are the governments' strength of will,
their character and abilities.

These three considerations introduce uncertainties that
make it difficult to gauge the amount of resistance to be
faced and, in consequence, the means required and the
objectives to be set.

Since in war too small an effort can result not just in
failure but in positive harm, each side is driven to outdo
the other, which sets up an interaction.

Such an interaction could lead to a maximum of effort if

such a maximum could be defined.   But in that case all
proportion between action and political demands would be
lost: means would cease to be commensurate with ends, and
in most cases a policy of maximum exertion would fail on
account of the domestic problems it would raise.

In this way the belligerent is again driven to adopt a
middle course.   He would act on the principle of using no
greater force, and setting himself no greater military aim,
than would be sufficient for the achievement of his political purpose.   To turn this principle into practice he must
renounce the need for absolute success in each given case,
and he must dismiss remoter possibilities from his calculations.[119]

As the demands of logical necessity would require, everywhere that the will to resist is taken as a function of armed
forces as the *essential* strategic centre of gravity may now
be transformed by the superior requirements of the political
world because 'war is not an act of senseless passion but is
controlled by its political object, [thus] the value of this
object must determine the sacrifices to be made for it in *magnitude* and also in *duration*'.[120]   This means that the real
world will hold a variety of objects that may serve the will
to resist on the condition that if 'we do not aim at destroying the opposing army, and if we are convinced that the enemy
does not seek a brutal decision, but rather *fears* it',[121] then
seizure of provinces, and disruption of the opposing alliances, among others, can lead to advantage that may be enough to
make the enemy fear for the final outcome.   Here, the theoretical extreme gives way to the imperatives of the political
world:

We can now see that in war many roads lead to success, and
that they do not all involve the opponent's outright

defeat.   They range from *the destruction of the enemy's
forces, the conquest of his territory, to a temporary occupation or invasion, to projects with an immediate political
purpose, and finally to passively awaiting the enemy's
attacks*.   Any one of these may be used to overcome the
enemy's will: the choice depends on circumstances.[122]

The reduction in the absolute form of all military activity
to its unitary concept of the single engagement, in which its
sole aim is the destruction of the enemy's armed forces as the
principal instrument and the centre of the will to resist, can
all dissolve in the political world: 'The fact that engagements do not always aim at the destruction of the opposing
forces, that their objectives can often be attained without
any fighting at all but merely by an evaluation of the situation, explains why entire campaigns can be conducted with
great energy even though actual fighting plays an unimportant
part in them'.[123]   Such a situation, unlike anything proposed
by the absolute form, is more 'a phase of true strategic
maneuver, and is certainly more or less characteristic of
all campaigns where a major decision is precluded by political
motives or the general state of affairs'.[124]   The influence
of the political world can, at times, be seen to dissolve the
imperatives inherent in the pure concept of war to the point
of highly limited wars stagnant in a pool of limited aims:

Thus interaction, the effort to outdo the enemy, the violent and compulsive course of war, all stagnate for lack of
real incentive.   Neither side makes more than minimal
moves, and neither feels itself seriously threatened.

Once this influence of the political objective on war is
admitted, as it must be, there is no stopping it;   consequently we must also be willing to wage such minimal wars,
which consist in *merely threatening the enemy*, with *nego-
tiations held in reserve*.

This poses an obvious problem for any theory of war that
aims at being thoroughly scientific.   All imperatives
inherent in the concept of a war seem to dissolve, and its
foundations are threatened.   But the natural solution soon
emerges.   As the modifying principle gains a hold on military operations, or rather, as the incentive fades away,
the active element gradually becomes passive.   Less and
less happens, and guiding principles will not be needed.
The art of war will shrivel into prudence, and its main
concern will be to make sure the delicate balance is not
suddenly upset in the enemy's favor and the half-hearted
war does not become a real war after all.[125]

The larger and more general reason why the absolute form
can frequently fall into this state of dissolution in the
political world, where before in the abstract world it reigned
without interruption, is that theory must always before all
else 'revert to the fact that war is a political act which
does not operate under a law quite of itself, or a true political instrument which does not operate itself, but is guided
by a hand.   This hand is politics.'[126]   The larger conception of war is, in the real world, seen as wholly saturated by
the liquid of politics:

War is not a self-dependent matter, but the continuation of
politics by other means, hence the principal features of
all great strategic plans are *for the most part of a poli-*
tical nature, and always the more they encompass the totality of war and state.   The whole plan of war results
directly from the political existence of both warring
states as well as from their relations with others.   The
plan of campaign results from the plan of war and is even,
if of course everything is confined to a theatre of war,
often identical with the same.   But even in the individual

parts of a campaign the political element is implicated and
indeed there is seldom any great act of war, such as a
battle, etc. where at least some influence of it was not
apparent. According to this view there can be no question
of a *purely military* valuation of a great strategic whole
as well as of a purely military plan of the same. That
this view is a quite necessary one, which, if one considers
only military history is *quite obvious*, certainly needs no
proof. But that it nevertheless has not yet been established is shown precisely in that until now people have
always wanted to separate the purely military element of a
great strategic plan from the political and to regard the
latter as something unseemly. *War is nothing other than
the continuation of political struggles by other means.* I
take this view as a basis for all strategy, and believe
that whoever refuses to recognize its necessity, does not
yet quite understand on what it depends. All military
history becomes intelligible by this principle, without it
everything is full of the greatest absurdities.[127]
Military history, experience and the real world are only
thereby rendered intelligible because they can remain beyond
the reach of the power of abstraction: 'Thus even if from
such problems [of the real world] we can abstract from a
number of things, because we imagine their powers neutralized,
we cannot do so however from those which call the act of war
itself into existence, which determine political purpose and
let the military objective be deduced from it, along with the
available means'.[128] War is given a unity in the political
world, where 'war does not advance relentlessly towards the
absolute, as theory would demand. Being incomplete and self-
contradictory, it cannot follow its own laws, but has to be
treated as a part of some other whole; the name of which is

policy' - and it is here that 'these contradictory elements
combine in real life'.[129]   This must remain everywhere the
cardinal point of view from which the conception of war should
be approached, as it alone yields an integrated view of all
phenomena:

Thus policy converts the overwhelmingly destructive element
of war into a mere instrument.   The terrible two-handed
sword that should be used with total strength to strike
once and no more, becomes the lightest rapier - sometimes
even a harmless foil fit only for thrusts and feints and
parries.

Thus the contradictions in which war involves that naturally timid creature, man, are resolved; if this is the
solution we choose to accept.

If war is part of policy, policy will determine its
character.   As policy becomes more ambitious and vigorous,
so will war, and this may reach the point where war attains
its absolute form.   If we look at war in this light, we do
not need to lose sight of this absolute: on the contrary,
we must constantly bear it in mind.

Only if war is looked at in this way does its unity reappear; only then can we see that all wars are things of
the *same* nature; and this alone will provide the right
criteria for conceiving and judging great designs.[130]

If we recall the nature of actual war, if we remember the
argument in Chapter 3 above - that the *probable character
and general shape of any war should mainly be assessed in
the light of political factors and conditions* - and that
war should often (indeed today one might say *normally*) be
conceived as an organic whole whose parts cannot be separa-
ted, so that each individual act contributes to the whole

and itself originates in the central concept, then it will
be perfectly clear and certain that the supreme standpoint
for the conduct of war, the point of view that determines
its main lines of action, can only be that of policy.[131]

Theory has now come around to the acceptance of gradations
of violence, 'that the art of war relates to all possible
gradations which the interests of politics can require'.[132]
Since 'generally speaking a military objective that matches
the political object in scale will, if the latter is reduced,
be reduced in proportion', it therefore follows 'that without
any inconsistency wars can have all degrees of importance and
intensity, ranging from a war of extermination down to simple
armed observation'.[133]   In a number of passages Clausewitz
states that war is to be thought of in only two different
ways, one as nothing more than a simple modification of the
other.   That is to say, 'since war can be thought of in two
different ways - its absolute form or one of the variant
forms that it actually takes - two different concepts of success arise';[134]   thus 'theory makes this distinction in the
application of the two concepts: all action must be based on
the former since it is the fundamental concept; the latter
can be used only as a modification justified by circumstances'.[135]   This suggests, as either a severe, slight or no
modification in the absolute form, that:

> In reality, most wars will probably fall between the two
> poles, sometimes approaching one, sometimes the other.
> The practical effect of these attributes [of limited war]
> becomes evident only as a modification, caused by their
> contrary action, in the *absolute form* of war.[136]

In his 'Note of July 1827' on plans for revising 'On War',
Clausewitz seems to move further away from this pre-eminence
of the absolute form by expressing the desire to develop

further the existence of the two types of war, and by imply-
ing that limited war is a wholly different form of war, not
simply evident as a modification in the absolute form:

> I regard the first six books, which are already in a clean
> copy, merely as a rather formless mass that must be thor-
> oughly reworked once more. The revision will bring out
> the two types of war with greater clarity at every point.
> All ideas will then become plainer, their general trend
> will be more clearly marked, their application shown in
> greater detail.
>
> War can be of two kinds, in the sense that either the
> objective is to *overthrow the enemy* - to render him politi-
> cally helpless or militarily impotent, thus forcing him to
> sign whatever peace we please; or *merely to occupy some of
> his frontier-districts* so that we can annex them or use
> them for bargaining at the peace negotiations.   Transi-
> tions from one type to the other will of course recur in my
> treatment; but the fact that the aims of the two types are
> quite different must be clear at all times, and their
> points of irreconcilability brought out.[137]

Whatever his revisions might have been, this simple
abstraction founded on, and held together as a logical proposition by the assumption that war is a wholly isolated act
from the political world, has all been swept *intact* into the
heart of theory and the real and political world with possible
modifications and final, though unfinished, corrections that
may well be 'Clausewitz's most impressive intellectual
achievement'.   These, however, have little substantive value
in restoring theory to a *free* consideration of the more elementary social and moral phenomena of which the conception of
war is the natural extension.   Indeed, Clausewitz not only
poisoned theory in giving an abstraction a full status (though

joined by external modifications) in reality by dropping its
offensive assumptions out of sight rather than maintaining
them throughout while properly applying the model, but from
here he elevated this in the real world to the point of being
wholly 'resulted from the transformation of politics'. He
went even further with this model into the intimacies of the
political world by making what had once been built on the
notion of a wholly isolated act from the political world, now
being driven into this same abstraction by policy itself:

Theory, therefore, demands that at the outset of a war its
character and scope should be determined on the basis of
the political probabilities. The closer these political
probabilities drive war toward the absolute, the more the
belligerent states are involved and drawn into its vortex,
the clearer appear the connections between its separate
actions, and the more imperative the need not to take the
first step without considering the last.[138]

In the real and political world war falls in between two
independent poles, being driven, as 'a political act which
does not operate under a law quite of itself, or a true political instrument which does not operate itself',[139] by the
'hand of politics' instead. The further policy drives war
in reality into the absolute form, 'then the more politics
and enmity coincide; the more the former is absorbed in the
latter; the simpler becomes the war; the more it proceeds
from the mere concept of might and destruction; the more it
corresponds to all requirements which one can logically
develop from these concepts; and the more all its parts have
association of a *necessity*. Such a war appears quite *unpolitical* and that is why it was considered as standard war. But
plainly the political principle is lacking just as little here
as in other wars; it only coincides completely with the con-

cept of might and destruction and disappears from view. [140]
In contrast, one has movement towards the opposite pole,
whereby 'the less intense the motives, the less will the
military element's natural tendency to violence coincide with
political directives', in which, 'as a result, war will be
driven further from its natural course, the political object
will be more and more at variance with the aim of ideal war,
and the conflict will seem increasingly *political* in character'.[141]   The notion that real war is driven into or between
one form and another by a hand not of its own but by that 'of
some other whole; the name of which is policy', is not so
much an introduction of the superiority of the real and political world into the purely military world in the abstract.
It is the poisoning of the former, and the remainder of theory
concerning real war, by the silent assumption on which the
latter was built, only once formally stated, then dropped out
of view.

Theory cannot run away from its own assumptions by which it
is given life in the first place.   What drives war into its
absolute form is the strength of the contract that Clausewitz
forgot about, not policy.   This flight from the tyranny of
forgotten assumptions is what Clausewitz was likely attempting in his later writings, as expressed in his 'Note of July
1827', moving further away from the absolute form by, on one
hand, making it more and more subject to, and a consequence
of the political world and, on the other, less necessary in
its own right by joining it, in almost equal weight, with the
notion of limited war.   Of course, the absolute form appears
quite unpolitical because, as standard war, it was earlier
built on that assumption.   This never left Clausewitz in
peace, as shown in the above-quoted reply to two strategic
exercises where he returns to the undeniable temptation to

reason about absolute war as if it were somehow unpolitical or
isolated.   And how could he find peace, already so burdened
with the earlier built-in, now latent, temptations of theory,
and a contradictory dedication to the concept of war as a
political act.   To such a concept the suggestion that the
political principle is absorbed by the (once isolated) neces-
sities of the absolute form, that they now coincide completely
and the former simply disappears from view, must seem quite
puzzling.   Again, the political act that does not appear as
a political act is explained by the surreptitious method
Clausewitz used in the description of this act.   Saying that
the political principle is lacking no less here cannot hope
to put the muddle right, in fact, it only makes matters worse.

Underneath all the statements to the contrary and the later
rewritings, amendments and intentions of further reworking,
Clausewitz, who may have felt he was working his way further
into the political principle, instead was progressively flood-
ing theory with a silent contract to reason about war as a
wholly isolated act not produced by previous events in the
political world - and the inviolability of social order that
it embraces.   Truly to drive theory straight into the heart
of the political principle is to drive it right down into its
most elementary concept of the fabric of social relations
inherent in all social order where power is everywhere aliena-
ted and concentrated for the conduct of war, as earlier explained.   This is a possibility which has threatened, and
should continue to threaten contemporary strategy, that
Clausewitzian theory is built to ignore, the illustration of
which is intended to open our eyes to where things seem to be
moving in the nuclear age.   Even in the discussion of 'people
in arms', insurrection is viewed in the classical concept very
reminiscent of Hua Fu's insistence that guerrilla warfare is

'only an auxiliary form of battle': 'We merely wish to add
that strategic plans for defence can provide for a general
insurrection in one of two ways: either as a last resort
after a defeat or as a natural auxiliary before decisive
battle'.[142]   Naturally, in this, social order is deemed
beyond the realm of concern:

> In the civilized parts of Europe, war by means of popular
> uprisings is a phenomenon of the nineteenth century.   It
> has its advocates and its opponents.   The latter object
> to it either on political grounds, considering it as a
> means of revolution, a state of legalized anarchy that is
> as much of a threat to the social order at home as it is
> to the enemy; or else on military grounds, because they
> feel that the results are not commensurate with the ener-
> gies that have been expended.
>
> The first objection does not concern us at all: here
> we consider a general insurrection as simply another means
> of war - in its relation, therefore, to the enemy.[143]

I conclude by way of an apology for having taken what may
appear as the long route through an excessive volume of quotations.   Although the purpose for doing so has, in fact,
left untouched, or only briefly sketched, many areas that
would too lightly serve its singular design, this volume of
quotations was necessary to express directly from the original
how Clausewitz lost sight of the crucial assumptions on which
he was working.   Such loss is illustrated in a related series
of methodological errors: (a) in the rigorous concern for
naive reality proper to a 'practical art' such as war he lost
grasp of the fact that the assumptions, distortions and errors
hidden in theory can come to dominate how we perceive, formulate and act in reality.   That is to say, such rigorous concern can never be relied on too heavily for checks particular-

ly to the pursuit of the logical extreme in abstraction, and
the gross assumptions needed to support this pursuit; (b)
moreover, one is less likely to take due note of the point
that the reality of the social activity that is war is a consequence of the social conditions from which it springs, particularly the vision or 'theory' of its conduct that men carry
into it; meaning that the real world, especially for any
social activity, is itself, quite apart from the theorist's
own assumptions concealed in how he thinks, made up of the
very same as brought into it by its human constituents. The
reality of war, like the whole of the social world, can be
held up in a state of fabrication by the thin but universally
accepted conventions that are carried into its conduct; (c)
Clausewitz assumed so much out of the heart of the social
reality that is war in the construction of the absolute form
that its remaining logic and propositions are so narrow, reductionist and necessarily obsessive that one is less likely
to keep in mind original assumptions in the resulting swift
currents of the logical extreme, and the real value of this
abstraction is found in what it passed over or left out, not
what it contained; (d) having only formally stated once the
cardinal assumptions of its isolation from the political world
by which the absolute form, as the general point of reference,
was constructed and held together as a viable proposition,
Clausewitz then lost these offending assumptions into the
recesses of theory in giving this simple abstraction a full
status in real war (joined by the possibility of modifications
and, later in almost equal weight, the notion of limited war)
as an indissoluble consequence of the transformation of politics, and a direct result of the driving influence of policy.
This spilled into the intimacies of the political and real
world and throughout the remainder of theory the now secret

temptation hidden away in the still wholly intact logic of the
absolute form to reason about war as if it were an isolated
act from the political world.   That is to say, the notion of
war is swallowed as a contractual affair held back from a
natural consideration of its own social and political roots,
in particular, as regards the inviolability of social order
at the heart of the problem and alienation of power for the
conduct of war.   All of these four methodological errors
lead to this one poor result.

As Clausewitz became more dedicated to the principle of
war as a political act, particularly in the later writings,
he appeared to draw further away from the emphasis on the
absolute form.   In reality, what happened was that he left
even further behind the more and more obviously offensive
assumptions by which this abstraction was built, in the hopes
of further imposing the rule of the political world into the
necessary logic of the absolute form, to the point of joining
it in almost equal weight with the concept of limited war.
Accept the original proposition of the isolated nature of the
absolute form and this ends the discussion of the political
principle, unless one progressively changes the whole conception itself as it is rendered into the real world.   Instead,
to plead the case of war as a political act, he chose to
elevate the simple abstraction without its vital conditions
and yet *entirely intact* (although now on a scale and joined
at the other pole by the notion of limited war) into a status
in reality it should never have enjoyed - even by his own ad-
mission only once recorded in the revised and finished first
chapter.   It hardly matters whether one can argue that he
viewed the absolute form as consisting of 10 or 90 per cent
of reality.   That is unimportant.   What is crucial is that
he made it a point in reality wholly intact, subject to pos-

sible modification and without its conditions; and after this
percentages are anyone's preference. Furthermore, he drove
the absolute form, again intact, right into the intimacies of
the political and social world by making it an indissoluble
consequence of the transformation of politics in general, and
a direct result of the driving force of policy in particular.

What may appear as 'perhaps Clausewitz's most impressive
intellectual and psychological achievement',[144] this is, the
theoretical acceptance of gradations of violence intended to
bring the abstraction further into the reality of the political world for which it could not account alone, instead
stained whatever there was left of theory with the everywhere
hidden temptations that war is to be conceived of as an isolated act. One cannot even look at this abstraction, with or
without modifications and whether one can be lured into
believing it is real or not, without falling into the unconscious temptation of thinking on the basis by which it was
built and looks plausible. Even if we can be persuaded to
see the absolute form as more than a simple abstract representation of reality and accompanied by all its possible
modifications, the problem is that, as was stated only once,
should such an unlikely event occur it is still a contractual
fabrication of varying degree, a kind of military dream-world
held together by all simultaneously and continually agreeing
to view war as largely an isolated act. That is to say, all
must agree not to reach down and touch in the depths of the
political and social world the moral and social phenomena of
which war is the natural extension. The instant this is done
'reality' suddenly becomes the contractual fabrication it
always was, which can go on only as long as all, unconsciously
or otherwise, honour the contract Clausewitz mentioned only
once.

On the one hand, Clausewitz was held back by the silent
temptation hidden in every corner of reasoning to see war as
an isolated act that so eloquently expresses how classical
theory, ever since, could never flow into a free consideration
of the very roots of its own political insight into the nature
of war that is the mortal challenge to theory today.   On the
other hand, the irony of this is that he actually foretold in
those conditions underlying the theory the entire revisionist
critique and the dissolution of our classical heritage as best
illustrated in the revelations of the Chinese case on which
this critique is based.   To my limited knowledge, it is the
only paragraph in the entire classical tradition that strikes
down the reasoning which, in one form and in one degree or
another, came to influence our heritage, for the contractual
fabrication it always was.   And this is the essence of revisionist theory which simply takes its lead from Clausewitz's
sadly inconsistent recognition of the assumptions used to
build this abstraction and his pursuit held back, as a consequence, from its natural direction of enquiry into the notion
of war as a political act - which should naturally raise all
manner of political and sociological considerations.   Revisionism may appear unfamiliar, hard to pull together and with
little solid foundation in the history of strategic thought
(this lack encouraged by my earlier and rather blanket hostil-
ity to classical reasoning, but this was simply a way of setting things up).   Rather it grows, with the expository aids
of the Chinese case, directly out of classical reasoning.
Strategic revisionism had already been hinted and poked at by
Clausewitz because the conditions he presented for his own
theory, along with the belated pursuit of the political principle, point the way along which the Chinese case first stumbled towards its real practice over a century later.   It is

not sufficient to state that the absolute form is an abstraction, *one must state in detail the contractual basis by which it is an abstraction, that is, its isolation from the political world.* This is Clausewitz's most prophetic theoretical achievement (the implications of which have never been at all appreciated) because in a backhanded way it suddenly opens up the contractual frontiers of theory to a host of elementary and social matters that would in any event, one day, push their way into the heart of theory. His one fleeting comment that for the absolute form to 'ever be the case in practice' required that war be a wholly isolated act from the political world is the heart of a revisionist theory in a nutshell. Clausewitz did point the way towards general theory here and in the belated pursuit of the political principle. And if this is correct, and if the Chinese case along with others, notably in South-east Asia and southern Africa, are, in one form and degree or another, a living confirmation of his little-worked, partly conscious and yet most astute prophecy, then how can contemporary strategy fail in its duty to its own history and innate nature, if not our security in time of war that has fewer and fewer options left in the nuclear age, to rethink entirely.

By way of a final remark I return to the proposition that best pulls together our classical heritage, many elements of which, particularly the hidden ones, are still tacitly influential today, at least in so far as they hold theory back from a free flow into the intimacies of the social world:

> For over a hundred years the theory of strategy has taught that the object in war is to break the war-will of the enemy and that the method of achieving this object is to disorganize his armed forces by battle.[145]

Now it must surely be possible to see this contractual

abstraction, its partly hidden structure of reasoning along
with its concomitant theoretical flesh for what it always was,
as Clausewitz admitted only once and then forgot.   Only recently, particularly in the nuclear age, the reality of war
and its theory of strategy that returns to violence as an
instrument of policy has been forced to put right the muddles
of the last century and the better half of this century by an
inexorable dissolution towards its free state in which the
war-will is a true function of moral and social order.   Here
is found the free solution, not only to the mounting challenge
to contemporary strategy in the nuclear age where violence has
few remaining avenues of application left, but also to the
century-old theoretical dilemma which has always held back a
classical theory secretly despising the very political and
social world in which it was born and was intended to serve.

For those who care to listen, present-day theorists will
not like being told that the way they have been taught to
reason is a contractual fabrication; and if they escaped the
rigours of classical training they may still resist, by a
latent inclination, the rather out-of-the-way conclusion that
the weight of our classical heritage and the undercurrents by
which it still circulates throughout contemporary strategy are
little more.   If my slender talents cannot persuade, then a
return to Clausewitz for a good re-read, now much easier in
the recent translation, along with a cold look at where politically motivated violence seems more than ever headed, might.

Notes

1 SOCIAL ORDER AND STRATEGIC THEORY

1 These being a mass of people, their states of mind in terms of deeply embedded values and commitments, and related patterns of behaviour and socialization. This notion of social resources for the prosecution of war would vanish if it rested solely on a mass of people without mention of their moral and social capacities to conform to the social order through which they conduct war, along with the process of socialization, in which, for our purposes, these capacities are acquired.

2 Martin Wight, 'Systems of States', Leicester University Press, 1977, p. 135. The following discussion of legitimacy is based on this source.

3 Carl von Clausewitz, 'On War', ed. Anatol Rapoport, Harmondsworth, Penguin Books, 1968, p. 119.

2 THE SOCIAL PREMISE OF PROTRACTED WAR

1 Mao Tse-tung, 'Selected Military Writings', 2nd ed., Peking, Foreign Languages Press, 1966, pp. 210-11.
2 Ibid., p. 159.
3 Ibid., p. 143.
4 Ibid., p. 103.
5 Ibid., p. 136.
6 Ibid., p. 132.
7 Ibid., p. 117.
8 Ibid., pp. 113-14.
9 Ibid., p. 114.
10 Ibid., p. 136.
11 Ibid., p. 174.
12 Ibid., p. 176.

13 Ibid., p. 167.
14 Ibid., pp. 167-8 [brackets are added].
15 Ibid., p. 171.
16 Ibid., p. 172.
17 Ibid., p. 170.
18 Ibid.
19 Ibid., p. 171.
20 Ibid., p. 174.
21 Ibid., p. 213.
22 Ibid., pp. 213-14.
23 Ibid., p. 214.
24 Ibid., p. 279 [brackets are added].
25 Ibid., p. 212.
26 Ibid., p. 247.
27 Ibid., p. 54.
28 Ibid., p. 213 [brackets are added].
29 Ibid., p. 167.
30 Ibid., p. 72.
31 Ibid.
32 Ibid., p. 247.
33 Ibid., p. 216.
34 Ibid., p. 246.
35 Ibid., p. 214.
36 Ibid. [brackets are added].
37 Ibid., p. 121.
38 Ibid., pp. 247-8.
39 Ibid., p. 217.
40 Ibid., p. 261.

3 THE DEATH OF CLASSICAL THEORY

1 Roger A. Leonard (ed.), 'A Short Guide to Clausewitz on War', London, Weidenfeld & Nicolson, 1967, pp. 15-16 [brackets are added].
2 Michael Howard, The Classical Strategists, in 'Adelphi Papers', No. 54, February 1969, p. 18.
3 André Beaufre, 'An Introduction to Strategy', London, Faber & Faber, 1965, pp. 28 and 23-4.
4 E.J. Kingston-McCloughry, 'War in Three Dimensions: The Impact of Air-Power Upon the Classical Principles of War', London, Jonathan Cape, 1949, pp. 9 and 13 [brackets are added].
5 J.F.C. Fuller, 'Machine Warfare', Washington, The Infantry Journal, 1943, p. 96.
6 Samuel P. Huntington, Guerrilla Warfare in Theory and Policy, in Franklin M. Osanka (ed.), 'Modern Guerrilla Warfare: Fighting Communist Guerrilla Movements, 1941-1961', New York, Free Press, 1962, p. xvi.

4 STRATEGIC REVISIONISM

1 Concluding remarks by Anatol Rapoport in Carl von Clausewitz, 'On War', ed. Anatol Rapoport, Harmondsworth, Penguin Books, 1968, p. 412.
2 Ibid., p. 119.
3 Ibid., p. 173, p. 133 [emphasis added] and p. 342.
4 Ibid., p. 119.

5 THE CHINESE THEORY OF LAND REVOLUTION

1 Please note the following abbreviations: CCC: the
   'Ch'en Ch'eng Collection, (Shih-sou tzu-liao shih kung-
   fei tzu-liao) 1931-7', microfilm, 21 reels, available at
   the Hoover Institution, Stanford University; URI: Union
   Research Institute, Hong Kong.
2 For historical background to the land revolution period
   see John E. Rue, 'Mao Tse-tung in Opposition 1927-1935',
   Stanford University Press, 1966; and Tso-liang Hsiao,
   'Power Relations Within the Chinese Communist Movement,
   1930-1934: A Study of Documents', Seattle, University
   of Washington Press, 1961.
*3 'Theories of the Agrarian Revolution' (section 2), con-
   tained in 'A Collection of Red Bandit Reactionary Documents (Ch'ih-fei fan-tung wen-chien hui-pien)', compiled
   under sponsorship of General Ch'en Ch'eng, 1935, as held
   in handwritten copy on file in the URI, Hong Kong, vol.
   6, pp. 896-7.
4 Mao Tse-tung, 'Selected Military Writings', 2nd ed.,
   Peking, Foreign Languages Press, 1966, pp. 77-152,
   153-86, and 187-267.
5 Tso-liang Hsiao, 'The Land Revolution in China, 1930-
   1934: A Study of Documents', Seattle, University of
   Washington Press, 1969, p. 293; see also Mao Tse-tung,
   'Selected Military Writings', p. 111.
6 For examples of Mao versus Li Li-san, the Russian Returned Students, and Chou En-lai, see Tso-liang Hsiao,
   'Power Relations', pp. 16-18, 202-7, and 230-47.
7 Mao Tse-tung, 'Selected Works', vol. I, Peking, Foreign
   Languages Press, 1965, p. 123.
8 Tso-liang Hsiao, 'The Land Revolution', p. 202.
9 Ibid., p. 209.
10 Ibid. [emphasis added].
11 Ibid., pp. 202-3.
12 F.T.C. Yu, 'Mass Persuasion in Communist China', New
   York, Praeger, 1964, p. 14 [emphasis added].
13 C. Brandt, B. Schwartz and J. Fairbank, 'A Documentary

History of Chinese Communism', New York, Atheneum, 1966, p. 227.

*14 Mass Work in the White Areas (section 4), contained in 'A Collection of Red Bandit Reactionary Documents', vol. 4, pp. 480-91.

15 Tso-liang Hsiao, 'The Land Revolution', p. 164.

16 Ibid., p. 175.

17 Ibid., p. 166.

18 Ibid., p. 147.

19 Ibid.

20 Ibid., p. 205.

21 Ibid., pp. 203-5 [brackets added].

22 Ibid., p. 219.

*23 The Land Investigation Movement (section 7), contained in 'A Collection of Red Bandit Reactionary Documents', vol. 6, pp. 950-1.

24 Tso-liang Hsiao, 'The Land Revolution', pp. 214, 219, 238-9, 244-5, 252.

25 Ibid., p. 219.

*26 Ibid., pp. 219, 225; also The Land Investigation Movement (section 7), contained in 'A Collection of Red Bandit Reactionary Documents', vol. 6, p. 951.

*27 The Land Investigation Movement (section 7), contained in 'A Collection of Red Bandit Reactionary Documents', vol. 6, p. 952 [brackets added].

28 Tso-liang Hsiao, 'The Land Revolution', p. 249.

*29 'Outline of the Land Investigation Movement (Ch'a-t'ien yün-tung ti kai-k'uang)', published by the Kiangsi Provincial Committee of the Central Committee of the Party, September 1933, CCC reel No. 17 [no visible pagination].

*30 Teng T'o, To Strengthen Ideological Tasks, to Develop Ideological Struggle, in 'Study (Hsüeh Hsi)', vol. IV, No. 9, 16 August 1951, p. 17.

31 Tso-liang Hsiao, 'The Land Revolution', p. 222.

32 Ibid., p. 219.

33 Ibid., p. 226.

34 Ibid., p. 241.

35 Ibid., p. 243.

*36 The Land Investigation Movement (section 7), contained in 'A Collection of Red Bandit Reactionary Documents', vol. 6, p. 950.

37 Tso-liang Hsiao, 'The Land Revolution', p. 203.

38 Ibid., pp. 100-1.

*39 Mao Tse-tung, 'Ch'ang-kang Hsiang Survey', contained in Mao Tse-tung, 'Rural Survey of Districts (Nung-ts'un tiao-cha)', Ho-chien, Hopei Province, Hsin-hua shu-tien, 10 August 1947.

*40 Ibid., p. 95.

*41 Ibid., p. 95 [brackets added].
*42 Ibid., p. 106.
 43 Tso-liang Hsiao, 'The Land Revolution', p. 209.
*44 Mao Tse-tung, 'Ch'ang-kang Hsiang Survey', p. 107.
*45 Ibid., p. 127.
*46 The Puppet Children's Corps Organization (section 7),
     contained in 'A Collection of Red Bandit Reactionary
     Documents', vol. 3, p. 324.

6 BLOCK-HOUSE AND GUERRILLA WARFARE

 1 The recent opening of the 'Ch'en Ch'eng Collection' and
    recent appearance of the 'Tsunyi Resolutions' in trans-
    lation (see below, Note 7) have brought forward the
    strategist Hua Fu as the central figure in this dispute,
    few of whose writings on strategy have been, to my know-
    ledge, substantially translated and published for Western
    readers until now.   For outside discussions of Hua Fu,
    see sources given in Notes 4 and 7.   Please note the
    following abbreviations: CCC: the 'Ch'en Ch'eng Collec-
    tion, (Shih-sou tzu-liao shih kung-fei tzu-liao) 1931-
    1937', microfilm, 21 reels, available at the Hoover
    Institution, Stanford University; and URI: Union
    Research Institute, Hong Kong.
 2 Tso-liang Hsiao, 'Power Relations Within the Chinese Com-
    munist Movement, 1930-1934: A Study of Documents',
    Seattle, University of Washington Press, 1961, pp. 210-
    11.
 3 Ibid., pp. 220-1.
 4 Chi-hsi Hu, Hua Fu, the Fifth Encirclement Campaign and
    the Tsunyi Conference, in 'The China Quarterly', No. 43,
    July-September 1970, pp. 40-1; see especially footnote
    37.
 5 Tso-liang Hsiao, 'Power Relations', p. 221.
 6 The case argued by Chi-hsi Hu, see Note 4 above.
 7 The alternative suggested by Jerome Ch'en (translator),
    Resolutions of the Tsunyi Conference, in 'The China
    Quarterly', No. 40, October-December 1969, pp. 1-38.
*8 Some of these are in my files in partial translation or
    summarized in entirety, including articles in: 'Red Star
    (Hung-hsing)', Nos 29, 33, 39, 40 and 60, and 'Struggle
    (Tou-cheng)', No. 24, CCC reels Nos 16 and 18.
 9 Tien-wei Wu, The Kiangsi Soviet Period, in 'Journal of
    Asian Studies', No. 2, February 1970, p. 410.   This is
    a useful bibliographical review on the Ch'en Ch'eng
    Collection - surprisingly, however, not a mention of
    Hua Fu.

*10 Chou En-lai, Fight to the End for Territory, for Freedom, and for the Soviet Political Power!, in 'Red Star (Hung-hsing)', No. 39, 29 April 1934, p. 1, CCC reel No. 16 [one *li* = one-third English mile].

11 Jerome Ch'en, Resolutions of the Tsunyi Conference, pp. 2-3.

*12 The Bandit Army's Tactics under the 'Block-house Warfare' (section 5), contained in 'A Collection of Red Bandit Reactionary Documents (Ch'ih-fei fan-tung wen-chien hui-pien)', compiled under sponsorship of General Ch'en Ch'eng, 1935, as held in handwritten copy on file in the URI, Hong Kong, vol. 11, pp. 1851-2 [brackets added]

*13 The Guerrilla Tactics of the Bandit Army (section 4), contained in 'A Collection of Red Bandit Reactionary Documents', vol. 11, pp. 1844-6.

14 Tso-liang Hsiao, 'Power Relations', pp. 296-7.

15 Chi-hsi Hu, Hua Fu, the Fifth Encirclement Campaign and the Tsunyi Conference, p. 31.

16 Jerome Ch'en, Resolutions of the Tsunyi Conference, p. 14.

17 Ibid.

18 Ibid., p. 14.

19 Ibid., p. 6.

20 Ibid.

21 Ibid., p. 13.

22 Ibid., p. 7.

23 Ibid., p. 5.

24 Ibid., p. 4.

25 Ibid., p. 8.

26 Ibid., p. 6.

27 Ibid., p. 7.

28 Ibid., pp. 3-4.

29 Ibid., p. 7.

30 Ibid., p. 4.

31 Mao Tse-tung, 'Selected Military Writings', Peking, Foreign Languages Press, 1963, pp. 130-1. [This translation, better suited for our purposes, differs slightly in this earlier 1963 edition.]

32 Ibid., pp. 210-15.

*33 Although vague references were made to the social content of guerrilla warfare, one, that is, embracing armed land revolution (see Chou En-lai's articles in 'Red Star (Hung-hsing)', No. 60, 20 August 1934, and in 'Struggle (Tou-cheng)', No. 24, 29 August 1933; see also the editorial in 'Red Star' (Hung-hsing)', No. 55, 25 July 1934; and On the Party's Work in the Far and Near Rear Lines of the Enemy in 'Struggle (Tou-cheng)', No. 64, 16 June 1934; and 'Order Number Eight (Ti pa hao)' issued by the

General Political Department of the Red Army, 5 January
1934, on CCC reel No. 7; finally, see Ch'en Yün's
article in 'Struggle (Tou-cheng)', No. 72, 23 September
1934) it would appear that this social content was, for
the most part, left to one's imagination.   This is the
case with Ch'en Yi's article in 'Red Star (Hung-hsing)',
No. 48, 15 June 1934, being perhaps the most detailed
and forceful plea for the efficacy of guerrilla warfare
in the 5th Campaign.   See CCC reel No. 16 for 'Red Star'
and No. 18 for 'Struggle'.

*34 Hua Fu, An Urgent Problem of the Revolutionary War, in
     'Revolution and War (Ko-ming yü chan-cheng)', No. 2,
     April 1934, pp. 1-3.   CCC reel No. 16 [brackets con-
     cerning *li* and regular armed force and emphasis added].
*35 Hua Fu, More on Tactical Principles, in 'Revolution and
     War (Ko-ming yü chan-cheng)', No. 4, 18 May 1934, pp. 8-
     11.   CCC reel No. 16 [one *li* = one-third English mile].
*36 Hua Fu, Combat all Misinterpretations of our Tactics, in
     'Revolution and War (Ko-ming yü chan-cheng)', No. 4, 18
     May 1934, p. 6.   CCC reel No. 16.
*37 Ch'en Yün, Work Methods and Organizational Methods in the
     Guerrilla Zones (Zones Occupied by the Enemy), in
     'Struggle (Tou-cheng)', No. 72, 23 September 1934, p. 1.
     CCC reel No. 18 [emphasis added].
*38 Chou En-lai, A New Situation and a New Victory, in 'Red
     Star (Hung-hsing)', No. 60, 20 August 1934, p. 2.   CCC
     reel No. 16.

7 THE CINDERELLA OF CLASSICAL THEORY

1 Samuel P. Huntington, Guerrilla Warfare in Theory and
   Policy, in Franklin M. Osanka (ed.), 'Modern Guerrilla
   Warfare: Fighting Communist Guerrilla Movements, 1941-
   1961', New York, Free Press, 1962, p. xvi.
2 Ibid., p. xviii.
3 Ibid., p. xxi.
4 Mao Tse-tung, 'Selected Military Writings', 2nd ed.,
   Peking, Foriegn Languages Press, 1966, p. 277.   Pointed
   out here is that, on balance, taking as a whole the
   stages of strategic retreat and stalemate, guerrilla warfare is primary.   This does not contradict other discussions of the primacy of mobile warfare in the initial
   strategic retreat which, in the final tally of both
   stages, is less important.
5 Mao Tse-tung, 'Selected Works', vol. IV, Peking, Foreign
   Languages Press, 1961, p. 118.
6 William Hinton, 'Fanshen: A Documentary of Revolution in

a Chinese Village', New York, Random House, Vintage Books, 1966, p. 201.

7 Ibid.; see also Isabel Crook and David Crook, 'Revolution in a Chinese Village: Ten Mile Inn', London, Routledge & Kegan Paul, 1959, pp. 178-9.

8 William Hinton, 'Fanshen', p. 17 [brackets added].

9 Ibid., pp. 124-5.

10 Ibid., pp. 130-1.

11 Ibid., p. 146 [brackets added].

12 Ibid., p. 155 [brackets added].

13 Ibid., p. 200 [brackets added].

14 Ibid., p. 202.

15 Ho Kan-chih, 'A History of the Modern Chinese Revolution', Peking, Foreign Languages Press, 1959, pp. 467-539.

16 Mao Tse-tung, 'Selected Military Writings', pp. 219-20 [brackets added].

17 Jack Belden, 'China Shakes the World', New York, Monthly Review Press, 1970, p. 359.

18 Mao Tse-tung, 'Selected Military Writings', p. 213 [brackets added].

*19 Available at the Hoover Library in: Chin-Ch'a-Chi hsin-hua shu-tien (ed.), 'Land Reforms and Rectifications of the Party (T'u-ti kai-ko yü cheng-tang)', n.p., Hsin-hua shu-tien, 1948.

*20 Available at the Hoover Library in: Chieh-fang she (ed.), 'On Land Policy in New Liberated Areas (Lun hsin chieh-fang ch'ü t'u-ti cheng-ts'e)', n.p., Hsin-hua shu-tien, 1949.

*21 Ibid., pp. 11-15.

*22 Directive of the CC of the CCP on 1948 Land Reform and Party Rectification Work, contained in Chieh-fang she (ed.), 'On Land Policy in New Liberated Areas', pp. 9-10.

23 Mao Tse-tung, 'Selected Works', vol. IV, p. 251.

24 Ibid., p. 273.

25 Isabel Crook and David Crook, 'Revolution in a Chinese Village: Ten Mile Inn', p. 145.

26 William Hinton, 'Fanshen', pp. 285-6 [brackets added].

27 Ibid., p. 411 [brackets added].

*28 Directive of the CC of the CCP on Work of Land Reform and Party Rectification in Old Liberated and Semi-old Liberated Areas, contained in Chin-Ch'a-Chi hsin-hua shu-tien (ed.), 'Land Reforms and Rectifications of the Party'.

*29 Ibid., p. 4 [brackets added].

*30 Ibid., pp. 1-4.

31 Jack Beldon, 'China Shakes the World', pp. 48-50 [brackets added].

32 Ibid., p. 205.

33 Ibid., pp. 219-20.
34 Ibid., p. 228.
35 Ibid., pp. 233-4 [brackets added].
36 Ibid., p. 275.
37 Ibid., p. 413.
*38 Lu Feng-hsiang (ed.), Summary of the Guerrilla Warfare
     for the Past Nine Months and Future Tasks, contained in
     'Work Correspondence, No. 32: Special Issue on Guerrilla
     Warfare (Kung-tso t'ung-hsün, 32: yu-chi chan-cheng
     chuan-hao)', n.p., Hopeh-Shantung-Honan Committee of the
     CCP, June 1947, pp. 5-6 [second brackets and emphasis
     added].
*39 Ibid., p. 11 [brackets and emphasis added].
*40 Directive on Developing Guerrilla Warfare Behind Enemy
     Lines and Making Preparations for Launching a Guerrilla
     War, contained in 'Work Correspondence, No. 32: Special
     Issue on Guerrilla Warfare', p. 57.
*41 Summary of the Guerrilla Warfare for the Past Two Months
     (from part of February to part of April 1947) and Future
     Tasks, contained in 'Work Correspondence, No. 32:
     Special Issue on Guerrilla Warfare', p. 33.
*42 Ibid., pp. 31-2.
*43 Ibid., p. 33.
*44 Lu Feng-hsiang (ed.), Summary of the Guerrilla Warfare
     for the Past Nine Months and Future Tasks, contained in
     'Work Correspondence, No. 32: Special Issue on Guerrilla
     Warfare', p. 22 [first bracket added].
*45 Summary of the Guerrilla Warfare for the Past Two Months
     (from part of February to part of April 1947) and Future
     Tasks, contained in 'Work Correspondence, No. 32: Special
     Issue on Guerrilla Warfare', p. 29 [emphasis added].
*46 Ibid., p. 32 [brackets and emphasis added].
*47 Lu Feng-hsiang (ed.), Summary of the Guerrilla Warfare
     for the Past Nine Months and Future Tasks, contained in
     'Work Correspondence, No. 32: Special Issue on Guerrilla
     Warfare', p. 12.
*48 Summary of the Guerrilla Warfare for the Past Two Months
     (from part of February to part of April 1947) and Future
     Tasks, contained in 'Work Correspondence, No. 32:
     Special Issue on Guerrilla Warfare', p. 34.

8 CLAUSEWITZ AND SILENT CONTRACT

1 Klaus Knorr, 'On The Uses of Military Power in the
   Nuclear Age', Princeton University Press, 1966, p. 38.
2 Herman Kahn, 'On Escalation: Metaphors and Scenarios',
   New York, Praeger, 1965, p. 95 [brackets added].

3 Concluding remarks by Anatol Rapoport in Carl von Clausewitz, 'On War', ed. Anatol Rapoport, Harmondsworth, Penguin Books, 1968, p. 413.
4 Michael Howard, The Transformation of Strategy, in
  'Brassey's Annual', 1972, p. 8 [author quoting Robert
  McNamara].
5 Philip Green, 'Deadly Logic: The Theory of Nuclear
  Deterrence', Ohio State University Press, 1966, p. 77.
6 Michael Howard, Military Power and International Order,
  in 'International Affairs', No. 3, July 1964, pp. 398-9
  and p. 403.
7 Of the recent work published in English on the classical
  strategists, two stand out for their contribution to the
  study of nineteenth-century military theory: John I.
  Alger, 'Antoine-Henri Jomini: A Bibliographical Survey',
  West Point, United States Military Academy, 1975. In
  the foreword by Peter Paret it is suggested that
  'Jomini's basic ideas on war are few in number and relatively straightforward', which is one reason why the
  present study will pass over his writings, some of which
  show in its most elementary form the effects of contract,
  particularly the 'Traité de grande tactique', Paris,
  1805-6, and 'Traité des grandes opérations militaires',
  Paris, 1811. Also of importance is the discussion of
  primary and secondary sources on Clausewitz's extensive
  writings on military history and theory, correspondence,
  and work on other subjects such as politics and education contained in Peter Paret, 'Clausewitz and the
  State', Oxford, Clarendon Press, 1976.
8 A new translation has just become available that was not
  published at the time of writing of the earlier chapters:
  Michael Howard and Peter Paret (edited and translated),
  Carl von Clausewitz, 'On War', Princeton University
  Press, 1976. This latest translation will be quoted
  from now on.
9 It is not the purpose here to trace these threads through
  their constituent writings, which have received an admir-
  able treatment in: Peter Paret, 'Clausewitz and the
  State', p. 206; see also bibliography pp. 445-7.
10 Carl von Clausewitz, Zwei Briefe des Generals von Clausewitz: Gedanken zur Abwehr, in 'Militärwissenschaftliche
   Rundschau' (special issue), II, 1937.
11 Carl von Clausewitz, 'Nachrichten über Preussen in seiner
   grossen Katastrophe; Kriegsgeschichtliche Einzelschriften', X, Berlin, 1888.
12 Carl von Clausewitz, 'On War', Book II, ch. 5, p. 164.
13 Peter Paret, 'Clausewitz and the State', pp. 328-9.
14 Carl von Clausewitz, 'Hinterlassene Werke des Generals

Carl von Clausewitz über Krieg und Kriegführung', Berlin, Ferdinand Dümmler, 1832-7.

15 Peter Paret, 'Clausewitz and the State', p. 152.
16 Carl von Clausewitz, 'On War', Book IV, ch. 3, p. 229.
17 Ibid., Book II, ch. 2, p. 144.
18 Ibid., preface, p. 61.
19 Ibid., Book II, ch. 6, p. 170.
20 Ibid., Book II, ch. 5, p. 165 [emphasis in original unless stated otherwise for all Clausewitz references].
21 Ibid., p. 156.
22 Ibid.
23 Ibid., p. 158 [brackets added].
24 Ibid., p. 157.
25 Ibid.
26 Ibid., p. 156.
27 Ibid.
28 Peter Paret, 'Clausewitz and the State', p. 152.
29 Carl von Clausewitz, 'On War', Book II, ch. 6, p. 170, and ch. 5, p. 165.
30 Peter Paret, 'Clausewitz and the State', p. 354 [brackets added].
31 Carl von Clausewitz, 'On War', Book VIII, ch. 2, p. 581 [brackets added].
32 Ibid., Book VIII, ch. 1, pp. 577-8.
33 Ibid., Book II, ch. 5, p. 158.
34 Ibid., Book II, ch. 2, p. 141.
35 Ibid., Book II, ch. 5, pp. 157-8.
36 Ibid., Book VI, ch. 8, p. 388.
37 Ibid., p. 389.
38 Ibid., Book I, ch. 1, p. 78.
39 Ibid., Book VIII, ch. 2, p. 580.
40 Ibid., Book I, ch. 1, p. 87.
41 Ibid., Book VIII, ch. 6, p. 605.
42 Ibid., Book VII, ch. 1, p. 523.
43 Of the recent work published in English on Clausewitz, see Peter Paret, 'Clausewitz and the State', for discussions of such analytic devices as the theory of purpose and means, concepts of friction, genius and chance, the nature of the dialectical argument; and the range of secondary propositions, the tendency of military action to escalate, the interdependence of attack and defence, the notion of the 'culminating point' and the superiority of the defence, among others.
44 Carl von Clausewitz, 'On War', Book I, ch. 1, p. 75.
45 Ibid., p. 76.
46 Ibid., p. 78.
47 Ibid., p. 87 [square brackets added].
48 Ibid., Book VIII, ch. 3, p. 582.

49 Ibid., Book I, ch. 2, p. 91.
50 Ibid., p. 90.
51 Ibid., Book IV, ch. 3, p. 229.
52 Ibid., Book I, ch. 2, p. 97.
53 Ibid., Book V, ch. 6, p. 529.
54 Ibid.
55 Ibid.
56 Ibid., Book VIII, ch. 9, p. 617.
57 Ibid., p. 619.
58 Ibid., p. 617.
59 Ibid., Book VIII, ch. 4, pp. 595-6 [brackets added].
60 Ibid., p. 597.
61 Ibid., Book I, ch. 1, p. 78; see conditions (a) and (b).
62 Ibid., Book VI, ch. 27, pp. 485-7.
63 Ibid., Book I, ch. 1, p. 78.
64 Ibid., p. 82.
65 Ibid., Book III, ch. 16, p. 216.
66 Ibid., Book IV, ch. 1, p. 225.
67 Ibid., Book IV, ch. 3, p. 227.
68 Ibid., Book IV, ch. 11, p. 258.
69 Ibid., Book VI, ch. 30, p. 516.
70 Ibid., Book VI, ch. 28, p. 489.
71 Ibid., Book III, ch. 1, p. 181.
72 Ibid., Book IV, ch. 4, p. 230.
73 Ibid., Book II, ch. 1, p. 129.
74 Ibid., p. 128.
75 Ibid., Book IV, ch. 9, p. 250 [brackets added].
76 Ibid., Book I, ch. 2, p. 96.
77 Ibid., p. 95.
78 Ibid., Book II, ch. 2, p. 143.
79 Ibid., Book I, ch. 2, p. 99.
80 Ibid.
81 Ibid., Book I, ch. 1, p. 78.
82 Ibid., Book IV, ch. 3, p. 228.
83 Ibid.
84 Ibid., Book VI, ch. 28, pp. 488-9.
85 Ibid., Book V, ch. 14, p. 338.
86 Ibid., Book III, ch. 12, p. 205.
87 Ibid., p. 206.
88 Ibid.
89 Ibid., Book III, ch. 13, p. 211.
90 Ibid., Book III, ch. 12, p. 209.
91 Ibid., Book VIII, ch. 9, p. 624.
92 Ibid., Book IV, ch. 6, p. 238.
93 Ibid., Book VIII, ch. 4, p. 598.
94 Ibid., Book III, ch. 11, p. 204.
95 Ibid., Book VI, ch. 28, p. 489 [brackets added].
96 Ibid., Book VII, ch. 15, p. 546.

97   Ibid., Book IV, ch. 11, p. 259.
98   Ibid., Book III, ch. 8, p. 196.
99   Ibid., Book VII, ch. 8, p. 194.
100 Ibid., Book IV, ch. 5, p. 236.
101 Ibid., Book I, ch. 1, p. 78.
102 Ibid., Book III, ch. 16, p. 217.
103 Ibid., Book VIII, ch. 2, p. 580.
104 Ibid., Book VIII, ch. 6, p. 610.
105 Ibid., Book I, ch. 1, p. 87.
106 Peter Paret, 'Clausewitz and the State', p. 380 [brackets added].
107 Carl von Clausewitz, 'On War', Book VIII, ch. 2, p. 579.
108 Ibid. [brackets added].
109 Ibid.
110 Ibid., pp. 580-1 [brackets added].
111 Peter Paret, 'Clausewitz and the State', see particularly pp. 356-81 and 147-68.
112 Carl von Clausewitz, 'On War', Book VIII, ch. 3, p. 593.
113 Ibid., Book I, ch. 2, p. 99.
114 Ibid., Book I, ch. 1, p. 79.
115 Ibid., Book I, ch. 2, p. 91.
116 Ibid., Book I, ch. 1, pp. 80-1.
117 Ibid., Book VI, ch. 8, p. 388.
118 Ibid., Book VII, ch. 3, p. 585.
119 Ibid.
120 Ibid., Book I, ch. 2, p. 92 [brackets added].
121 Ibid.
122 Ibid., p. 94.
123 Ibid., p. 96.
124 Ibid., Book VI, ch. 30, p. 513.
125 Ibid., Book VIII, ch. 6, p. 604.
126 Carl von Clausewitz, Zwei Briefe des Generals von Clausewitz: Gedanken zur Abwebr, p. 8.
127 Ibid., p. 6.
128 Ibid., p. 7 [brackets added].
129 Carl von Clausewitz, 'On War', Book VIII, ch. 6, pp. 606 and 605.
130 Ibid., p. 606.
131 Ibid., p. 607.
132 Carl von Clausewitz, Zwei Briefe des Generals von Clausewitz: Gedanken zur Abwebr, p. 8.
133 Carl von Clausewitz, 'On War', Book I, ch. 1, p. 81.
134 Ibid., Book VIII, ch. 3, p. 582.
135 Ibid., p. 583.
136 Ibid., Book VI, ch. 30, p. 501 [brackets added].
137 Ibid., p. 69.
138 Ibid., Book VIII, ch. 3, p. 584.
139 Carl von Clausewitz, Zwei Briefe des Generals von Clausewitz: Gedanken zur Abwebr, p. 8.

140   Ibid.
141   Carl von Clausewitz, 'On War', Book I, ch. 1, p. 88.
142   Ibid., Book VI, ch. 26, p. 483.
143   Ibid., p. 479.
144   Peter Paret, 'Clausewitz and the State', p. 380.
145   E.J. Kingston-McCloughry, 'War in Three Dimensions: The
      Impact of Air-Power upon the Classical Principles of
      War', London, Jonathan Cape, 1949, p. 9.

Appendix A

HOW TO ANALYZE THE CLASSES

Adopted by the Eight-County Conference on the Land
Investigation Drive, 17-21 June 1933, and
Approved by the Central Government of the
Chinese Soviet Republic, 10 October 1933
(Taken from Tso-liang Hsiao, 'The Land Revolution', pp. 254-7.)

1   WHAT IS MEANT BY A LANDLORD?

[A landlord] owns land (irrespective of amount), but he does
not labor himself or [at best] engages in supplementary labor
only.   He lives solely on exploitation.

The form of exploitation by a landlord is primarily the
form of land rent (including the school-land rent) through
which he exploits the peasants.   In addition, he may lend
money, hire labor, or engage in industry and commerce.   But
the exploitation of the peasants by means of land rent is the
main form of exploitation by a landlord.   The management of
landholdings of public bodies is also a kind of exploitation
through land rent.

The small landlords exploit more ruthlessly than [other]
landlords.   Some landlords, though having become bankrupt,
still do not labor themselves after bankruptcy but live by
fraud and robbery or by receiving aid from their relatives and

271

friends - these people shall still be classified as landlords.

Warlords, bureaucrats, village bosses, and bad gentry are the political representatives of the landlord class. They are the most ruthless of the landlords. The landlord class is the principal enemy of the land revolution. The policy of the Soviets toward the landlords is to confiscate all their land and [other] property and to annihilate the landlord class.

Those who help landlords collect rent and manage property and who live on the exploitation of peasants by landlords shall be treated as landlords. Those who live wholly or mainly on exploitation by usury are called usurers. Though these people are not landlords, it is necessary to confiscate all their property in order to suppress usurers, since usury is a sort of feudalistic exploitation.

2 WHAT IS MEANT BY A RICH PEASANT?

A rich peasant generally owns land. But in some cases he owns only a part of the land [he cultivates] and rents the other part [from others]. In other cases, he owns no land whatever and rents all the land [from others]. (The last-listed cases are relatively few.) Generally speaking, the rich peasant owns better means of production and circulating capital and engages in labor himself, but he constantly depends on exploitation as a part or, in some cases, even a major part of his means of livelihood.

The form of exploitation by a rich peasant lies primarily in exploitation through the hiring of labor (hiring long-term laborers). Besides, he may rent out a part of his land for extorting land rent, or lend money, or engage in commerce and small-scale industry. Most rich peasants also manage landholdings of public bodies. But there are also

rich peasants in China who usually labor themselves and hire
no laborers, but who exploit the peasants in the form of land
rent, loan interest, and so on.   The exploitation by rich
peasants is constant and, in many cases, major in character.

The policy of the Soviets toward the rich peasants is to
confiscate their land.   But only the surplus parts of their
draft cattle, farm implements, and houses are to be confiscated.   They are still to be assigned labor land allotments of
a poorer quality.

3 WHAT IS MEANT BY A MIDDLE PEASANT?

Many a middle peasant owns land.   In some cases he owns only
a part of the land [he cultivates] and rents the other part
[from others].   In other cases he owns no land whatever and
rents all the land [from others].   Invariably he has suitable
implements of his own.   He depends entirely or for the most
part on his own labor [for his living].   In general, he does
not exploit others; in many cases he is exploited by others
in the form of a small part of land rent, loan interest, and
so on.   But the middle peasant generally does not sell his
labor power.   Some middle peasants (including the well-to-do
middle peasants) exploit others in a measure, but such exploitation is by no means constant and major in character.   All
these people are middle peasants.

The policy of the Soviets toward the middle peasants is to
enter into a solid alliance with them.   Without their consent, the land of the middle peasants shall not be subject to
equal redistribution.   Those middle peasants who do not own
enough land shall be allotted the same amount of land as the
poor peasants and hired farm hands.

4   WHAT IS MEANT BY A POOR PEASANT?

In some cases a poor peasant owns a part of the land [he cul-
tivates] and some incomplete implements; in others he owns no
land whatever but only some incomplete implements.   In general, he has to rent land [from others] to till and is exploited by others through land rent, loan interest, and the hiring
out of part of his labor (the poor peasant, in general, has
to sell a part of his labor power).   All these people are
poor peasants.

     In land redistribution, the poor peasants should obtain the
same benefits as the middle peasants and hired farm hands.
The small amount of land and the few farm implements they
originally own shall not be confiscated.

5   WHAT IS MEANT BY A WORKER?

[A worker] generally owns no land and implements at all.   In
some cases he owns a very small part of land and implements.
He depends entirely or chiefly on the sale of his labor power
for his living.   This is the worker (including the hired farm
hand).

     In the course of land revolution, all workers of the rural
districts should be allotted the same amount of land as the
poor peasants and middle peasants.   The very small part of
land and implements which some of the workers may originally
own shall not be confiscated.   There are cases in which the
workers are working in the cities [Chinese original a little
involved], leaving their families behind in the countryside
with land to let and money to lend.   If the families do not
rely on the collecting of rent as the main means of subsistence, their land shall not be confiscated and they shall all
be allotted land as ordinary peasants.   [On the other hand,]

their land shall be subject to confiscation if their families
rely on the collecting of rent and the lending of money as the
main means of subsistence.   In the latter case, the wives and
children shall be allotted land while the workers themselves
are not to receive any land because they are in the cities.

Appendix B

STOP LAND REFORM IN THE NEW LIBERATED AREAS AND
CARRY OUT RENT AND INTEREST REDUCTION

('West Honan Daily News', editorial, 24 August 1948)

Land reform is our Party's basic policy during the stage of
the New Democratic Revolution. Only by thoroughly carrying
out land reform and really achieving land-to-the-tiller can
the peasants who form over 80 per cent of the nation's population achieve emancipation; the feudal system which obstructs
the development of China's social economy be destroyed; the
social basis of imperialist aggression towards China be eliminated; China's agricultural production be developed; industry and trade prosper; the basis for the nation's industrial-
ization be established, and, finally, can democracy and freedom be ensured. And only then can an independent, mighty and
prosperous, free and united new China have a future. Therefore the land reform policy should not be carried through by
our Party and army alone. All other patriotic parties and
military men should join in our effort. Not only should the
workers, peasants and all labouring people support the land
reform policy, but also industrialists and merchants should
favour it. As for the landlords, land reform uproots the
exploiting feudal land system and eliminates the landlord
class which lives on unearned income by relying on this system; but it does not advocate the elimination of landlord
elements physically. Furthermore, land reform is to turn

these landlord elements into labourers who live on their own
toil or into merchants and industrialists, thereby changing
them from useless persons into persons of use to society.
This is the road of rebirth for landlord elements.

The importance and righteousness of land reform cannot be
disputed. Why then do we now stop land reform in the new
liberated areas in the Central Plains and replace it with rent
and interest reduction? The reason for this change is
because preparatory work for land reform has not yet been
fully conducted in most parts of the Central Plains, and not
because the land reform policy is incorrect, nor because land
reform could not be implemented in the Central Plains. We
shall carry out land reform in the new liberated areas in the
Central Plains and, in the future, even in all new liberated
areas throughout the country - this is our Party's and army's
firm and steadfast basic policy, and we don't have to conceal
it from anybody. However, we should know that the appropriate environment and sufficient preparatory work are needed
for putting land reform into effect. Ideologically, the
peasants should have a high political consciousness and confidence in the victory of the revolution, while organizationally they should have their own core leadership consisting of
tenant peasants, poor and middle peasants - this should be our
main preparatory work. Examining our work in the new liberated areas in the Central Plains, it is obvious that such preparatory work has not yet been done. In the new liberated
areas in the Central Plains, the majority of the peasants were
not well prepared both ideologically and organizationally.
The political consciousness of the common peasants has not yet
been raised and their confidence in the revolution has not yet
been established. Although they live in poverty, they lack
knowledge about the source of their poverty. Although they

desperately need land, they still lack a deep understanding
about the concept of 'land and one's original home'.   Although they warmly support the People's Liberation Army, they
are still doubtful about how long the People's Liberation Army
can last.   Although they deeply hate the rule of Chiang Kai-
shek's KMT and the oppression of the bandit Chiang, they still
have scruples about smashing his rule and his power at the
basic level.   Genuine peasant associations of tenant peasants,
poor and middle peasants are not yet fully organized; and a
selfless core of cadres who are revered by the local people is
not yet fostered in great numbers.   Therefore, during the
land reform in the new liberated areas struggle was carried
out by only a small number of activists, while the broad
masses were still adopting a wait-and-see attitude.   If we
now conduct equal distribution of land, unhealthy tendencies
such as coercion and commandism, taking everything into one's
own hands and even corrupting the fruits of the struggle by a
handful of people will inevitably occur.   In some regions,
land reform was controlled by rascals, local pests and oppor-
tunists who used this opportunity to carry out revenge and to
become wealthy; and therefore they conducted struggles at
random, confiscated at random, violated our policies and created panic, in which the broad masses of poor peasants gained
very little.   Such is the general situation of the land
reform in the new liberated areas in the Central Plains.   Of
course, there are individual villages where the masses were
really mobilized and where land reform was carried out well,
but the general situation is that reform was conducted in name
only, or at random, or even not carried out at all.   Why is
this?   This is the inevitable result of poor preparatory
work.   Such a land reform is of little interest to the
majority of the peasants, and, moreover, of no advantage to

the entire social production.   This is the reason why the
Central Plains Bureau of the CCP decided, in accordance with
the instructions of the CCP's Central Committee, to stop land
reform in the new liberated areas in the Central Plains and
replace it with the policy of rent and interest reduction.
Such a policy will reduce the rent and interest burden of the
peasants, improve their livelihood, and will bring about initial development of agricultural production.   Furthermore,
during the rent and interest reduction struggle we can raise
the political consciousness of the peasants and improve their
organizational strength.   At the same time we must persuade
the landlords to carry out the rent and interest reduction
ordinance, and encourage and assist them gradually to engage
themselves in labour.   This rent and interest reduction,
which is a policy of gradual reform, is the preparatory step
for a thorough land reform in the future, and is therefore
within the actual class interest of the broad masses of the
peasantry at present in the Central Plains.   It is obviously
wrong to be reluctant to stop land reform and to be dissatis-
fied with the new rent and interest reduction policy.   The
entire Party organization and army of the Central Plains must
correctly assess the validity of the Central Bureau's policy
of stopping land reform and conducting rent and interest reduction.   This policy must be resolutely carried out so as
to unite the people of all strata, to win over all forces
which can be won over, and to neutralize all forces which can
be neutralized.   This way we can diminish unnecessary
obstacles and form a broad anti-US, anti-Chiang patriotic
united front, and fight for a total victory of the People's
Liberation War.   However, on the other hand, we must retain
the benefits already obtained by the peasants.   In the old
liberated areas which have been through the rent and interest

reduction movement and the liquidation of enemy agents movement during the War of Resistance or during the early period
of the People's Liberation War, land reform must be continued;
whereas in the new liberated areas occupied during the great
advance [strategic counter-offensive] of last year [1947],
land reform must be stopped and replaced with rent and interest reduction.   But in villages in the new liberated areas
where land reform has been carried out and where the land has
been distributed to the peasants, the government must guarantee their land ownership and prohibit the landlords from forcing the peasants to return the land.   Landlords who defy this
prohibition must be severely punished.   As for the movable
property of the landlords which has been distributed, the government must not force the people to return it.   Only when
the peasants voluntarily return the land and movable property
should the government not intervene.   As for the property of
middle peasants which should not be confiscated and the indus-
trial and commercial enterprises of landlords and rich
peasants which have been confiscated, these should be returned
to the original owners or they should be compensated.   Continue land reform in the old liberated areas;   stop land
reform in the new liberated areas and replace it with rent and
interest reduction while retaining the benefits already gained
by the peasants - this will be our Party's basic policy in the
Central Plains for a considerable length of time.   We hope
that all our Party comrades together with the broad masses
will do their utmost in carrying through this policy so that
the fifty million people in the Central Plains can walk the
level road towards total emancipation!

Appendix C

IMPORTANT DOCUMENTS ON THE LAND REFORM MOVEMENT DURING
THE FIRST HALF OF 1947 ISSUED BY THE DISTRICT PARTY
COMMITTEE
(Published by the Hopeh-Shantung-Honan District Party
Committee, June 1947)
[Extract from pages 73 and 74 of the Chinese original]

THE JOIN-THE-ARMY MOVEMENT SIGNIFIES THE CONTINUED ADVANCE OF
THE LAND REFORM MOVEMENT

(1) Regions where land reform has been relatively thorough-
going: landlords guilty of heinous crimes have been either
executed or arrested and their land and portable property have
been thoroughly redistributed into the hands of the peasantry.
Through struggles, both violent and non-violent, the status of
the landlords has been totally overturned and trampled on to
the ground. With the consciousness of the basic multitude of
the masses raised to unprecedented heights, the forces of the
proletariat have dominated the rural areas where the political
leadership of the proletariat has been fully realized. The
masses consciously accepted the task of joining the army, from
the distribution of land to the protection of it, and from the
transformation of theory into practical action to the eventual
unfolding of a dynamic and vigorous mass join-the-army movement. In particular, it was in those regions where, out of
mass indignation, the landlords were struggled against and the
despotic ones killed that the masses were even more active and
resolute in joining the army. This is not to say one can get
peasants to join the army just by killing landlords or towing

them around, but rather it points to the fact that the masses
have become consciously aware that merely executing despots
and bringing to submission the bad landlords (looked upon as
the little Old Chiangs by the masses) is still not a conclu-
sive solution to the problem, since there still is the big Old
Chiang at large - in other words, the struggle made its turn
from a showdown with individual landlords to the showdown with
the landlord class.

(2) In regions where land reform has not been thorough-
going, Party policy has not been carried through to the
masses, who accordingly have not been able readily to accept
the task of joining the army: when preliminary discussions
were held in the respective villages after the meeting of
labour heroes and model workers, or the peasants' meeting,
only a minority of the activists were enthusiastic in joining
the army while the majority of the masses kept to a 'wait-and-
see' attitude. Actually, in some cases it was due to landlords spreading rumours and in other cases the result of
sabotage by enemy agents (such as the case of Lint'ou in Fan
county). In certain cases it was also because the peasants
were not given their fair share of distribution - hence the
stagnancy in the raising of their consciousness and the
absence of any land protection demands. As matters stand,
the deepening of the join-the-army movement could only be
solved by meeting the actual needs of the masses:

1 By continuing to clear away stumbling blocks.
2 By intensifying the review [land investigation].
3 By getting the masses to redress grievances and air complaints.
4 By continuing to distribute the fruits of struggle where
  it has not been done fairly.
In a word, it all amounts to the continued struggle against

the feudal influence of the landlords.   The task of getting peasants to join the army may take more time to fulfil, but it will also plunge the [land] struggle against feudal forces into greater depth.

(3) The join-the-army movement is the summarization of the land reform movement.

Appendix D

Zwei Briefe des Generals von Clausewitz:

Gedanken zur Abwehr

[Extract from pages 6-11 of the German original]

War is not a self-dependent matter, but the continuation of
politics by other means; hence the principal features of all
great strategic plans are *for the most part of a political
nature*, and always the more they encompass the totality of
war and state.   The whole plan of war results directly from
the political existence of both warring states as well as from
their relations with others.   The plan of campaign results
from the plan of war and is even, if of course everything is
confined to a theatre of war, often identical with the same.
But even in the individual parts of a campaign the political
element is implicated and indeed there is seldom any great act
of war, such as a battle, etc. where at least some influence
of it was not apparent.   According to this view there can be
no question of a *purely military* valuation of a great strategic whole as well as of a purely military plan of the same.
That this view is a quite necessary one, which, if one considers only military history is *quite obvious*, certainly needs no
proof.   But that it nevertheless has not yet been established
is shown precisely in that until now people have always wanted
to separate the purely military element of a great strategic
plan from the political and to regard the latter as something
unseemly.   *War is nothing other than the continuation of*

political struggles by other means.   I take this view as a
basis for all strategy, and believe that whoever refuses to
recognise its necessity, does not yet quite understand on what
it depends.   All military history becomes intelligible by
this principle, without it everything is full of the greatest
absurdities.

Now how is it possible to draw up a plan of campaign, be it
for one theatre of war or for several, without stating the
political situation of the states and their relation to each
other?

Every great military plan arises from such a mass of *individual* circumstances, which determine it thus and not otherwise, that it is impossible to so determine a fictitious case
as the real one would be.   Here we do not want to think only
of small matters, but of very *great essentials* which notwith-
standing have almost never been considered until now.   For
example, people often compare Bonaparte with Frederick the
Great; sometimes indeed without thinking much about the fact
that the one had five, the other forty million subjects.   But
I want only to point out a quite different, much more unre-
markable and yet very essential distinction, that Bonaparte
was an usurper who had won his enormous power through a kind
of continuous game of chance and who during the greater part
of his hazardous career did not even have an inheritance, but
that Frederick the Great administered a true patrimony.   If
both had been created exactly the same in their personality by
nature, was it possible that both acted in the same way for
that reason?   Certainly not, and one can certainly not measure the two with the same scale for this single reason.   Thus
it is not possible to so construct a fictitious case that one
could say what has been omitted was unimportant.   But one can
certainly imagine a number of circumstances of the kind, that

they are exactly alike in both armies and states and mutually
neutralize each other. The solution of such problems will
then be nothing other than a *useful exercise*, and that which
was determined as the best in so doing cannot be used for *real
cases*. Thus even if from such problems we can abstract a
number of things, because we imagine their powers neutralized,
we cannot do so however from those which call the act of war
itself into existence, which determine political purpose and
let the military objective be deduced from it, along with the
available means. This final objective of the whole military
act, that of the individual campaign, in so far as the two are
identical, is thus the most important and the first thing
about which the strategist must concern himself, for all axes
of the plan run to this objective or at least are determined
by it. Yet it is plainly something quite different if I have
and may have the intention of *overcoming* the enemy, disarming
him and forcing him to accept my conditions of peace, or if I
must be satisfied with placing myself at an advantage by the
conquest of a small tract of land, of a stronghold, etc., in
order to keep this in peace or to offer it in exchange. The
extraordinary circumstances of Bonaparte and France have,
since the Revolution, almost always and everywhere allowed him
to secure the first, and that is why people hit upon the idea
of considering his plans and the actions *which arose from them
as the general norms*. But therewith the whole of earlier
military history would be summarily dismissed. This is
folly. If we wish to deduce the art of war from military
history, and that is indisputably the only way it can be
accomplished, then we must not underestimate the testimony of
military history. Thus if, perhaps, we find that of 50 wars
49 were of the second kind, i.e. with a restricted objective,
and not aimed at the suppression of the enemy, then we must

surely believe that this is in the nature of the matter and
does not originate in false views, lack of energy, etc. every
time. Thus we should not allow ourselves to be induced to
consider war as a mere act of might and destruction and, by
logical consequence, to draw from this simple concept a series
of conclusions which no longer coincide with the appearances
of the real world at all; instead we must revert to the fact
that war is a political act which does not operate under a law
quite of itself, or a true political instrument which does not
operate itself, but is guided by a hand. This hand is politics. The more politics stems from noble intentions which
include the whole and the interest which encompasses its existence, and the more the question is posed of existence and
non-existence mutually, then the more politics and enmity
coincide; the more the former is absorbed in the latter; the
simpler becomes the war; the more it proceeds from the mere
concept of might and destruction; the more it corresponds to
all requirements which one can logically develop from these
concepts; and the more all its parts have association of a
necessity. Such a war appears quite *unpolitical* and that is
why it was considered as standard war. But plainly the political principle is lacking just as little here as in other
wars; it only coincides completely with the concept of might
and destruction and disappears from view.

After these developments I do not need to prove that there
can be wars where the objective is yet more insignificant, a
mere threat, an armed negotiation, or, in cases of alliances,
a merely feigned action. It would be quite unphilosophical
to maintain that these military actions had nothing more to do
with the art of war. As soon as it is seen that the art of
war must concede that from a rational point of view there can
be wars which do not have the extreme, the suppression and

destruction of the enemy, for an objective, then it is also
apparent that the art of war relates to all possible gradations which the interests of politics can require. In relation to politics, the problem and intent of the art of war is
chiefly to prevent politics requiring things *which are opposed
to the nature of war*, committing out of ignorance of the
effects of the instrument an error in the use of the same.

I therefore insist that everywhere where a strategic plan
is to be possible, the military objective of both parties be
determined. This objective results chiefly from the great
political relationship of both sides to each other and to
those of the remaining states which can take an interest in
the action. Without taking due account of these things,
such a plan is a mere combination of certain circumstances of
time and space, which are directed towards an *arbitrarily
assumed* objective, a battle, a siege, etc., and which, in so
far as the objective cannot be shown as a necessary or better
objective, can be refuted and contested by other plans, without these other plans being nearer the absolute truth. This,
then, is also the story of all strategic discussions until
now. Everyone turns in an arbitrarily described circle; no-
one seeks by his arguments to reach that point from which the
whole action arose, where the actual motive of the same lies
and where its logical conclusions can only begin. Successful and pertinent strategic actions are the work of tact in
generals of genius, penetrating and estimating with one glance
a mass of circumstances. This tact is sufficient for action,
but plainly not for discussion, however much more noble that
may be than every laborious development of matters.

You will see from this, my valued friend, how little I
actually know how to set about your problem. Above all, I
must ask: have the Austrians the intention, or could they

have the intention, of overcoming and disarming Prussia with
150,000 men, or will they be satisfied with a limited objective?   In the Seven Years War they would have been able to do
the first without hesitation; the way to it was chiefly
through Saxony and Lusatia to Berlin.   The Austrians at that
time let slip their opportunity.   This was rated with justi-
fication as a great mistake, and in the same way it was regarded as a mistake that they directed their operations more
to Silesia than Lusatia.   But if the circumstances are such
that there can be no question of suppressing the Prussian
military state, then the operation through lower Lusatia in
the direction of Berlin is no longer the *most appropriate* and
consequently no longer the most *dangerous* for Prussia.   You
will very easily perceive that if there can be circumstances
in which Austria has just sufficient power to gain possession
of a tract of land with a single or a few strongholds, in
which only *such a moderate plan promises success*, whereas a
greater plan, because it transcends the balance of power,
promises *none*, I say then that the Austrians' moderate plan
would be the most dangerous for Prussia also.   Thus you see
that in the problem, as well as in both solutions, this point
assigns itself a generality which it does not have, a mistake
which is made constantly in strategy, and which results in
general strategical arguments almost always proving useless
in practice.   The greatest danger for Prussia can only be
determined when one knows what the objective of the Austrians
can be or will be, and in the problem in question, this objective could in the present task only follow from a determination of the great political circumstances or it had to be
arbitrarily determined as a date of the problem.   In the task
as well as the solutions importance is obscurely, that is
without being clearly stated, attributed to the capital, which

in practice it cannot have.   The Seven Years War certainly
proves this adequately.   Furthermore the notion was thereby
effective, since because of the direction of the Austrian
thrust the Prussian monarchy is split into two great masses
as it were, because if the army was beaten and ruthlessly pursued it would have to decide either to retreat across the Oder
or to withdraw across the Lower Elbe.   This is a very serious
point - but of course only against an enemy who can carry
through this great project.   For there is certainly no question that for the Austrians such an operation, which is
flanked on the right side of Bohemia by Silesia and on the
other by the strongholds of the Elbe, is a *very difficult one*,
which can only succeed if a *vast superiority* compensates for
the difficulties.   But the problem does not seem to point to
this superiority at all;   rather it appears to take a kind of
equality of power as its basis.

It seems to me, however, that in *this* problem, a useless
value is attributed to that point which is the most dangerous
line of operation for the Austrians.   Attack and defence are
reciprocally determined in their expedience.   However, for
theory, and this is the general view, the series of notions
arising through it must nevertheless begin somewhere.   This
is quite correct.   According to my belief it should begin
with defence, partly because all arrangements existing in
peace time for the state of war are directed chiefly towards
defence (and this precedes attack) and partly because the
arrangements for defence generally call into existence those
for attack first, without which it would have no facts.
Defence, on the other hand, does not lack these facts even
without attack, because they lie in the form and the situation
of the country.   For the completely general question, the
first steps in defence must therefore develop from the nature

of things; in the *individual case, however, this is by no means always necessary*, but only so if one cannot recognize the enemy's intention sufficiently early in order to make the necessary counter-preparations. Now this does not seem to me to be the case here at all. Whether the Austrians direct their main power on Silesia or Saxony will be discovered early enough by the direction of their marches, the layout of their depots, the mobilization of their army service corps and by other information. Whether they will advance on one or the other bank of the Elbe, this can *possibly* be concealed until the last moment. This alternative is however exceedingly weak for us, for the slightest movement to the right or left makes it even. If we gather, which according to mere dislocation is the most natural, our three divisions standing in Silesia respectively at Neisse, Liegnitz and Sprottau, the II and III corps with guards in lower Silesia and the IV corps on the right bank of the Elbe at Torgau, we can act, for the further arrangement, completely in accordance with news which we will certainly receive from the direction of the enemy's main force in order to lead our main force against it. That is why the problem seems to me quite uselessly incorporated in the field of speculative consideration. Where concrete circumstances decide, there need to be no further question of those, which only too often degenerate into subtleties. Should the question of the greatest weakness of the Prussian military state be discussed, then the problem would have to be a quite different one.

After I have shown in this way, first, that the problem is much too incomplete to allow a solution which would have a certain inbuilt necessity, and, second, that the point which to a certain extent is made the basis of the solution (namely, that the most dangerous of lines of operations would in practice never have constituted the basis of our measures), I will now examine the individual points of the second solution *historically*, because the logical connection is too tenuous for a logical refutation itself.

Selected bibliography

I CHINESE LANGUAGE SOURCES [* indicates that the Chinese
original and translation in part or entirety are lodged in my
files]

'A Collection of Important Documents of Communist Bandits'
Land Policy (Kung-fei t'u-ti cheng-ts'e chung-yao wen-chien
hui-pien)', compiled by Chung-lien Publishing House,
December 1947.

'A Collection of Reactionary Documents (Fan-tung wen-chien
hui-pien)', compiled by the KMT Headquarters, Fourteenth
Division of the Army, March 1932; CCC reel No. 19.

* 'A Collection of Red Bandit Reactionary Documents (Ch'ih-
fei fan-tung wen-chien hui-pien)', compiled under sponsorship of General Ch'en Ch'eng, 1935, as held in handwritten
copy on file in the URI, Hong Kong.

* 'A Study of the Strategy and Tactics of Communist Bandits
(Kung-fei chan-lueh chan-shu chih yen-chiu)', published by
the Research Institute on Revolutionary Practice, Taiwan,
October 1953.

* 'Build Red Block-houses in Order to Smash the Enemy (Kou-
chu ch'ih-se pao-lei fen-s'ui ti'-jen)', issued by the
Political Department of the Eastern Route Army, 29 October
1933; CCC reel No. 3.

'Ch'en Ch'eng Collection (Shih-sou tzu-liao shih kung-fei
tzu-liao), 1931-7', compiled by General Ch'en Ch'eng,
microfilm, 21 reels, available at the Hoover Institution,
Stanford University, California.

* Ch'en Yi. Lessons Drawn by Units Assuring the Defence of
Fortified Posts, in 'Revolution and War (Ko-ming yü chan-
cheng)', No. 4 (18 May 1934); CCC reel No. 16.

* Ch'en Yi. Review on the Guerrilla Warfare in the North-
western Front during this Recent Period, in 'Red Star
(Hung-hsing)', No. 48 (15 June 1934); CCC reel No. 16.

* Ch'en Yün. Work Methods and Organizational Methods in the Guerrilla Zones (Zones Occupied by the Enemy), in 'Struggle (Tou-cheng)', No. 72 (23 September 1934); CCC reel No. 18.

* Chieh-fang she (ed.). CCP Central Committee Directive on 1948 Land Reform and Party Rectification Work, in 'On Land Policy in New Liberated Areas (Lun hsin chieh-fang ch'ü t'u -ti cheng-ts'e)', n.p.: Hsin-hua shu-tien, 1949.

* Chieh-fang she (ed.). Stop Land Reform in the New Liberated Areas and Carry Out Rent and Interest Reduction, in 'On Land Policy in New Liberated Areas (Lun hsin chieh-fang ch'ü t'u-ti cheng-ts'e)', n.p.: Hsin-hua shu-tien, 1949.

* Chin-Ch'a-Chi hsin-hua shu-tien (ed.). Directive of the Central Committee of the CCP on Work of Land Reform and Party Rectification in Old Liberated and Semi-old Liberated Areas, in 'Land Reforms and Rectifications of the Party (T'u-ti kai-ko yü cheng-tang)', n.p.: Hsin-hua shu-tien, 1948.

* Chin—Ch'a-Chi jih-pao she (ed.). 'Peasants Arise to Divide the Land (Ch'üan-T'i nung-min ch'i-lai p'ing-fen t'u-ti)', n.p.: Hsin-hua shu-tien, 1948.

* Chou En-lai. A New Situation and a New Victory, in 'Red Star (Hung-hsing)', No. 60 (20 August 1934); CCC reel No. 16.

* Chou En-lai. Although Kuang-ch'ang Has Fallen, We Must Smash the Enemy at all Costs!, in 'Red Star (Hung-hsing)', No. 40 (5 May 1934); CCC reel No. 16.

* Chou En-lai. Fight to the End for Territory, for Freedom, and for the Soviet Political Power!, in 'Red Star (Hung-hsing)', No. 39 (29 April 1934); CCC reel No. 16.

* Chou En-lai. Our Victory in the 5th Campaign - On Protracted War, in 'Red Star (Hung-hsing)', No. 33 (18 March 1934); CCC reel No. 16.

* Chou En-lai. Report at the National Political Work Conference, in 'Red Star (Hung-hsing)', No. 29 (18 February 1934); CCC reel No. 16.

* Chou En-lai. The Urgent Tasks of the Red Army of the Central Region in Smashing the Enemy's 5th Encirclement and Suppression, in 'Struggle (Tou-cheng)', No. 24 (29 August 1933); CCC reel No. 18.

* Ch'un Ming and Yi Feng. Introduction on the Tunnel Warfare Developed by the Fifth Sub-region, in 'Work Correspondence, No. 32: Special Issue on Guerrilla Warfare (Kung-tso t'ung hsün, 32: Yu-chi chan-cheng chuan-hao)', n.p.: Hopeh-Shantung-Honan Committee of the CCP, June 1947.

* Directive on Developing Guerrilla Warfare Behind Enemy Lines and Making Preparations for Launching a Guerrilla War (Regional Party Committee, 20 November 1946), in 'Work

Correspondence, No. 32: Special Issue on Guerrilla Warfare (Kung-tso t'ung-hsün, 32: Yu-chi chan-cheng chuan-
hao)', n.p.: Hopeh-Shantung-Honan Committee of the CCP,
June 1947.

* Hua Fu. An Urgent Problem of the Revolutionary War, in
'Revolution and War (Ko-ming yü chan-cheng)', No. 2 (April
1934); CCC reel No. 16.

* Hua Fu. Combat all Misinterpretations of Our Tactics, in
'Revolution and War (Ko-ming yü chan-cheng)', No. 4 (18 May
1934); CCC reel No. 16.

* Hua Fu. More on Tactical Principles, in 'Revolution and
War (Ko-ming yü chan-cheng)', No. 4 (18 May 1934); CCC
reel No. 16.

* 'Important Documents Concerning Land Reforms Issued in the
First Half of 1947 by the Hopeh-Shantung-Honan Committee of
the CCP (I-chiu-szu-ch'i-nien shang-pan-nien lai ch'ü tang-
wei Kuan-yü t'u-kai yün-tung te chung-yao wen-chien)',
n.p.: Hopeh-Shantung-Honan Committee of the CCP, June
1947.

* Li Chen-yang. Some Impressions on the Land Reform in the
Guerrilla Zone of Chiahsiang-Chining, in 'Work Correspondence, No. 32: Special Issue on Guerrilla Warfare (Kung-
tso t'ung-hsün, 32: Yu-chi chan-cheng chuan-hao)', n.p.:
Hopeh-Shantung-Honan Committee of the CCP, June 1947.

* Li Fu. Summary Report on the Land Reform Movement During
Guerrilla Warfare in Hushi, in 'Work Correspondence, No.
32: Special Issue on Guerrilla Warfare (Kung-tso t'ung-
hsün, 32: Yu-chi chan-cheng chuan-hao)', n.p.: Hopeh-
Shantung-Honan Committee of the CCP, June 1947.

* Lu Feng-hsiang (ed.). Summary of the Guerrilla Warfare
for the Past Nine Months and Future Tasks, in 'Work Correspondence, No. 32: Special Issue on Guerrilla Warfare
(Kung-tso t'ung-hsün, 32: Yu-chi chan-cheng chuan-hao)',
n.p.: Hopeh-Shantung-Honan Committee of the CCP, June
1947.

* Mao Tse-tung. Ch'ang-Kang Hsiang Survey, in 'Rural Survey
of Districts (Nung-ts'un tiao-cha)', Ho-chien, Hopei Province: Hsin-hua shu-tien, 1947.

* Mao Tse-tung. On Culture and Education of the Soviet, in
'Patriot Chü Ch'iu-pai (Hsün kuo lieh shih Chü Ch'iu-pai)',
n.p., 1936.

* Mao Tse-tung. 'Rural Survey of Districts (Nung-ts'un
tiao-cha)', Ho-chien, Hopei Province: Hsin-hua shu-tien,
1947.

* On the Party's Work in the Far and Near Rear Lines of the
Enemy (editorial letter to the guerrilla zones), in
'Struggle (Tou-cheng)', No. 64 (16 June 1934); CCC reel
No. 18.

* 'Order Number Eight (Ti pa hao)', issued by the General
  Political Department of the Red Army, 5 January 1934;
  CCC reel No. 7.
* 'Outline of the Land Investigation Movement (Ch'a-t'ien
  yün-tung ti kai-k'uang)', published by the Kiangsi Provin-
  cial Committee of the Central Committee of the Party,
  September 1933; CCC reel No. 17.
* P'eng Teh-huai. Letter to a Division Commander, in 'Rev-
  olution and War (Ko-ming yü chan-cheng)', No. 9 (10 Septem-
  ber 1934); CCC reel No. 16.
* Raise the Task of Developing Guerrilla Warfare to the
  Highest Political Level (editorial), in 'Red Star (Hung-
  hsing)', No. 55 (25 July 1934); CCC reel No. 16.
  'Red China (Hung-se Chung-hua)', published by the Provis-
  ional Central Government, Central Soviet Area, Kiangsi,
  1931-4; CCC reels Nos 16 and 18.
* 'Red Star (Hung-hsing)', published by the General Political
  Department of the Red Army, Central Soviet Area, 1933-4;
  CCC reel No. 16.
* 'Revolution and War (Ko-ming yü chan-cheng)', published by
  the Military Revolutionary Commission of the Central Gov-
  ernment of the Chinese Soviet Republic, 1933-4; CCC reel
  No. 16.
* 'Struggle (Tou-cheng)', published by the Party Press Committee, Central Bureau, Soviet Areas, Kiangsi, 1933-4;
  CCC reel No. 18.
* 'Struggle (Tou-cheng)', published by the Huatung Bureau of
  the Central Committee of the CCP, No. 56, 1946. (Although
  to be found in the Hoover Library as above, it is, in fact,
  Li Yü's September 1945 report on the mass line and the mass
  movement in Shantung given to the second Conference on mass
  work.)
* Summary of the Guerrilla Warfare for the Past Five Months
  in Hopeh-Shantung-Honan and Present Tasks (2 March
  1947), in 'Work Correspondence, No. 32: Special Issue on
  Guerrilla Warfare (Kung-tso t'ung-hsün, 32: Yu-chi chan-
  cheng chuan-hao)', n.p.: Hopeh-Shantung-Honan Committee
  of the CCP, June 1947.
* Summary of the Guerrilla Warfare for the Past Two Months
  (from part of February to part of April 1947) and Future
  Tasks (Regional Party Committee), in 'Work Correspondence,
  No. 32: Special Issue on Guerrilla Warfare (Kung-tso
  t'ung-hsün, 32: Yu-chi chan-cheng chuan-hao)', n.p.:
  Hopeh-Shantung-Honan Committee of the CCP, June 1947.
* Teng T'o. To Strengthen Ideological Tasks, to Develop
  Ideological Struggle, in 'Study (Hsüeh Hsi)', vol. IV, No.
  9 (16 August 1951).
* 'The Chinese Communist Party and the Agrarian Revolution

(Chung-kuo kung-ch'an tang yü t'u-ti ko-ming)', Hong Kong: Cheng-pao, n.d.
* The Experience of Shengli County in Continuing the Land Investigation Movement (editorial), in 'Struggle (Tou-cheng)', No. 61 (26 May 1934); CCC reel No. 18.
* 'Work Correspondence, No. 24 (Kung-tso t'ung-hsün, 24)', n.p.: Po-Hai District Party Committee of the CCP, July 1947.
* Yang P'ei.   The Armed Work Team of Chining, in 'Work Correspondence, No. 32: Special Issue on Guerrilla Warfare (Kung-tso t'ung-hsün, 32: Yu-chi chan-cheng chuan-hao)', n.p.: Hopeh-Shantung-Honan Committee of the CCP, June 1947.

II WESTERN LANGUAGE SOURCES

ALGER, John I., 'Antoine-Henri Jomini: A Bibliographical Survey'.   West Point: United States Military Academy, 1975.
ALMOND, G. and COLEMAN, James S. (eds), 'The Politics of the Developing Areas'.   Princeton University Press, 1960.
ARENDT, Hannah, 'On Revolution'.   New York: Viking Press, 1963.
ARON, Raymond, 'The Century of Total War'.   Translated by E. Dickes and O. Griffiths.   London: Derek Verschoyle, 1954.
ARON, Raymond, The Evolution of Modern Strategic Thought, in 'Problems of Modern Strategy I'. 'Adelphi Papers', No. 54 (February 1969), pp. 1-17.
ATKINSON, Alexander, Chinese Communist Strategic Thought: The Strategic Premise of Protracted War, in 'Journal of the Royal United Services Institute for Defence Studies', vol. 118, No. 1 (March 1973), pp. 60-4.
ATKINSON, Alexander, Social War - The Death of Classicalism in Contemporary Strategic Thought?, in 'Journal of the Royal United Services Institute for Defence Studies', vol. 119, No. 1 (March 1974), pp. 43-8.
BADCOCK, C.R., 'Lévi-Strauss: Structuralism and Sociological Theory'.   London: Hutchinson, 1975.
BARBER, Bernard, Structural-Functional Analysis: Some Problems and Misunderstandings, in 'American Sociological Review' No. 2 (April 1956), pp. 129-35.
BARRY, Brian (ed.).   'Power and Political Theory: Some European Perspectives'.   London: John Wiley, 1976.
BAYLIS, J., BOOTH, K., GARNETT, J. and WILLIAMS, P., 'Contemporary Strategy: Theories and Policies'.   London: Croom Helm, 1975.
BEAUFRE, André, 'An Introduction to Strategy'.   Translated by R.H. Barry.   London: Faber & Faber, 1965.

BEAUFRE, André, 'Deterrence and Strategy'. Translated by R.H. Barry. London: Faber & Faber, 1965.

BEAUFRE, André, 'Strategy of Action'. Translated by R.H. Barry. London: Faber & Faber, 1967.

BECKER, H. and BOSKOFF, A. (eds), 'Modern Sociological Theory in Continuity and Change'. New York: Dryden Press, 1957.

BELDEN, Jack, 'China Shakes the World'. New York: Monthly Review Press, 1970.

BIDWELL, Shelford, 'Modern Warfare: A Study of Men, Weapons and Theories'. London: Allen Lane, 1973.

BIERSTEDT, Robert, An Analysis of Social Power, in 'American Sociological Review', No. 6 (December 1950), pp. 730-8.

BLACK, Max (ed.), 'The Social Theories of Talcott Parsons'. Englewood Cliffs: Prentice-Hall, 1961.

BLAU, Peter M., 'Exchange and Power in Social Life'. New York: John Wiley & Sons, 1964.

BLOOMFIELD, L. and LEISS, A., 'Controlling Small Wars: A Strategy for the 1970s'. London: Allen Lane, Penguin Press, 1970.

BOND, Brian, 'Liddell Hart: A Study of his Military Thought'. London: Cassell, 1977.

BRANDT, C., SCHWARTZ, B. and FAIRBANK, J., 'A Documentary History of Chinese Communism'. New York: Atheneum, 1966.

BRAUN, Otto, 'Chinesische Aufzeichnungen (1932-1939)'. Berlin: Dietz, 1973.

BRODIE, Bernard, 'Strategy in the Missile Age'. Princeton University Press, 1965.

BRODIE, Bernard, Technology, Politics and Strategy, in 'Problems of Modern Strategy II'. 'Adelphi Papers', No. 55 (March 1969), pp. 21-9.

BRODIE, Bernard, 'War and Politics'. London: Cassell, 1974.

BRODIE, Bernard and BRODIE, F.M., 'From Crossbow to H-Bomb', 2nd ed., rev. Bloomington: Indiana University Press, 1973.

BUCHAN, Alistair, 'War in Modern Society: an Introduction'. London: Watts, 1966.

BUCK, John L. 'Land Utilization in China'. Shanghai: The Commercial Press, 1937.

BUCKLEY, Walter, Social Stratification and the Functional Theory of Social Differentiation, in 'American Sociological Review', No. 4 (August 1958), pp. 369-75.

CAEMMERER, Rudolf von, 'The Development of Strategical Science during the 19th Century'. Translated by Karl von Donat. London: Hugh Rees, 1905.

CHAO Kuo-chun, 'Agrarian Policy of the Chinese Communist Party, 1921-1959'. London: Asia Publishing House, 1960.

CHASSIN, Lionel M., 'The Communist Conquest of China: A History of the Civil War, 1945-1949'. Translated by T. Osato and L. Gelas. Cambridge: Harvard University Press, 1965.

CH'EN, Jerome, 'Mao and the Chinese Revolution'. London:
Oxford University Press, 1965.

CH'EN, Jerome, Resolutions of the Tsunyi Conference, in 'The
China Quarterly', No. 40 (October-December 1969), pp. 1-38.

CHEN Po-ta, 'Notes on Ten Years of Civil War, 1927-1936'.
Peking: Foreign Languages Press, 1954.

CLAUSEN, John A. (ed.), 'Socialization and Society'. Boston:
Little, Brown, 1968.

CLAUSEWITZ, Carl von, 'Hinterlassene Werke des Generals Carl
von Clausewitz über Krieg und Kriegführung', vols I-X. Berlin:
Ferdinand Dümmler, 1832-7.

CLAUSEWITZ, Carl von, 'Nachrichten über Preussen in seiner
grossen Katastrophe; Kriegsgeschichtliche Einzelschriften',
X, Berlin, 1888.

CLAUSEWITZ, Carl von, Zwei Briefe des Generals von Clausewitz:
Gedanken zur Abwehr, in 'Militärwissenschaftliche Rundschau',
(special issue) II, 1937.

CLAUSEWITZ, Carl von, 'Principles of War'. Translated by
Hans Gatzke. London: Bodley Head, 1943.

CLAUSEWITZ, Carl von, 'On War'. Edited by Anatol Rapoport.
Harmondsworth: Penguin Books, 1968.

CLAUSEWITZ, Carl von, 'On War'. Edited and translated by
Michael Howard and Peter Paret. Princeton University Press,
1976.

CLAUSEWITZ, Carl von, 'The Campaign of 1812 in Russia'.
Translator not listed. Westport: Greenwood Press, 1977.

COHEN, Percy S., 'Modern Social Theory'. London: Heinemann,
1968.

COLIN, J.L.A., 'The Transformations of War'. Translated by
L.H.R. Pope-Hennessy. Westport: Greenwood Press, 1977.

CROOK, Isabel and CROOK, David, 'Revolution in a Chinese
Village: Ten Mile Inn'. London: Routledge & Kegan Paul,
1959.

DAVIS, Kingsley, The Myth of Functional Analysis as a Special
Method in Sociology and Anthropology, in 'American Sociological Review', No. 6 (December 1959), pp. 757-72.

DAVIS, Kingsley and MOORE, W.E., Some Principles of Stratification, in 'American Sociological Review', No. 2 (April 1945),
pp. 242-9.

DELBRÜCK, Hans, 'History of the Art of War Within the Framework of Political History', vol. I. Translated by W.J.
Renfroe. Westport: Greenwood Press, 1975.

DEUTSCH, Karl, Social Mobilization and Political Development,
in 'American Political Science Review', No. 3 (September
1961), pp. 493-514.

DONNELL, John C., Pacification Reassessed, in 'Asian Survey',
No. 8 (August 1967), pp. 567-76.

DURKHEIM, Emile, 'The Division of Labor in Society'. Translated by George Simpson. New York: Free Press, 1964.

DURKHEIM, Emile, 'The Elementary Forms of the Religious Life'. Translated by J.W. Swain. London: George Allen & Unwin, 1971.

DURKHEIM, Emile, 'Moral Education'. Translated by E. Wilson and H. Schnurer. New York: Free Press, 1973.

EARLE, Edward M. (ed.), 'Makers of Modern Strategy: Military Thought from Machiavelli to Hitler'. Princeton University Press, 1943.

EKEH, Peter P., 'Social Exchange Theory'. London: Heinemann, 1974.

ELLIOTT-BATEMAN, M., 'Defeat in the East: The Mark of Mao Tse-tung on War'. London: Oxford University Press, 1967.

ELLIOTT-BATEMAN, M. (ed.), 'The Fourth Dimension of Warfare', vol. 1. Manchester University Press, 1970.

EMERSON, R., Power-dependence Relations, in 'American Sociological Review', No. 1 (February 1962), pp. 31-41.

FULLER, J.F.C., 'Machine Warfare'. Washington: The Infantry Journal Inc., 1943.

FULLER, J.F.C., 'The Decisive Battles of the Western World: And Their Influence Upon History', vols I-III. London: Eyre & Spottiswoode, 1956.

FULLER, J.F.C., 'The Conduct of War 1789-1961'. London: Eyre & Spottiswoode, 1961.

GARNETT, John (ed.), 'Theories of Peace and Security: A Reader in Contemporary Strategic Thought'. London: Macmillan, 1970.

GITTINGS, John, 'The Role of the Chinese Army'. London: Oxford University Press, 1967.

GOULDNER, A.W., 'The Coming Crisis of Western Sociology'. London: Heinemann, 1971.

GREEN, Philip, 'Deadly Logic: The Theory of Nuclear Deterrence'. Ohio State University Press, 1966.

HALPERIN, Morton H., 'Limited War in the Nuclear Age'. London: John Wiley & Sons, 1963.

HEILBRUNN, Otto, 'Partisan Warfare'. London: Allen & Unwin, 1962.

HEILBRUNN, Otto, 'Warfare in the Enemy's Rear'. London: Allen & Unwin, 1963.

HINTON, William, 'Fanshen: A Documentary of Revolution in a Chinese Village'. New York: Random House, Vintage Books, 1966.

HO Kan-chih, 'A History of the Modern Chinese Revolution'. Peking: Foreign Languages Press, 1959.

HOBBES, Thomas, 'Leviathan'. Edited by M. Oakeshott. Oxford: Blackwell, 1960.

HOFHEINZ, Roy, The Peasant Movement and Rural Revolution:
Chinese Communists in the Countryside 1923-1927, PhD disserta-
tion, Department of History, Harvard University, 1966.
HOFHEINZ, Roy, The Ecology of Chinese Communist Success:
Rural Influence Patterns, 1923-1945, in 'Chinese Communist
Politics in Action'.   Edited by A. Doak Barnett.   Seattle:
University of Washington Press, 1969.
HOLMES, Rodger, 'Legitimacy and the Politics of the Knowable'.
London: Routledge & Kegan Paul, 1976.
HOMANS, George C., 'Social Behaviour: Its Elementary Forms'.
London: Routledge & Kegan Paul, 1961.
HOWARD, Michael, 'The Franco-Prussian War: The German Inva-
sion of France, 1870-1871'.   London: Rupert Hart-Davis,
1962.
HOWARD, Michael, Military Power and International Order, in
'International Affairs', No. 3 (July 1964), pp. 397-408.
HOWARD, Michael (ed.), 'The Theory and Practice of War'.
London: Cassell, 1965.
HOWARD, Michael, 'Strategy and Policy in Twentieth-Century
Warfare'.   Colorado: United States Air Force Academy, 1967.
HOWARD, Michael, The Classical Strategists, in 'Problems of
Modern Strategy I'. 'Adelphi Papers', No. 54 (February 1969),
pp. 18-32.
HOWARD, Michael, 'Studies in War and Peace'.   London: Temple
Smith, 1970.
HOWARD, Michael, The Transformation of Strategy, in 'Brassey's
Annual' (1972), pp. 1-9.
HSIAO Tso-liang, 'Power Relations Within the Chinese Commu-
nist Movement, 1930-1934:   A Study of Documents'.   Seattle:
University of Washington Press, 1961.
HSIAO Tso-liang, 'The Land Revolution in China, 1930-1934:   A
Study of Documents'.   Seattle: University of Washington
Press, 1969.
HSÜEH, Chün-tu, 'The Chinese Communist Movement, 1921-1937'.
An Annotated Bibliography of Selected Materials in the Chinese
Collection of the Hoover Institution.   Stanford: Hoover
Institution, 1960.
HSÜEH, Chün-tu, 'The Chinese Communist Movement, 1937-1949'.
An Annotated Bibliography of Selected Materials in the Chinese
Collection of the Hoover Institution.   Stanford: Hoover
Institution, 1962.
HU, Chi-hsi, Hua Fu, the Fifth Encirclement Campaign and the
Tsunyi Conference, in 'The China Quarterly', No. 43 (July-
September 1970), pp. 31-46.
IRVINE, Dallas D., The French Discovery of Clausewitz and
Napoleon, in 'Journal of the American Military Institute', vol.
4 (1940), pp. 143-61.

ISAACS, Harold Robert, 'The Tragedy of the Chinese Revolution', 2nd ed., rev.   Stanford University Press, 1961.

JANOWITZ, Morris, Toward a Redefinition of Military Strategy in International Relations, in 'World Politics', No. 4 (July 1974), pp. 473-508.

JOHNSON, Chalmers A., 'Peasant Nationalism and Communist Power'.   Stanford University Press, 1962.

JOHNSON, Chalmers A., 'Revolutionary Change'. Boston: Little, Brown, 1966.

JOMINI, Antoine H., 'Traité de grande tactique', vols I, II and V.   Paris: Giguet et Michaud, Magimel, 1805-6.

JOMINI, Antoine H., 'Traité des grandes opérations militaires' vols I-VI.   Paris: Magimel, 1811.

JOMINI, Antoine H., 'Précis de l'art de la guerre'.   Paris: Anselin, G. Laguionie, 1838.

JOMINI, Antoine H., 'The Art of War'.   Translated by G.H. Mandell and W.P. Graighill.   Westport: Greenwood Press, 1971.

KAHN, Herman, 'On Thermonuclear War'.   Princeton University Press, 1960.

KAHN, Herman, 'Thinking About the Unthinkable'.   New York: Horizon Press, 1962.

KAHN, Herman, 'On Escalation: Metaphors and Scenarios'.   New York: Praeger, 1965.

KATAOKA, Tetsuya, Communist Power in a War of National Liberation: The Case of China, in 'World Politics', No. 3 (April 1972), pp. 410-27.

KINGSTON-McCLOUGHRY, E.J., 'War in Three Dimensions: The Impact of Air-Power Upon the Classical Principles of War'. London: Jonathan Cape, 1949.

KISSINGER, H.A., 'Nuclear Weapons and Foreign Policy'.   New York: Harper & Brothers, 1957.

KITSON, Frank, 'Low Intensity Operations'.   London: Faber & Faber, 1971.

KNORR, Klaus, 'On the Uses of Military Power in the Nuclear Age'.   Princeton University Press, 1966.

KNORR, K. and READ, T. (eds), 'Limited Strategic War'. London: Pall Mall Press, 1962.

KUO, Warren, 'Analytical History of the Chinese Communist Party', vols I-IV.   Taipei: Institute of International Relations, 1968-71.

LASSWELL, Harold D. and KAPLAN, A., 'Power and Society: A Framework for Political Inquiry'.   New Haven: Yale University Press, 1950.

LEONARD, Rodger A. (ed.), 'A Short Guide to Clausewitz on War', London: Weidenfeld & Nicolson, 1967.

LÉVI-STRAUSS, C., 'The Elementary Structures of Kinship'.

Translated by J. Bell and J. von Sturmer.   Boston: Beacon Press, 1969.

LIDDELL HART, B.H., 'Foch: the Man of Orleans'.   London: Eyre & Spottiswoode, 1931.

LIDDELL HART, B.H., 'The British Way in Warfare'.   London: Faber & Faber, 1932.

LIDDELL HART, B.H., 'The Ghost of Napoleon'.   London: Faber & Faber, 1933.

LIDDELL HART, B.H., 'The Strategy of Indirect Approach'. London: Faber & Faber, 1941.

LIU, F.F., 'A Military History of Modern China, 1924-1949'. Princeton University Press, 1956.

LÖTVEIT, Trygve, 'Chinese Communism 1931-1934: Experience in Civil Government'.   Scandinavian Institute of Asian Studies Monograph Series No. 16, 1973.

LUKES, Steven, 'Power: A Radical View'.   London: Macmillan, 1974.

MAO Tse-tung, 'On Guerrilla Warfare'.   Translated by Samuel Griffith.   New York: Praeger, 1961.

MAO Tse-tung, 'Selected Works', vols I-IV.   Peking: Foreign Languages Press, 1961-5.

MAO Tse-tung, 'Basic Tactics'.   Translated by Stuart Schram. New York: Praeger, 1966.

MAO Tse-tung, 'Selected Military Writings', 2nd ed.   Peking: Foreign Languages Press, 1966.

MARTIN, Laurence, 'Arms and Strategy'.   London: Weidenfeld & Nicolson, 1973.

MARTIN, Laurence, The Utility of Military Force, in 'Force in Modern Societies: Its Place in International Politics'. 'Adelphi Papers', No. 102 (1973), pp. 14-21.

McCUEN, John J., 'The Art of Counter-Revolutionary War: The Strategy of Counter-insurgency'.   London: Faber & Faber, 1966.

MENNELL, Stephen, 'Sociological Theory: Uses and Unities'. London: Nelson, 1974.

MORGENTHAU, Hans J., 'Politics Among Nations: The Struggle for Power and Peace', 2nd ed., rev.   New York: Alfred A. Knopf, 1954.

MULKAY, M.J., 'Functionalism, Exchange and Theoretical Strategy'.   London: Routledge & Kegan Paul, 1971.

MYERS, Ramon H., 'The Chinese Peasant Economy: Agricultural Development in Hopei and Shantung, 1890-1949'.   Cambridge: Harvard University Press, 1970.

NADEL, S.F., 'The Theory of Social Structure'.   London: Cohen & West, 1957.

NORTH, Robert C., 'Moscow and Chinese Communists'.   Stanford University Press, 1953.

OSANKA, Franklin M. (ed.), 'Modern Guerrilla Warfare: Fighting Communist Guerrilla Movements, 1941-1961'.   New York: Free Press, 1962.

OSGOOD, Robert E., The Reappraisal of Limited War, in 'Problems of Modern Strategy I'. 'Adelphi Papers', No. 54 (February 1969), pp. 41-54.

PAGET, Julian, 'Counter-Insurgency Campaigning'.   London: Faber & Faber, 1967.

PARET, Peter, 'French Revolutionary Warfare from Indochina to Algeria: The Analysis of a Political and Military Doctrine'. London: Pall Mall Press, 1964.

PARET, Peter, Clausewitz: A Bibliographical Survey, in 'World Politics', No. 2 (January 1965), pp. 272-85.

PARET, Peter, 'Yorck and the Era of Prussian Reform, 1807-1815'.   Princeton University Press, 1966.

PARET, Peter, Education, Politics, and War in the Life of Clausewitz, in 'Journal of the History of Ideas', No. 3 (July-September 1968), pp. 394-408.

PARET, Peter, 'Clausewitz and the State'.   Oxford: Clarendon Press, 1976.

PARET, Peter and SHY, John W., 'Guerrillas in the 1960s'. London: Pall Mall, 1962.

PARKINSON, Roger, 'Clausewitz: A Biography'.   London: Wayland, 1970.

PARSONS, Talcott, 'The Social System'.   London: Routledge & Kegan Paul, 1951.

PARSONS, Talcott, 'The Structure of Social Action', 2nd ed. New York: Free Press, 1961.

PEPPER, Suzanne, 'Civil War in China: The Political Struggle, 1945-1949'.   Berkeley: University of California Press, 1978.

PIKE, Douglas, 'Viet Cong'.   Cambridge: MIT Press, 1966.

RADCLIFFE-BROWN, A.R., 'Structure and Function in Primitive Society'.   London: Cohen & West, 1952.

REX, John, 'Key Problems of Sociological Theory'.   London: Routledge & Kegan Paul, 1961.

RUE, John E., 'Mao Tse-tung in Opposition 1927-1935'.   Stanford University Press, 1966.

RUNCIMAN, W.G., 'Sociology in its Place and Other Essays'. Cambridge University Press, 1970.

SCHELLING, T.C., 'Arms and Influence'.   New Haven: Yale University Press, 1966.

SCHRAM, Stuart, 'The Political Thought of Mao Tse-tung'. New York: Praeger, 1963.

SCHRAM, Stuart, 'Mao Tse-tung'.   Harmondsworth: Penguin Books, 1966.

SCHURMANN, Franz, 'Ideology and Organization in Communist China'.   Berkeley: University of California Press, 1966.

SELDEN, Mark, 'The Yenan Way in Revolutionary China'. Cambridge: Harvard University Press, 1971.

SIMMEL, Georg, 'Conflict' and 'The Web of Group-Affiliations'. Translated by K. Wolff and R. Bendix. Chicago: Free Press, 1955.

SKIDMORE, William, 'Theoretical Thinking in Sociology'. Cambridge University Press, 1975.

SMEDLY, Agnes, 'Battle Hymn of China'. New York: Alfred A. Knopf, 1943.

SNOW, Edgar, 'Red Star Over China'. London: Victor Gollancz, 1937.

SWARUP, Shanti, 'A Study of the Chinese Communist Movement'. Oxford: Clarendon Press, 1966.

TANHAM, George K., 'Communist Revolutionary Warfare from the Vietminh to the Viet Cong'. New York: Praeger, 1967.

THOMPSON, Robert, 'Defeating Communist Insurgency: Experiences from Malaya and Vietnam'. London: Chatto & Windus, 1966.

THOMPSON, Robert, 'Revolutionary War in World Strategy 1945-1969'. London: Secker & Warburg, 1970.

TOWNSEND, James R., 'Political Participation in Communist China'. Berkeley: University of California Press, 1967.

TRINQUIER, Roger, 'Modern Warfare: A French View of Counterinsurgency'. Translated by Daniel Lee. London: Pall Mall Press, 1964.

TRYTHALL, Anthony J., 'Boney Fuller: The Intellectual General 1878-1966'. London: Cassell, 1977.

WALLWORK, Ernest, 'Durkheim: Morality and Milieu'. Cambridge: Harvard University Press, 1972.

WHITSON, William W., 'The Chinese High Command: A History of Communist Military Politics, 1927-1971'. London: Macmillan, 1973.

WIGHT, Martin, 'Systems of States'. Leicester University Press, 1977.

WRIGHT, Quincy, 'A Study of War'. University of Chicago Press, 1942.

WU, Tien-wei, The Kiangsi Soviet Period, in 'Journal of Asian Studies', No. 2 (February 1970), pp. 395-412.

YU, F.T.C., 'Mass Persuasion in Communist China', New York: Praeger, 1964.

Printed in the United States
by Baker & Taylor Publisher Services